Reptiles and Amphibians of the Amazon

Florida A&M University, Tallahassee
Florida Atlantic University, Boca Raton
Florida Gulf Coast University, Ft. Myers
Florida International University, Miami
Florida State University, Tallahassee
University of Central Florida, Orlando
University of Florida, Gainesville
University of North Florida, Jacksonville
University of South Florida, Tampa
University of West Florida, Pensacola

University Press of Florida

Gainesville Tallahassee Tampa Boca Raton Pensacola Orlando Miami Jacksonville Ft. Myers

REPTILES AND AMPHIBIANS OF THE AMAZON

An Ecotourist's Guide

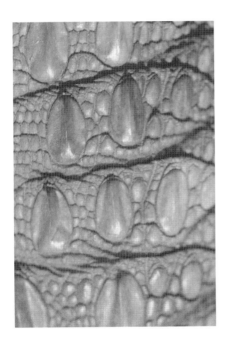

R. D. Bartlett
and Patricia P. Bartlett

Library of Congress Cataloging-in-Publication Data
Bartlett, Richard D., 1938–
Reptiles and amphibians of the Amazon: an ecotourist's guide /
R. D. Bartlett and Patricia P. Bartlett.
p. cm.
Includes bibliographical references (p.).
ISBN 0-8130-2623-7 (pbk.: alk. paper)
1. Reptiles—Amazon River Watershed—Identification. 2. Amphibians—
Amazon River Watershed—Identification. I. Bartlett, Patricia Pope, 1949–
II. Title.

QL657.A44B37 2003
597.9'09811—dc21   2003040241

The University Press of Florida is the scholarly publishing agency
for the State University System of Florida, comprising Florida A&M
University, Florida Atlantic University, Florida Gulf Coast University,
Florida International University, Florida State University, University
of Central Florida, University of Florida, University of North Florida,
University of South Florida, and University of West Florida.

University Press of Florida
15 Northwest 15th Street
Gainesville, FL 32611-2079
http://www.upf.com

Contents

Species

Amphibians

Caecilians

Family Caeciliidae
 1. *Oscaecilia bassleri*, Bassler's slender caecilian
 2. *Siphonops annulatus*, Amazonian ringed caecilian

Family Typhlonectidae
 3. *Typhlonectes compressicauda*, common aquatic caecilian

Salamanders

Family Plethodontidae
 4. *Bolitoglossa altamazonica*, Amazon climbing salamander
 5. *Bolitoglossa peruviana*, dwarf climbing salamander
 6. *Bolitoglossa* species, black-bellied climbing salamander

Toads, Frogs, and Treefrogs

Family Bufonidae
 7. *Atelopus flavescens*, cayenne harlequin toad
 8. *Atelopus pulcher*, Amazon harlequin toad
 9. *Atelopus spumarius spumarius*, common harlequin toad
 10. *Bufo ceratophrys*, eyelashed forest toad
 11. *Bufo dapsilis*, sharp-nosed toad
 12. *Bufo glaberrimus*, Peruvian smooth-sided toad
 13. *Bufo guttatus*, eastern smooth-sided toad
 14. *Bufo margaritifer*, crested forest toad
 15. *Bufo marinus*, common giant toad
 16. *Dendrophryniscus minutus*, orange-bellied leaf toad

Family Centrolenidae

Family Dendrobatidae

Family Hylidae

Hemiphractine treefrogs

Hyline treefrogs

Subfamily Telmatobiinae

Subfamily Leptodactylinae

Family Microhylidae

Family Pipidae
  122. *Pipa pipa*, common Suriname toad
  123. *Pipa snethlageae*, Utinga Suriname toad
Family Pseudidae
  124. *Pseudis paradoxa*, paradox frog
Family Ranidae
  125. *Rana palmipes*, Neotropical green frog

Reptiles

Crocodilians

Family Crocodylidae
  126. *Caiman crocodilus* ssp., spectacled caiman
  127. *Caiman (Melanosuchus) niger*, black caiman
  128. *Paleosuchus palpebrosus*, dwarf caiman
  129. *Paleosuchus trigonatus*, smooth-fronted caiman

Turtles and Tortoises

Pleurodine turtles

Family Chelidae
  130. *Chelus fimbriatus*, matamata
  131. *Phrynops geoffroanus tuberosus*, spotted toad-headed turtle
  132. *Phrynops gibbus*, lesser toad-headed turtle
  133. *Phrynops nasutus*, common toad-headed turtle
  134. *Phrynops raniceps*, Amazon toad-headed turtle
  135. *Phrynops rufipes*, red-faced toad-headed turtle
  136. *Platemys platycephala melanonota*, western twist-necked turtle
Family Pelomedusidae
  137. *Peltocephalus dumerilianus*, big-headed river turtle
  138. *Podocnemis expansa*, giant river turtle
  139. *Podocnemis erythrocephala*, red-spotted river turtle
  140. *Podocnemis sextuberculata*, Amazon river turtle
  141. *Podocnemis unifilis*, yellow-spotted river turtle

Cryptodirine turtles

Family Kinosternidae
  142. *Kinosternon leucostomum*, white-lipped mud turtle
  143. *Kinosternon scorpioides scorpioides*, Amazon mud turtle
Family Emydidae
  144. *Rhinoclemmys punctularia punctularia*, Amazon wood turtle

Family Testudinidae
    145. *Chelonoidis (Geochelone) carbonaria*, red-footed tortoise
    146. *Chelonoidis (Geochelone) denticulata*, yellow-footed tortoise

Amphisbaenians

Family Amphisbaenidae
    147. *Amphisbaena alba*, giant amphisbaenian
    148. *Amphisbaena fuliginosa*, banded amphisbaenian

Lizards

Family Gekkonidae
    149. *Gonatodes concinnatus*, collared forest gecko
    150. *Gonatodes humeralis*, bridled forest gecko
    151. *Pseudogonatodes guianensis*, Amazon pygmy gecko
    152. *Hemidactylus mabouia*, tropical house gecko
    153. *Thecadactylus rapicaudus*, turnip-tailed gecko
Family Gymnophthalmidae
    154. *Alopoglossus angulata*, large-scaled forest lizard
    155. *Alopoglossus atriventris*, black-bellied forest lizard
    156. *Arthrosaura reticulata reticulata*, reticulated creek lizard
    157. *Bachia vermiformis*, brown worm lizard
    158. *Cercosaura ocellata bassleri*, black-striped forest lizard
    159. *Gymnophthalmus underwoodi* complex, spectacled forest lizard
    160. *Iphisa elegans*, glossy shade lizard
    161. *Leposoma parietale*, common forest lizard
    162. *Micrablepharis maximiliana*, blue-tailed glossy lizard
    163. *Neusticurus ecpleopus*, common streamside lizard
    164. *Prionodactylus argulus*, elegant eyed lizard
    165. *Prionodactylus oshaughnessyi*, white-striped eyed lizard

Iguanian lizards: Families Hoplocercidae, Iguanidae, Polychrotidae, and Tropiduridae

Family Hoplocercidae
    166. *Enyalioides laticeps*, Amazon forest dragon
    167. *Enyalioides palpebralis*, horned forest dragon
Family Iguanidae
    168. *Iguana iguana*, great green iguana
Family Polychrotidae
    169. *Anolis bombiceps*, blue-lipped forest anole
    170. *Anolis fuscoauratus fuscoauratus*, slender anole
    171. *Anolis nitens scypheus*, yellow-tongued forest anole

172. *Anolis nitens tandae,* blue-throated anole
173. *Anolis ortonii,* Amazon bark anole
174. *Anolis punctatus,* Amazon green anole
175. *Anolis trachyderma,* common forest anole
176. *Anolis transversalis,* banded tree anole
177. *Polychrus acutirostris,* sharp-nosed monkey lizard
178. *Polychrus marmoratus,* common monkey lizard

Family Tropiduridae

179. *Stenocercus fimbriatus,* western leaf lizard
180. *Tropidurus (Plica) plica,* collared tree runner
181. *Tropidurus (Plica) umbra ochrocollaris,* olive tree runner
182. *Tropidurus (Uracentron) azureum azureum,* eastern green thornytail
183. *Tropidurus (Uracentron) flaviceps,* Amazon thornytail
184. *Uranoscodon superciliosus,* diving lizard

Family Scincidae

185. *Mabuya nigropunctata,* black-spotted skink

Family Teiidae

186. *Ameiva ameiva,* Amazon whiptail
187. *Cnemidophorus lemniscatus* complex, rainbow whiptail
188. *Crocodilurus amazonicus (lacertinus),* crocodile tegu
189. *Dracaena guianensis,* northern caiman lizard
190. *Kentropyx altamazonica,* cocha whiptail
191. *Kentropyx pelviceps,* forest whiptail
192. *Tupinambis merianae,* black and white tegu
193. *Tupinambis teguixin,* golden tegu

Snakes

Family Aniliidae

194. *Anilius scytale scytale,* coral pipesnake
195. Families Leptotyphlopidae and Typhlopidae, thread snakes and blind snakes

Family Boidae

196. *Boa constrictor constrictor,* red-tailed boa
197. *Boa constrictor imperator,* common boa
198. *Corallus caninus,* emerald tree boa
199. *Corallus hortulanus,* Amazon tree boa
200. *Epicrates cenchria cenchria,* Brazilian rainbow boa
201. *Epicrates cenchria gaigei,* Peruvian rainbow boa
202. *Eunectes murinus murinus,* green anaconda

Family Colubridae
203. *Atractus latifrons*, wedge-tailed earth snake
204. *Atractus* species cf. *collaris*, ring-necked earth snake
205. *Atractus* species, white-naped earth snake
206. *Atractus torquatus*, rusty earth snake
207. *Chironius exoletus*, common whipsnake
208. *Chironius fuscus*, olive whipsnake
209. *Chironius scurrulus*, rusty whipsnake
210. *Clelia clelia clelia*, common mussurana
211. *Dendrophidion dendrophis*, tawny forest racer
212. *Dipsas catesbyi*, ornate snail-eating snake
213. *Dipsas indica indica*, big-headed snail-eating snake
214. *Dipsas variegata variegata*, variegated snail-eating snake
215. *Drepanoides anomalus*, Amazon egg-eating snake
216. *Drymarchon corais corais*, yellow-tailed cribo
217. *Drymoluber dichrous*, common glossy racer
218. *Erythrolamprus aesculapii aesculapii*, common false coral snake
219. *Helicops angulatus*, banded South American water snake
220. *Helicops leopardinus*, spotted water snake
221. *Hydrodynastes gigas*, giant false water cobra
222. *Hydrops martii*, coral mud snake
223. *Imantodes cenchoa*, common blunt-headed tree snake
224. *Imantodes lentiferus*, Amazon blunt-headed tree snake
225. *Leptodeira annulata annulata*, common cat-eyed snake
226. *Leptophis ahaetulla nigromarginatus*, black-skinned parrot snake
227. *Liophis breviceps breviceps*, tricolored swamp snake
228. *Liophis reginae semilineatus*, common swamp snake
229. *Liophis typhlus typhlus*, velvety swamp snake
230. *Mastigodryas boddaertii*, tan racer
231. *Oxybelis aeneus*, brown vine snake
232. *Oxybelis (Xenoxybelis) argenteus*, green-striped vine snake
233. *Oxybelis fulgidus*, green vine snake
234. *Oxyrhopus formosus*, yellow-headed calico snake
235. *Oxyrhopus melanogenys melanogenys*, black-headed calico snake
236. *Oxyrhopus petola digitalis*, banded calico snake
237. *Oxyrhopus trigeminus*, Brazilian calico snake
238. *Philodryas viridissimus viridissimus*, emerald palmsnake
239. *Pseudoboa coronata*, Amazon scarlet snake
240. *Pseudoboa neuwedii*, eastern scarlet snake
241. *Pseudoeryx plicatilis*, dusky mud snake

242. *Pseustes poecilonotus polylepis*, common bird snake
243. *Pseustes sulphureus sulphureus*, giant bird snake
244. *Rhinobothryum lentiginosum*, Amazon ringed snake
245. *Siphlophus cervinus*, common liana snake
246. *Spilotes pullatus pullatus*, tiger rat snake
247. *Taeniophallus brevirostris*, short-nosed leaf-litter snake
248. *Thamnodynastes pallidus*, common mock viper
249. *Tripanurgos (Siphlophus) compressus*, red vine snake
250. *Xenodon rhabdocephalus rhabdocephalus*, common false viper
251. *Xenodon severus*, giant false viper
252. *Xenopholis scalaris*, flat-headed snake

Family Elapidae
253. *Leptomicrurus narduccii melanotus*, northwest black-backed coral snake
254. *Leptomicrurus scutiventris*, pygmy black coral snake
255. *Micrurus albicinctus*, white-banded coral snake
256. *Micrurus averyi*, black-headed coral snake
257. *Micrurus filiformis*, slender coral snake
258. *Micrurus hemprichii ortonii*, orange-ringed coral snake
259. *Micrurus langsdorffi*, Langsdorff's coral snake
260. *Micrurus lemniscatus helleri*, western ribbon coral snake
261. *Micrurus lemniscatus lemniscatus*, eastern ribbon coral snake
262. *Micrurus putumayensis*, sooty coral snake
263. *Micrurus remotus (=psyches)*, remote coral snake
264. *Micrurus spixii obscurus*, western Amazon coral snake
265. *Micrurus spixii spixii*, central Amazon coral snake
266. *Micrurus surinamensis surinamensis*, aquatic coral snake

Family Viperidae
267. *Bothriopsis bilineata bilineata*, eastern striped forest pit viper
268. *Bothriopsis bilineata smaragdina*, western striped forest pit viper
269. *Bothriopsis taeniata taeniata*, speckled forest pit viper
270. *Bothrops atrox*, South American lancehead (fer-de-lance)
271. *Bothrops brazili*, velvety lancehead
272. *Bothrops hyoprora*, Amazonian hog-nosed lancehead
273. *Crotalus durissus dryinas*, Amazonian rattlesnake
274. *Crotalus durissus terrificus*, tropical rattlesnake
275. *Lachesis muta muta*, Amazon bushmaster

Foreword

Do you ever let your mind wander to a place just out of reach? Have you seen the fossils of extinct creatures in museums and wondered what they were really like? Have you been teased by thoughts of what our human ancestors might have seen when they first came to this continent—creatures now gone from memory, represented only by the largest and hardiest in the fossil record? What of the smaller ones that left no fossils? What wonderful fauna escaped our grasp by mere moments on the grand scale of time? How ironic that creatures that survived and evolved over millions of years should have ceased to exist mere moments before we became aware of them.

They are gone, but others remain. Even today there are still great tracts of primeval forest, as yet hardly changed by human hands but in danger of slipping from our grasp in another human generation or two. Here life teems in myriad varieties, millions of niches filled with specialized life forms, known and unknown, awaiting our curious glance. How many of these creatures will pass without notice into extinction? Who will document their existence before they are gone? Let future generations not wonder why we did not take advantage of our opportunity to explore and learn what treasures lived among us.

The authors of this book, Dick and Patti Bartlett, have taken advantage of their opportunities. For many years, Dick and Patti, as a team, have sought to know the creatures who share the planet with us and to publish their findings in informative books, articles, and documentary photos. Their perseverance has given us some of the most complete field guides to North American herpetofauna ever published. They have now turned their sights on the strange and little-known reptiles and amphibians of the Amazon Basin, laying the groundwork for future explorers to add to our knowledge of this fragile environment.

Dick and Patti know the value of ecotourism. Trained scientists are in limited supply and cannot hope to explore all the possible habitats in this vast region. Therefore, disciplined and informed amateur observers are of great value to the scientific world. Many eyes are better than a few, and new creatures are constantly being brought to light by determined amateur observers. It is often said that we cannot preserve what we do not know exists, and this applies to both obscure flora and fauna and to entire ecosystems. As tourists gain insight into the vast Amazon Basin, its beauty and treasures become personal, and worth preserving. Awareness of these environments is essential if we are to bear witness to their value to humankind. Armed with this guide, the keen observer will better understand the diversity of this wonderful ecosystem and will be able to speak on its behalf to the world that will decide its future.

Dennis Cathcart
Tropiflora Nursery, Inc.

Acknowledgments

We are indebted to Albert Slugocki, Margaret Slugocki, and Devon Graham, of Margarita Tours/Project Amazonas, for their efforts to show us the diversity of the Amazon and its wildlife. Our Peruvian forest guides, Cesar Peña, Segundo Rios, Segundo Mesia, and Asuncion "Ashuco" Perez, proved most adept at bringing us to the forest and the forest to us. Bill Lamar and longtime friend Rob MacInnes of Glades Herp, Inc., were ideal and enthusiastic tour leaders on my (RDB) first ecotour. Guillermo Guerra provided many hours of companionship and the vehicles that facilitated road hunting along the Iquitos–Nauta highway.

In their dual roles as natural history photographers and tropical researchers Jim Castner, Harry W. Greene of Cornell University, Brice Noonan of the University of Texas at Arlington, Janalee P. Caldwell of the Sam Noble Oklahoma Museum of Natural History, R. Wayne Van Devender of Appalachian State University, and Leo Nico graciously provided photographs and/or comments that added much to the accuracy of our coverage. Likewise, A. J. Calisi; Dave Schleser and Dave Roberts of Nature's Images; Carl Franklin, Ruston Hartgeden, and Richard Reams of the Dallas Zoo; Bill Love of Blue Chameleon Ventures; Bruce Morgan; Dennis Sheridan; Bob Thomas of Loyola University; and Laurie J. Vitt of the Sam Noble Oklahoma Museum of Natural History graciously supplied us with information, photographs, or both to round out our coverage. John D. Lynch of the Universidad Nacional de Colombia helped with the identification of the frogs of the genus *Eleutherodactylus*. To all: thank you!

Glenn Novotny of Seaside Reptiles; Marcus Breece; Bill Samples and Cliff Gibbens of CB Distributors; Derek Rader, Chris Miller, Larry Marshall, and Mark Pulawski allowed us to photograph poison frogs in their keeping; our appreciation is extended to all.

Thanks are due Lynn Kirkland, former curator of reptiles at the St. Augustine Alligator Farm, who allowed us off-display access to upgrade our photos of the black caiman. Thanks, too, to Tom Davis for providing photo opportunities.

The talents of Dale Johnson, illustrator and computer wizard, can be seen in the several line drawings and computer renderings.

We are additionally indebted to friends such as Brad Smith, Mike Manfredi, Lisa Manfredi, Rick Buss, Pauline Ho, Scott Cushnir, Sandy Oldershaw, Tom Tyning, and Mark Salvato. The camaraderie they and others who have accompanied us to the Peruvian rainforests provided added greatly to our enjoyment.

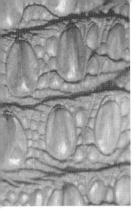

Introduction

Commercial ecotours offer opportunities to view rainforest habitats from Belém, Brazil, to La Paz, Bolivia, and from Quito, Ecuador, to Iquitos, Peru. You can travel in austerity or in comfortable multideck boats. Since our objective is to photograph the plants and animals of the areas we visit, we prefer (and promote) tours that interact directly with the rainforest. We ply remote rivers on smaller boats, visit river edge villages, bunk in tents pitched on sleeping platforms, and spend hours by both day and night walking seldom trodden trails.

Once considered among the most inaccessible regions on earth, today the Amazon Basin is an easily reached and popular ecotour destination. Many tours focus broadly on wildlife or plants; others offer more specialized excursions. Providers of the latter may specifically seek orchids, bromeliads, birds, reptiles and amphibians (herps), insects, fish, or mammals. Since absolute exclusivity is impossible, most ecotourists willing to leave the comfort of their boat have a broad-spectrum experience. If at night you walk trails looking for owls you will see frogs, and while seeking epiphytic plants on sun-dappled limbs you are likely to encounter lizards or snakes. For many observers, the whole experience is far more rewarding than any single part. Even if you choose not to leave your boat, your guide may be able to show you not only flowering plants and potoos perched on river edge snags, but treefrogs, tree boas, and caiman as well. Biodiversity is the keyword, and to observe and enjoy is your goal.

Some 40 years ago when I (RDB) first visited the Amazon Basin to search out reptiles, amphibians, and fish—long before the word "ecotour" had been coined—the area *was* remote. Vast expanses of pristine rainforest surrounded Leticia (Colombia), Manaus (Brazil), and Iquitos (Peru). The airports were tiny, open-air affairs served sporadically by propeller-driven airplanes of questionable vintage and even more questionable mechanical reliability. Although I found the entire region entrancing, my interest centered on Amazonian Peru. Eventually, due to everyday pressures, my trips to the Neotropics occurred less and less often, and finally ceased.

A hiatus of nearly 20 years had occurred when in 1995 I learned about a reptile and amphibian photography trip to the Iquitos region. Since the study of reptiles and amphibians had long been my forte, I quickly signed up.

It was a wonderful reintroduction to the region. Iquitos had become the epicenter for truly interactive ("get down and dirty") ecotours. I found that although jets had replaced the prop planes of old, the airport was still tiny, and if you landed in the rain you got soaked walking from ramp to terminal (have your camera well protected!). Iquitos had grown from a sleepy little Amazonian town to a bustling city with a population of about 500,000. Dwellings now sat where once towering rainforest trees had reigned supreme, and somehow, the Amazon River seemed just a little smaller. But despite these changes I felt immediately at ease, and I liked the experience so well that I decided to visit the area again in 1996, this time with Patti.

Since then, Patti and I have led our own herp photography tours to the Iquitos area of Peru. We have also visited Colombia's Putumayo region; been up-Amazon and down-Amazon; visited remote villages on the Rios Napo, Apayacu, and other exotic-sounding rivers; and seen countless wonderful beasts. But Iquitos is our staging ground, and each time we journey there we find a few herp species new to us.

Although some pessimists say that a group of ecotourists on a weeklong trip might, with luck, find 50 species of reptiles and amphibians, we have never failed to see less than 60, and when we travel for a fortnight we often nearly double that number. The many mammals, birds, and insects we see as well are an added bonus. Hundreds of species of butterflies, moths, grasshoppers, and beetles flit overhead, dot the trail margins, land on our screened sleeping enclosures, and drink from mud puddles at our feet.

We travel by boat up and down the Amazon and its tributaries, visit oxbow lakes, and stay at rainforest lodges. We hike far into the rainforest on intervillage trails by both day and night, with guides and without. In this flat land, walking is usually easy, especially in primary and old secondary forests, where understory plant growth is thwarted by the canopy of boughs high overhead.

On every journey into the jungle we find and photograph reptiles, amphibians, and insects. Most of the species we see are not "pet trade" creatures, and we have been hard-pressed to identify some. Our fellow travelers often know less than we do. These identification problems led to the idea behind this guide—a simple pictorial directory, if you will—to more than 250 of the reptiles and amphibians of the region. This guide is not intended to be a complete chronicle of the herpetofauna of the Amazon Basin. It is intended to help ecotourists identify some of the more frequently seen species as well as a handful that are somewhat less common.

Many ecotour companies regularly or occasionally mount reptile-watching trips or have staff herpetologists available. Besides the more normal tour packages of trail walks and boat trips, some companies offer access to canopy walkways or conduct rainforest workshops. Many advertise in the classified sections of reptile hobbyist magazines or have web sites. Tour companies that seriously commit to bringing their clients into contact with wildlife employ knowledgeable tour leaders; many are affiliated with zoos, museums, or universities and have a passion for Amazonian herpetofauna. With leaders such as these you can uncover and share the secrets of the Amazonian forests.

When planning your trip, research your tour company to ensure that its programs are suited to your interests and abilities. Then go and enjoy yourself. A visit to the Amazon Basin is truly an experience of a lifetime. Patti and I hope to see you there.

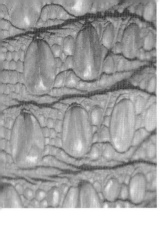

1

Before You Go

When to Go

Although much of the Amazonian herpetofauna is active year-round, many species are more active at certain times of the year than at others due to rainfall and temperature differences (see table 1). Thus, when you travel to the Amazon Basin—be it Bolivia, Peru, Ecuador, Colombia, Brazil, or the Guianas—the dates you select should depend largely on what you hope to see.

For example, many of the frogs are most easily seen when they gather in breeding congresses in newly formed pools and freshened *cochas* (oxbows) at the advent of the rainy season. Similarly, the snakes that eat frogs and their eggs are more apt to be visible during the periods when frogs are most actively breeding.

Many terrestrial species may be more concentrated and more easily found when rising waters have driven them to isolated patches of elevated dry forest (terra firma). Conversely, aquatic snakes, lizards, and turtles are more concentrated during the dry season, when water levels are low and water holes and rivers are reduced.

If you wish to actively search for Amazonian herps (reptiles and amphibians), select a tour company that can offer expertise in such activities. Make your tour company, and especially your individual tour leaders, aware of what you want to see, and seek their advice.

Table 1. Temperatures and rainfall by month

	Iquitos, Peru			Belém, Brazil		
	Rainfall (inches/cm)	Maximum Temperature °F/C	Minimum Temperature °F/C	Rainfall (inches/cm)	Maximum Temperature °F/C	Minimum Temperature °F/C
Jan.	14.6/37.2	80/27	70/21	—	89/31	72/22
Feb.	9.5/24.3	82/28	68/20	—	88/30	72/22
Mar.	24.3/61.9	84/29	70/21	—	88/30	72/22
Apr.	13.3/34.0	81/27.5	68/20	—	89/31	72/22
May	12/30.6	80/27	70/21	—	89/31	72/22
June	9.9/25	80/27	70/21	10.5/26.7	90/32	72/22
July	14.4/36.7	82/28	70/21	11.4/29.1	90/32	72/22
Aug.	8.7/22	79/26.5	68/20	9.9/25.2	90/32	72/22
Sept.	9.9/25.2	82/28	68/20	10.5/26.7	90/32	72/22
Oct.	16.6/42.2	82/28	68/20	8.7/22.2	90/32	72/22
Nov.	20.9/53	81/27.5	70/21	6.3/21.3	90/32	70/21
Dec.	14.4/36.7	82/28	70/21	16.1/41.1	90/32	72/22

What to Take

Deciding what to take on a trip to the Amazon may seem like packing for a trip to Mars. You don't want to neglect any eventuality, and pretty soon your "pack this" stack looks like the Washington Monument. But wait; the basic list is smaller than you might think.

Personal Items

Passport: A passport is essential. Your main post office has passport applications. Expect the process to take four weeks, but allow six. Find out whether a visa is necessary, and allow sufficient time to apply for and receive it if you need one. Some countries have web sites where visitors can download a visa application.

Clothing: The Amazon Basin can be hot, but you need to balance the heat factor against the protection factor. You can go the minimalist route and tour in shorts, athletic shoes, and a tee shirt. You will be cooler, but you probably won't be comfortable in the field because of the insects. Your tour operators may tell you that the biting insects (BSD's, for bloodsucking diptera) are no worse than anywhere in the United States, but when the mosquitoes swarm, you will find small comfort in that piece of information. Like the New Yorker who finds himself more badly bitten by Florida mosquitoes than a native Floridian, newcomers to the Amazon may find that they are the preferred hosts. Insect repellent helps, but the repellent can be instantaneously fatal to amphibians and uncomfortable for reptiles. *Never* handle reptiles or amphibians with repellent on your hands!

You may be hot, but you may also be more comfortable wearing a hat (one with a soft, floppy brim will help keep mosquitoes from buzzing closely around your ears), lightweight long pants, and a three-quarters-sleeved or long-sleeved shirt. Blue jeans are slow to dry once wet, although many people choose to wear them.

Most tour companies provide laundry service, but if you take laundry soap (dishwashing liquid works fine), a sink stopper, and a twisted elastic clothesline, you will be able to wash and attempt to dry soiled clothing almost anywhere.

Wearing a waist or fanny pack makes it possible for you to keep your cash, passport, field notebook, and pen handy and yet safe, whether you are in the jungle or in a town.

Socks: Take plenty of socks—the thick kind. They not only protect you from the rubbing of wet shoes but will also help prevent ant bites if you blunder into an ant procession. Ants (and mosquitoes, for that matter) can easily bite through thin socks.

Shoes: Many people wear knee-high rubber boots. These not only keep your feet dry but also provide protection against insect bites (ants can't crawl up the rubber). If you don't like boots, footwear can be either well-broken-in hiking boots or athletic shoes. Taking a spare pair or two will allow drying between hikes.

Sunscreen: Especially if you are taking any medication that increases sun sensitivity, sunscreen is important. After applying it, wash your hands carefully with soap and water before you touch any plants or animals.

Medications: Call your doctor or local health department to find out what inoculations and prophylactic medications are required or recommended for your destination. Your health care professional may suggest booster shots, an antimalarial regime, or an antibiotic to avoid gastrointestinal problems; be aware that some antibiotics will sensitize you to the sun.

A few basic medications and first-aid supplies can make a world of difference to you or a companion. If you are traveling in a group, you can almost count on someone else needing a simple treatment for a cut or scrape. Take a supply of aspirin or a Tylenol-type painkiller, anti-diarrhea pills, antibiotic powder that can be sprinkled over a cut or abrasion, adhesive bandages, gauze pads and adhesive tape, and moleskin for blisters.

Be certain to take your own prescription medications, and carry enough for the entire trip plus a few days.

Changing money: Although your bank can supply you with Peruvian currency, money exchange is also easily accomplished in Peru or in the airport before you leave your country. It's helpful to have at least some local currency in hand when you arrive to pay taxi fares and so forth. It is important that the cash you intend to change into Peruvian currency in Peru be nontorn, unmarked, and in otherwise excellent condition.

Field Equipment

Flashlights: Take two flashlights in case you accidentally drop one over the side of a canoe (it has happened to us). Keep a spare bulb for each at hand, perhaps in your waist pack. If your bulb blows on the trail at night, you can't go back to your tent or cabin to replace it.

Batteries: Flashlight batteries are not easy to find in Peru. Although they are heavy, we suggest that you take a fresh set of flashlight batteries for each night you intend to be in the field and plenty to keep any appliances (such as cameras and flash units) activated. Before packing, remove one battery from your flashlight or reverse its direction so your flashlight can't accidentally get turned on in your suitcase.

Camera: Film buffs will find that a single-lens reflex camera with changeable lenses and a bracket-held flash unit is the best bet for macrophotography. Field photography (larger plants and habitats) will not require the flash (although an "in-camera" flash may be very handy). A 28–49-mm wide-angle lens is an excellent choice for overviews of the forest, and a 100–105-mm macro lens will allow close-ups of insects, reptiles, amphibians, and small plants. Photographing mammals or birds will require a telephoto lens and, usually, a tripod. Needless to say, ask permission before you photograph individuals. If you prefer digital photography, take enough memory chips and batteries for your camera.

Film: Take plenty! We use an ISO-50 film for macrophotography and ISO-200 to ISO-400 for normal rainforest photography.

Trade items: T-shirts and baseball caps are popular trade items. Harmonicas, crayons, and other school supplies are also of value to the villagers. The children love yo-yos. You can trade for native handicrafts such as shell and nut necklaces, carved figures, or paintings, but steer clear of wild animal products. Cash, in local currency, almost always works.

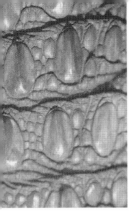

2

How to Use This Guide

In the following pages you will find descriptions and pictures of more than 250 representative species of snakes, lizards, "worm lizards" (we will refer to these properly as amphisbaenians), turtles, crocodilians, tailless amphibians (frogs, toads, and treefrogs), salamanders, and caecilians found in the Amazon Basin. Some are common, some are uncommon, and some are considered rare. We include information on most of the commonly seen species in an easy-to-use format. Rather than a complicated key, we offer photographs and simple comments to help you identify these creatures.

We have opted to list and discuss the Amazon Basin herpetofauna in the traditional manner, divided by classes (amphibians and reptiles), families, genera, species, and subspecies. To avoid confusion we use the current scientific name for each species and race as well as offering a common name. In the many cases where no common name exists, we offer a descriptive one. Changes in *both* types of name may occur in the future.

While many species are quite distinctive in appearance, others can be confusingly alike. Many have two or more color phases, and many of the amphibians are capable of undergoing chameleon-like changes in color or pattern. Some species are so variable that more than one picture is necessary.

All of the species and subspecies we discuss are numbered and listed in the species list that begins this book. The numbers assigned there coincide with the numbers used in both the text and the photographs. If you know or have a good idea of the identity of the species you are researching, begin with the species list. If you are unsure of the identity, begin your research at the family overviews in the text.

Virtually everyone knows that most snakes lack legs (the boas and anacondas retain vestiges of rear external legs in the form of a movable spur on each side of the anus), but few realize that there are other legless reptiles and amphibians as well. Some lizards have legs so short that they are not easily visible; amphisbaenians have no external legs and are annulated like earthworms. Caecilians, which come in both aquatic and terrestrial forms, also lack legs. The aquatic caecilians have smooth, shiny, scaleless skin; the terrestrial forms have moist, shiny, annulated bodies. There are even attenuate fish that look superficially like amphibians. Among these are electric eels, lungfish, and synbranchid eels (see photos F1, F2, and F3). Don't give up on an attempted identification before checking the photos of these fish *and* of other short-legged lizards such as the gymnophthalmids. Many short-legged lizards are mistaken for snakes because they rely on side-to-side, snakelike undulations to move.

Do not be disappointed if you have trouble identifying some of the frogs. Their overlapping and variable characteristics make the frogs of the genus *Eleutherodactylus* (family Leptodactylidae) notoriously difficult to identify. In many cases it may be possible only to identify them to genus and to eliminate a few of the more divergent species. Even the experts are confused by the eleutherodactylines.

Most treefrogs climb. In fact, some are canopy dwellers that seldom descend to where they can be seen. But other anurans (tailless amphibians), such as the rain frogs (family Leptodactylidae) and the poison-dart frogs (family Dendrobatidae), are also proficient climbers. Even toads (family Bufonidae) may climb to a height of several feet. Check the pictures of all when attempting to identify that frog or toad found sitting on an elevated flat leaf or on a limb.

Sometimes a lizard can act like a crocodilian. Read the accounts of the caiman lizard, the crocodile tegu, and the true tegus if you have found a crocodilian that does not look quite as it should.

In sum, when searching for Neotropical herpetofauna, look high, look low, look past the obvious, and always, *always,* look with caution.

Remember that this guide merely *represents* the herpetofauna known to exist in the region. Shown here are the species you are most likely to encounter—and which we have encountered; but the species you find may not be included in these pages. In that case, seek the expertise of your tour leader.

We recommend several publications to all ecotourists interested in the herpetofauna of the Amazon Basin, all written by researchers who have spent far more time in the region than we ever shall.

Martha L. Crump provides an academician's perspective of a Neotropical herpetofauna in *Quantitative Analysis of the Ecological Distribution of a Tropical Herpetofauna*. This monograph, published in 1971 by the University of Kansas's Museum of Natural History, includes information on the rainforest distributions of the reptiles and amphibians indigenous to the Guama Ecological Research Area near Belém, Brazil.

James R. Dixon and Pekka Soini have published two works of value to Amazon tourists. *The Reptiles of the Upper Amazon Basin, Iquitos Region, Peru. I. Lizards and Amphisbaenians* appeared in 1975. Its companion volume, *The Reptiles of the Upper Amazon Basin, Iquitos Region, Peru. II. Crocodilians, Turtles and Snakes* became available in 1977; both were published by the Milwaukee Public Museum. Like many academic papers published at that time, neither provides photos of the reptiles.

In 1978, William E. Duellman's *The Biology of an Equatorial Herpetofauna in Amazonian Ecuador* was published and quickly became noted for its coverage. Although Duellman's work centered in the vicinity of Santa Cecilia in Amazonian Ecuador, the ranges of many of the amphibians and reptiles he studied extend southward to (or beyond) Peruvian Amazonia. Although this is an academic work, it includes black-and-white photos of many of the species discussed. In 1989, another useful book, *The Venomous Reptiles of Latin America*, by Jonathan A. Campbell and William W. Lamar, became available.

The first popular book about the herpetofauna of Amazonian Peru appeared in 1994. Entitled simply *Guide to the Frogs of the Iquitos Region, Amazonian Peru*, it includes text and color photos of the frogs of Peruvian Amazonia. In it, authors Lily O. Rodriguez and William E. Duellman provide the first truly workable tool for nonacademic ecotourists.

And finally, *Guide des Serpents et Amphisbenes de Guyane* was published in 1998. Although it is in French, the author, Fausto Starace, provides English abstracts and photographs for the snakes and amphisbaenids of French Guiana. Many of these species occur elsewhere in the Amazon Basin.

A Note about Color

Reptiles and amphibians—especially the latter—vary in color both as species and individually. Significant day–night color changes occur routinely. For example, the Peruvian rainbow boa, *Epicrates cenchria gaigei,* usually dark and orangish by day, may take on a silvery sheen by night. The spotted treefrog, *Hyla punctata,* usually a bright green by day, may be distinctly red by night. When a description almost fits, consider the possibility of a day–night color change. There is always the possibility of encountering aberrantly colored individuals as well, of course.

A Note about Nomenclature

If you are new to the world of scientific nomenclature, a brief explanation may put you at ease. Scientific names are of Latin or Greek derivation. They can be binomial (two names) or trinomial (three names). The matamata, for example, bears the binomial name *Chelus fimbriatus* (*kee*-lus fim-bree-*ah*-tus). The binomial indicates that this turtle has not (in the eyes of taxonomists) subspeciated. The spotted treefrog, *Hyla punctata punctata* (*high*-la punk-*ta*-ta punk-*ta*-ta), bears a trinomial, indicating that in the eyes of systematists this small frog *has* subspeciated. The redundant specific and subspecific names tell us that *punctata* is the nominate race (i.e., the first subspecies described).

Looking at the Rainforest

Much of Amazonia is easily traversed. The rivers are your highways, and most of the land is flat or has a gently rolling topography. Low hills rise in some places, but these are easily climbed. Ravines along the intermittent streams are more of a challenge; most are spanned by slippery, narrow fallen trees in varying degrees of decomposition.

Habitats

When rainforests are discussed, the terms "secondary," "old secondary," and "primary" are often used. Respectively, these terms refer to young second-growth areas, old second growth, and the original uncut (often closed or nearly closed canopy) forest. The designation "terra firma" equates to high ground—land not subject to seasonal flooding. "*Varzea*" is seasonally flooded lowland or river edge forest. The term "*igapo*" may be used for stagnant swamplands, while "*aguajal*" designates more typical swampy areas. "*Capoeira*" merely means secondary growth.

Lightning strikes create natural burns that may be more extensive than openings created by humans. Tree falls in primary forests allow the sun to penetrate and generate rampant new growth and renewed (but temporary) opportunities for basking reptiles. Homesteading humans scar the rainforest with slash-and-burn techniques that are unsightly but quickly revert to forest when abandoned. Logging and clearing land for fossil fuel exploration create more serious and longer-lasting damage, but except where paved or polluted such areas may offer habitats for species that prefer disturbed areas. Village edges and river edge thickets can abound with wildlife.

Historically, much of Amazonas (including the Iquitos region, our principal area of research) lacked open savannas, but agriculture and homesteading have changed that. There are extensive farms throughout the area as well as abandoned plots, the latter in the process of reverting from bananas and manioc to razor grass and catbriers and then to new secondary forests. The progression begins with *Cecropia, Cassia, Sterculia*, and other fast-growing trees. If undisturbed, the taller trees will begin to interlace their upper branches and form a partially closed canopy. Palms and slower-growing hardwoods will then reappear, and the grasses will be replaced by such shade-loving plants as *Heliconia,* gingers, and various lianas.

In very old secondary forests, typical rainforest epiphytes such as bromeliads, orchids, aroids, and ferns recolonize both arboreal and terrestrial situations. The point at which secondary forest again becomes primary forest is arbitrary and open to interpretation—but at some point, if its progression remains unimpeded, the forest will regain its original species composition.

Primary forests are characterized by an enormous number of plant species, including a vast array of epiphytes and lianas colonizing a (usually) multitiered canopy. The trees are immense; subcanopy branching is uncommon, but stilting and buttressing are common. Very little light reaches the forest floor, and the herbaceous understory is largely nonexistent or restricted to the less densely shaded areas. A few typical shade-tolerant understory plant species of the primary forest are aroids, ferns, prayer plants, and palms. A rather thick cover of leaf litter is usually present.

During the rainy season, ephemeral ponds are present in forest floor depressions, ebbing between rains but rising, flowing, and interconnecting during periods of high water. These may become deep enough to provide aquatic highways for dugouts or small boats.

In Peruvian Amazonia, where rainfall averages about 120 inches a year, seasonally flooded lowlands are the norm. In normal years, "dry season" is merely a comparative term. But the reduced rainfall can mean that river levels may drop by 10 or more feet in a matter of days.

The lowlands may be submerged for nine or more months of each year, during which time floating carpets of water hyacinths, water lettuce, and other such water-dependent plant species develop. Emergent grasses and sedges abound in these areas, but except for some shrubs, woody plants are usually rather sparse.

The Neotropical rainforests are home to a vast number of species of animals and plants. Each species occupies its own niche, but each is interdependent on many other species as well, in either a literal or a metaphorical sense. Species have evolved diverse armaments, camouflages, and niche specificity to protect themselves from predators and help them compete with others seeking the same resources. Plants have evolved spines, thorns, poisons, and other passive deterrents. So, too, have the animals. The rainforests house caterpillars that mimic snakes, frogs that mimic lichens, snakes that mimic vines, lizards that mimic leaves, and turtles that mimic pond detritus.

Ecological niches are subdivided into more specific niches, and subdivided again. The more niches there are, the more types of life forms can exist. The more specific the ecological niche inhabited—for instance, a snake that eats frog eggs that are laid on low leaves—the less the competition.

When to Look

Different animals have different seasons of activity, and different periods of activity within those seasons. This both reduces competition and otherwise enhances survival. For example, a nocturnal activity pattern reduces (but does not eliminate) the likelihood of visually oriented predation and negates the desiccating effects of the heat of the day. Visually oriented predators and heliothermic (sun-dependent) species are diurnal—that is, active during the hours of daylight. To see that for yourself, walk a trail by day and then again by night. The creatures you encounter on the two walks will be completely different. Depending on what you are looking for, your time may be better spent at night. But don't avoid walking at night because the animals you are looking for are diurnal; you might find them as they sleep.

A nighttime walk reveals life forms completely unfamiliar to most of us. The insects alone may distract you from seeing anything else. You can see walking sticks 12 inches long and as big around as your thumb, yellow and lavender grasshoppers 6 inches long, and equally big tree crickets that are so thorny that you just know they can't be comfortably handled. Sleeping butterflies hang on the underside of leaves, and tailless whip scorpions ghost up and down trees.

When you get past the insect life you will probably find reptile and amphibian life abundant. Anoles nap stretched out atop leaf stems. Snail- and lizard-eating snakes prowl the shrubs in search of food. And even on dry nights, climbing salamanders and treefrogs may be common.

Where to Look

Reptiles and amphibians are very much where you find them—or where they find you. You can look long and hard in what may seem ideal habitat for a specific species and fail, only to stumble across that animal when you least expect it and at a most inopportune time. We have had insects, tree-frogs, snakes, and anoles literally fall into our laps as our boat brushed underneath limbs overhanging the rivers.

But whether you find many or few reptiles and amphibians, some places are apt to be more herpetologically productive than others. Edges—forest edges, trail edges, clearing edges, water edges, and even the grasses at the edges of buildings—are favored resting and basking areas for many reptiles and amphibians.

As you walk down a trail, look at the ground on both sides. Examine the tops of leaves and shrubs; look where the leaf joins the stem and at the boles of trees. If a fallen tree is beside or across the trail, look at the far side before you step over or place your hand atop or around it.

If you find a section of log small enough to turn, turn it temporarily to see what is underneath. Although you are likely to find only insects, you may be favored by the presence of a gecko, skink, toad, or snake. Always remember that pit vipers like to rest against logs and are amazingly well camouflaged. Be very careful. And always replace the log as you found it.

Look on the walls of your lodge and on village dwellings for anoles (by day) and geckos (by day or night). Tarantulas and snakes—sometimes sizable ones—find seclusion along the ridgepoles, in roof thatch, and in the toes of shoes. If the toilet tank is uncovered, check for frogs. Be thorough. Look twice—and remove nothing, whether living or of historic value! And always request permission before you begin looking around village dwellings, of course.

Use your ears when you are looking for animals. Many frogs and insects vocalize or stridulate during courtship or territoriality displays. Females are often drawn to the sounds. The more females he draws, the greater the male's chance of being successful at mating.

Not all reptile voices belong to animals you want to track indiscriminately. Male crocodilians bellow at dusk to warn other males away. Baby crocodilians offer guttural *awk*s as they begin to emerge from their eggs. The sound not only tells all the other babies in the nest that the hatching has begun, but also summons the attending mother. The mother often not only guards the nest from potential predators (human or otherwise) but also physically helps the babies hatch. She digs up the nest and gently mouths the eggs to speed hatching. She may then mouth-carry her young to water and may even remain with them as a combination guard and mobile sun deck. The parental care aspect of female crocodilians is fascinating, but a word of warning is in order. If you come across a crocodilian's nest—often a tidy heap of decaying vegetation about 2 feet high and 4 feet across, near water—and you hear nasal croaking, leave immediately. Mother may be nearby and is very likely to be intolerant of intruders.

At this point, another word of caution seems appropriate. Unless you are thoroughly familiar with the herpetofauna of the area, just look; don't pick up any animal. Superficial familiarity can be dangerous. The coral snakes, for example, are not always patterned like the species you may know from North America. And, just as in the United States, many species of harmless snakes in the Amazon Basin are every bit as gaudily colored as the brightest North American coral snake. Although rattlesnakes occur only in the eastern extremes of the Amazon Basin, some species of both harmless snakes and venomous snakes vibrate the tail to produce a whirring sound. Don't assume you have found a rattlesnake simply on the basis of a buzzing tail.

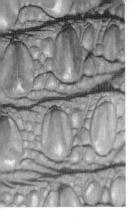

3

Overview

Amphibians and Reptiles

Amphibians and reptiles are two distinct classes of vertebrates. The amphibians are the more primitive of the two, having first appeared during the late Devonian period, some 360 million years ago. The earliest reptiles seem to have arisen from amphibians during the Upper Carboniferous period, some 45 million years later.

Both groups have been remarkably successful. There are some 11,000 species of amphibians and reptiles alive today, and more than 500 of these are found in the Amazon Basin. We hasten to add, however, that some are known only from a single specimen and others are still considered so rare that each sighting is cause for herpetological jubilation. Additional species are being described almost weekly. The anuran species—the frogs (this category includes the toads and treefrogs, of course)—are both the most numerous and the most diverse in appearance of the reptiles and amphibians in the Amazon Basin; lizards are a close second.

The Amphibians

What is an amphibian? Amphibian species vary from one another in so many respects that no description is simple. Amphibians are creatures of moist, but not necessarily wet, habitats. Most, but certainly not all, have a terrestrial adult stage and an aquatic larval stage. Amphibians lack true claws and external scales. Some have secretion-producing skin glands that help in providing and conserving moisture. The skin secretions of some species are very toxic. The eggs, contained in a gelatinous capsule, lack a shell. The males of most (and the females of some) frogs (anurans) have a true voice; it is often easier to identify a frog by its sound than by looking at it.

Some Amazonian amphibians are tiny, and none is truly large. When measured from snout to vent, the vast majority of the species are 6 inches (15 cm) or less in size.

There are three groups of amphibians: the caecilians, the salamanders, and the frogs. Although all three share certain characteristics, they are very different in external appearance. Representatives of all three groups occur in the Amazon Basin.

The Reptiles

Reptiles are usually clad in scales (sometimes in a leathery skin). The skin is dry (unless the specimen has been swimming or caught in the rain). If legs are present, the feet bear claws. If oviparous, the eggs are shelled, but some snakes and lizards bear live young.

Crocodilians vocalize loudly in croaks and grunts. Many geckos produce easily audible clicks, and anoles often squeak when stressed. Some snakes, some lizards, and turtles hiss when disturbed.

Reptiles of some type utilize virtually all habitats except the open sky. There are arboreal forms, aquatic forms, terrestrial types, and burrowers. Many species are at home in more than one habitat.

In size, reptiles range from tiny geckos, fully adult at an overall length of 2 inches (5 cm), to the green anaconda, which may exceed 25 feet (7.6 m) when adult. At 6 feet (1.8 m), the green iguana is the largest lizard. The black caiman regularly attains 12 feet (3.6 m) in total length. While most turtles seldom exceed 10 inches in shell length, a few, most notably the genus *Podocnemis*, hover near the 24-inch (70-cm) mark in carapace length.

Of the four major reptile groups—the turtles; the snakes, lizards, and worm lizards; the crocodilians; and the tuataras—all but the latter are represented in the Amazon Basin.

Three Amazonian Fish That Don't Look Like Fish; or, the Caecilian Look-alikes

"The animal I found looks like an aquatic caecilian, but I can't find it in this guide!"

Although we have not provided species accounts for the South American lungfish, the electric eel (and relatives), or the synbranchid eel, we have included a picture of each. Because of their attenuate morphology, these fish may initially be mistaken for caecilians.

A large adult lungfish, *Lepidosiren paradoxa,* may near 45 inches (114 cm) in length. It has two pairs of slender, leglike fins, one just behind the gill openings and the other near the vent. When moving along the bottom of a pond or through floating vegetation, the lungfish moves its fins like legs. This fish may be an unpatterned slaty black, or it may be liberally spangled with tiny light flecks. Lungfish have small but functional eyes. They are harmless (see photo F1).

The electric eel, *Electrophorus electricus,* has true pectoral fins (posterior to the gill opening) and a long ventral fin that is continually undulated when the fish is in motion. The belly, which is far anterior, tends to be a rich orange; otherwise the fish is black(ish). Baby electric eels are often seen in isolated rainforest pools. Adults are immense, nearing 6 feet (180 cm) in length. This is a potentially dangerous species. Although they use their ability to shock primarily to stun food, it is a very effective defense as well. Should you decide you want a closer look at one, do not try to catch even a baby with a metal-handled or wet-handled net (see photo F2).

The synbranchid eel, *Synbranchus marmoratus,* is unicolored olive when small. As an adult it bears a variable pattern of black flecks against a russet to brown ground color. The fins are reduced to rudimentary dorsal, ventral, and caudal fringes. Paired fins are lacking. There is only a single medial-ventral gill opening. This fish can and will bite if carelessly restrained. Adults may near 45 inches (114 cm in length) (see photo F3).

CLASS AMPHIBIA

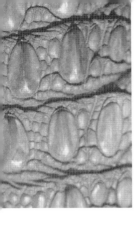

4

Caecilians

Two of the six caecilian families occur in our region of the Amazon: the terrestrial forms in the family Caeciliidae and the aquatic species in the family Typhlonectidae.

All caecilians are attenuate amphibians that lack legs, functional eyes, and a tail. The cloaca of the male is modified to enhance sexual contact. Caecilians have scalelike structures embedded beneath the epidermis. All have a pair of protrusible (although sometimes barely so) "tentacles" near the eye. The body may be ringed (annulated), imparting the appearance of an earthworm. Fertilization is internal.

Terrestrial caecilians are occasionally found beneath rotting logs or beneath leaf litter along pool edges; some are surface active during heavy rains. Aquatic caecilians can sometimes be found by turning mats of hyacinths, water lettuce, or other plants left behind on wet, muddy banks by seasonal lowering of water levels.

Terrestrial Caecilians: Family Caeciliidae

All members of this family are accomplished burrowers in terrestrial locales. In the Amazon Basin, the members of the genera *Caecilia* and *Siphonops* are of comparatively heavy girth; those of the genus *Oscaecilia* are very slender and attenuate. Foods include termites, earthworms, and other burrowing invertebrates. No caecilians are brightly colored, but on some the body rings are highlighted with a lighter color. The teeth—two rows in the upper jaw and one in the lower jaw—are recurved and sharp.

Genus *Oscaecilia;* Slender Caecilians

Very little is known about the members of this small tropical American genus. The species vary from moderately to excessively slender, have the eyes covered by bone, and are probably able to determine only light intensities rather than images. They seem to remain persistently beneath ground cover, and hence are seldom seen. The tentacle aperture is beneath the nostril. The head is no wider than the neck but is usually lighter in color than the body.

I. Bassler's Slender Caecilian

Oscaecilia bassleri

Size: Adults may near 3 feet (91 cm) in length.
Identifying features: A very slender, elongate, annulated, gray body typifies this remarkable amphibian. Because of its excessive slenderness, it is often mistaken for a giant earthworm. More than 280—often incomplete —body rings may be present. The head is lighter than the body in color, and the skin surrounding the nasal openings is white. The eyes are covered with bone and hence not visible externally. The head is not noticeably wider than the neck but is fairly deep posteriorly and shovel snouted.
Reproduction: The reproductive biology is unknown, but since this caecilian inhabits leaf litter and seems to have no ties to standing water, it is likely to be ovoviviparous.
Similar species: This is the most attenuate caecilian within its range.
Habitat/Range: *Oscaecilia bassleri* has been found in primary forest beneath moist leaf litter on the forest floor, amid fibrous surface roots of forest trees (again beneath leaf litter), and in and beneath decomposing logs. This species occurs in the northwestern Amazon Basin (Colombia, Ecuador, and Peru).

Genus *Siphonops;* Common Caecilians

This genus includes very typical-appearing caecilians of relatively robust to slender build. Some species are uniformly colored; others—*S. annulatus* and *S. paulensis* among them—have the body grooves marked with lighter pigment. Although they are usually persistently subterranean, *Siphonops* are occasionally seen traversing grassy areas or forest trails during wet weather. The eyes of most are rather well developed and readily discernible, and these caecilians may be capable of some degree of vision. The tentacle apertures are below and just anterior to the eye.

2. Amazonian Ringed Caecilian

Siphonops annulatus

Size: Heavy bodied; up to 17 inches (43 cm) long.

Identifying features: The ground color varies from slaty brown through slate blue to bluish black. All but the last few annuli are prominent, complete, and strongly outlined with white. There are fewer than 100 primary rings (those associated with the white outlining). The posteriormost annuli are usually interrupted dorsally. The head is somewhat flattened and slightly wider than the neck. Although covered with skin, the eyes are quite discernible and may be capable of at least limited vision.

Reproduction: Virtually nothing is known about the reproductive biology; this caecilian is thought to be ovoviviparous.

Similar species: This is the only prominently marked caecilian over most of its range. The look-alike Brazilian ringed caecilian has more than 100 primary annuli.

Habitat/Range: *Siphonops annulatus* is able to withstand somewhat drier habitat conditions than many other caecilians. It may be encountered in clearings as well as in secondary and primary forests. This is the most widespread caecilian of the Amazon Basin. It ranges from Bolivia and Brazil to Colombia, Ecuador, and the Guianas. It is not known to occur west of the Andes.

Comments: When discussing caecilians, herpetology texts usually discuss primary and secondary grooves, characteristics virtually impossible to determine on living examples. Nuchal (neck) collars are also discussed, and although far more easily seen than secondary grooves, are not pertinent to field identification.

Aquatic Caecilians: Family Typhlonectidae

The aquatic caecilians are attenuate, mud-colored, limbless amphibians with internal gills. The eyes are covered by skin but are readily visible and probably at least weakly functional. A low dorsal keel is present posteriorly. These caecilians are found in quiet waters, often in the shallows. As the seasonal floods recede, many are left in forest pools and muddy oxbow edges where they then burrow downward, following the moisture line or forming protective cocoons to await the next flood. Parchmentlike external gill membranes may be present at, but are usually resorbed immediately prior to, birth. Gill slits are present on larvae, but the lungs quickly become functional.

Genus *Typhlonectes;* Aquatic Caecilians

At least one species in this genus of aquatic Neotropical caecilians is more familiar to aquarists across the world than any other caecilian. This is *Typhlonectes compressicauda,* a creature widely sold in tropical fish stores as a "Sicilian" (caecilian) eel or rubber eel. This same creature is occasionally seen in ponds, oxbows, and slow-moving waters in the northwestern Amazon Basin. Because it lacks external eyes, limbs, and scales, this attenuate amphibian looks like nothing so much as a giant, heavy-bodied worm. It is entirely aquatic, burrowing deeply into the mud and aestivating when water levels drop. The head is only slightly wider than the neck. The teeth are many, small, and recurved. There are two rows in the upper jaw and a single row in the lower jaw. The body grooves are present but easily overlooked. The cloaca of the male is modified into a sucker to help retain contact during copulation. The six species in this genus are live-bearers.

3. Common Aquatic Caecilian

Typhlonectes compressicauda

Size: Adults are generally about 15 inches (38 cm) long; rarely up to 24 inches (60 cm).

Identifying features: Dorsally, laterally, and ventrally, this attenuate, eel-like creature is brownish gray to charcoal. There are neither fins nor limbs. Anteriorly and medially, the body is somewhat compressed from side to side. The posterior portion of the body is more noticeably compressed and is keeled (finned) dorsally. Lateral costal grooves are present. The eyes are represented by bluish spots. There is no tail. The lower jaw is partially countersunk. A very small and seldom seen protrusible tactile tentacle is present posterior to each nostril.

Reproduction: Females bear small numbers (commonly three to seven) of living young. Embryos have flat, parchmentlike, external gills that are usually resorbed prior to birth.

Similar species: This caecilian, the most widespread member of its genus, has a narrow, almost cylindrical head. The Colombian *T. natans* has a proportionally wider, flatter head and the body is compressed for its entire length.

Habitat/Range: These interesting amphibians may be found in quiet water situations throughout much of the northern Amazon Basin.

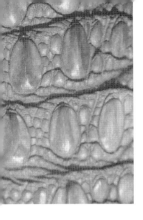

5

Lungless Salamanders

Family Plethodontidae

All of the salamanders of the Amazon region belong to this huge family, which is very well represented in North America but less diverse in Middle and South America. The plethodontids are unusual among vertebrates in having no lungs. They take in oxygen through the moist skin and mucous membranes. All are nocturnal, and they are often found on the leaves of low shrubs and herbaceous plants along trails and near forest clearings.

Genus *Bolitoglossa;* Climbing Salamanders and Web-Footed Salamanders

Although this genus comprises more than 70 species, at present only 2 species are known from the northwestern Amazon Basin. Both are small, and they are difficult to differentiate. At least one additional species, as yet undescribed, occurs in the basin.

The salamanders of this genus have webbed feet and a basal tail constriction (sometimes difficult to see) where the tail autotomizes (detaches as a defense mechanism). They are most often found on damp or humid nights when they ascend low, broad-leaved plants and terrestrial bromeliads to rest atop the leaves. There they are conspicuous. Perhaps they are foraging for minuscule insects, but most seem to be just sitting quietly and will often be in the same position if checked periodically through the hours of darkness. By dawn the salamanders are long gone, however, retired to some damp leaf axil or moisture-retaining crevice on the forest floor.

Females lay their eggs in damp, secluded crevices or leaf axils rather than in the water. The larvae develop entirely within the egg capsule and emerge as miniatures of the adults.

4. Amazon Climbing Salamander

Bolitoglossa altamazonica

Size: The adult is 3–3.5 inches (7.5–9 cm) in total length; the tail constitutes slightly *more* than half of the length.

Identifying features: Climbing salamanders vary from grayish to brownish in dorsal coloration. The head, tail, and limbs may be somewhat brighter than the trunk, which may be indistinctly lichenate or finely peppered with darker pigment. A darker or lighter vertebral stripe is occasionally present. The venter is gray peppered with lighter pigment. A rear-directed darker triangle may be present interorbitally. The tail is somewhat longer than the snout-to-vent length (a much-used measurement for reptiles and amphibians, usually abbreviated SVL), has a basal constriction, and is readily autotomized. The tan to orange eyes are bulbous and directed forward. Nasal cirri—slender projections that angle downward from each nostril—are present and are more prominent on sexually mature males.

Reproduction: Based on the eggs from three females that were being held overnight for photography, these salamanders produce small clutches (5–14) of rather large eggs. The eggs are probably placed in moist, dark tree cavities or the moisture- and debris-retaining axils of the leaves of such plants as bromeliads. It is likely that the female remains in attendance throughout the lengthy incubation. There is no free-swimming tadpole stage; the babies are miniatures of the adults at hatching.

Similar species: The Peruvian climbing salamander is very similar but proportionally more slender and smaller (2.5 inches, or 6 cm) when adult. A very similar-appearing salamander with a black venter that is also occasionally found in Amazonian Peru is an as yet undescribed species.

Habitat/Range: This small, arboreal, nocturnal salamander is often encountered at night on pathside vegetation. Most are from 1.5 to 6 feet (0.4–1.8 m) above the forest floor on broad-leaved plants or on the outer curves of the straplike leaves of huge terrestrial bromeliads. We have found them in both primary and secondary forests. The only specimen we found by day was tightly coiled in the basal between-leaf debris of a large terrestrial bromeliad. It was in contact with a clutch of 14 eggs. The range of this species has not yet been delineated. They are common throughout much of the northern Amazon Basin.

5. Dwarf Climbing Salamander

Bolitoglossa peruviana

Size: This slender plethodontid is a mere 2–2.25 inches (5–5.5 cm) in total length, with the tail constituting somewhat *less* than half.

Identifying features: The dorsum varies from russet to tan or deep brown and may be indistinctly lichenate or finely peppered with darker pigment. A dark triangle is often present on the crown of the head, apex directed rearward. A darker or lighter vertebral stripe is occasionally present. The venter is gray peppered finely with lighter pigment. The tail has a basal constriction and is readily autotomized. The tan to orange eyes are bulbous and directed forward. Nasal cirri are present and are more prominent on sexually mature males.

Reproduction: Gravid females produce up to 13 eggs. Other than clutch size, little is known of the reproductive biology. It may be that females, like other members of this genus, place the eggs in moisture- and debris-retaining axils of the leaves of such plants as bromeliads. It is likely that the female remains in attendance throughout incubation. The larval stages are spent in the eggs, with the babies emerging as miniatures of the adults.

Similar species: The Amazon climbing salamander is larger, more robust, and has a less finely peppered belly but is otherwise very similar externally. A third species (as yet unidentified) with a predominantly black venter is occasionally encountered in Amazonian Peru.

Habitat/Range: This web-footed, arboreal salamander is often encountered at night on pathside vegetation. We have found them in primary and secondary forests, most often 1–2 feet (30–60 cm) above the ground on broad-leaved plants. When seen, they are usually quietly coiled atop a leaf and will remain so for long periods. They are known to occur in northwestern Peru and in Ecuador.

6. Black-Bellied Climbing Salamander

Bolitoglossa species

Size: Adults are about 3 inches (7.5 cm) in total length, with the tail making up somewhat more than half of that.

Identifying features: These salamanders vary from grayish to brownish in dorsal coloration. The head, tail, and limbs may be somewhat brighter than the trunk, which may be finely peppered with darker pigment. A darker or lighter vertebral stripe is occasionally present. The venter is predominantly black. A rear-directed darker triangle may be present between the eyes. The tail has a basal constriction and is readily autotomized. The eyes are bulbous and directed forward. Nasal cirri are present and are more prominent on sexually mature males.

Reproduction: Unknown.

Similar species: The similar-sized Amazon climbing salamander and the smaller Peruvian climbing salamander have white-peppered gray bellies.

Habitat/Range: Like the other Amazonian plethodontids, this small, web-footed, arboreal salamander can be found at night on pathside vegetation, most often a few feet above the ground on the leaf surfaces of broad-leaved plants or terrestrial bromeliads. We have found them in primary and secondary forests in the Peruvian Amazon.

6

Toads, Frogs, and Treefrogs

The toads, frogs, and treefrogs, often referred to collectively as tailless amphibians (anurans), are well represented in the Iquitos region. Eight of the world's 20 families are found here. With the exception of the eleutherodactyline frogs, the hemiphractine treefrogs, and some pipid toads, all anurans of the region have a typical dual life that includes an aquatic larval (tadpole or polliwog) stage and a terrestrial adult stage. Some Amazonian anurans provide the tadpoles with such parental care as supplying infertile egg capsules as a food source.

Tadpoles are notoriously difficult to identify. They are tiny, and in many cases the lip structure and other obscure characteristics must be considered. For this reason, we have made no effort to provide a guide to tadpole identity.

Toads: Family Bufonidae

Most people are familiar with "hoptoads," if not by individual species then at least by general appearance. There are currently at least 10 kinds of true toads, genus *Bufo*, in the northwestern Amazon Basin. Several interesting forms await formal description. In addition, there are at least three species of *Atelopus*, or harlequin toads (with perhaps another form as yet undescribed), and a single leaf toad of the genus *Dendrophryniscus*.

The Amazonian *Bufo*s all have exposed parotid glands (often called shoulder glands), structures behind the head that produce and exude toxins. The tiny leaf toad lacks parotid glands. The aposematic colors of the harlequin toads indicate their bearers' unpalatability and toxicity.

The virulence of the glandular toxins is unknown in some toad species but is known to be significant in others (such as the cane toad, *Bufo marinus*). Always wash your hands thoroughly after handling a toad of any size or species.

Although many species of Bufonidae are seen only occasionally during most of the year, at the advent of the rainy season males and females gather in very large species-specific groups (called "congresses") for breeding.

Genus *Atelopus*; Harlequin Toads

This is a large genus of Neotropical anurans of diverse appearance. Only a few of the more than 65 species occur in the Amazon Basin. Most are between 1 and 1.5 inches in length (2.5–4 cm), but a few near or barely exceed 2 inches (5 cm). Many are montane species found in or along forest or grassland streams. There are some low-elevation rainforest species as well, and it is a sampling of these that we look at here. Depending on the species, the harlequin toads may be stubby and rough-skinned or smooth and lithe. Some are rather dull, but others are very brightly colored and intricately patterned. Today, for reasons as yet unknown, populations of many species—especially those from high elevations—have been reduced dramatically in numbers. A few species are hovering on the brink of extinction. Heightened ultraviolet levels and chytrid fungus infections are among the possible causes being carefully considered. Research facilities are developing herpetocultural (breeding) programs for some of the most severely endangered forms.

Many of the atelopid toads are primarily terrestrial; others prefer sites such as stream-swept rocks. Most are capable of climbing but are not particularly nimble when doing so. All feed on tiny insects and seem to have a "normal" anuran mode of reproduction. Atmospheric and climatic phenomena induce breeding. The eggs are laid and fertilized while pairs amplex in streams or other water sources. The tadpoles are aquatic, and metamorphosis occurs after several weeks of growth.

The forms discussed here are diurnally active and quite bold. The toxicity of the glandular skin secretions is not well known, but for your safety and the safety of the toads we suggest that you wash your hands both before and after handling them.

7. Cayenne Harlequin Toad

Atelopus flavescens

Size: Males attain a length of about 1 inch (2.5 cm); females reach about 1.5 inches (4 cm).

Identifying features: This is one of the long-legged, smooth-skinned atelopids. Most specimens have a pleasing yellow-orange dorsum. The yellow hue continues onto the lower sides, but the venter becomes pinkish (females) to pure pink (males) midventrally. Some specimens are duller, being tan to yellow-brown in hue. Darker reticulations may be present dorsally.
Voice: Periodic, occasionally rapidly repeated buzzes.
Reproduction: Breeding occurs along rainforest streams.
Similar species: Compared with other members of the genus, *Atelopus flavescens* is sharp-nosed and slender. Both A. *spumarius* and A. *pulcher* are strongly patterned dorsally.
Habitat/Range: This is essentially a tropical lowland rainforest frog of French Guiana and northern Brazil.

8. Amazon Harlequin Toad

Atelopus pulcher

Size: Females average 1.5 inches (4 cm) in length; males are smaller.
Identifying features: In Amazonian Peru this toad exhibits at least two distinctly different dorsal patterns and colors (perhaps two species are involved). The more common pattern involves a variably green dorsum bearing irregular dark reticulations. The other phase bears broad cream to yellow dorsolateral stripes (which contain rows of dark spots) against a brownish ground color. Similar patterns occur on the limbs. In both cases the venter is yellowish with black markings and the bottoms ("palms"?) of the feet and hidden areas of the thighs have bright orange flash marks (markings on the legs that are revealed, or "flashed," when the legs are extended). The skin is nearly smooth.
Voice: A series of buzzes.
Reproduction: Females lay small clutches of unpigmented eggs that contain predator-deterring neurotoxins. The tadpoles are aquatic and develop in rapidly flowing forest streams.
Similar species: In Amazonian Peru, only the tiny leaf toad, *Dendrophryniscus minutus*, also has orange palms, but it lacks dorsal and lateral flash colors.
Habitat/Range: The harlequin toad is diurnal and is encountered most often in primary forests densely carpeted in leaf litter. It is found both terrestrially (sitting atop mossy fallen logs) and on low leaves and erect mossy trunks. Those we have found were in Departamento Loreto, Peru. The exact range is unknown.
Comments: Although as brightly colored as many of the poison frogs, and probably as toxic as some, the harlequin toad is a very different

creature from these. Possibly because of susceptibility to a rapidly spreading chytrid fungus, many species of this widespread Neotropical genus are now greatly reduced in numbers, and some populations have apparently been extirpated.

9. Common Harlequin Toad

Atelopus spumarius spumarius

Size: Males attain a length of about 1 inch (2.5 cm); females reach about 1.5 inches (4 cm).

Identifying features: The dorsal ground coloration of this smooth-skinned atelopid is variable. Tannish green, olive, or variable brown are all typical; darker dorsal patterning is variable in both amount and contrast. The color and pattern continue well down onto the sides. The ventral coloration (including the palms and soles) tends to be yellow to pale yellow-orange, either with or without darker spotting. This beautiful, relatively slender frog has hind limbs of moderate length and a comparatively sharp nose.

Voice: Periodic, occasionally rapidly repeated buzzes.

Reproduction: Breeding occurs along rainforest streams.

Similar species: *Atelopus flavescens,* the only sympatric atelopid species in eastern South America, lacks strong patterning. *A. pulcher* tends to have a paler dorsal ground color and is a very bright red posteroventrally and on the palms and soles.

Habitat/Range: This is essentially a tropical lowland rainforest toad of the Guianas and Brazil; it may also occur farther to the west. The toads from the Peruvian Amazon region have recently been redesignated *A. pulcher.* The range of *A. pulcher* has not yet been precisely delimited.

Genus *Bufo;* True Toads

The anurans in this genus are the "hoptoads" that most of us first encountered as children. The more than 225 species occur in most parts of the world—Asia, Africa, Europe, North America, Central America, and South America all being strongholds.

As is the case with other anurans, some *Bufo* populations are in danger of extinction. Indeed, even after intense searches, some (such as the beautiful golden toad of Costa Rica's cloud forest) have not been seen in more than a decade.

For the most part, toads have a rather stubby appearance and hop rather than leap. Most have warty, glandular skin, but some are comparatively smooth and tubercle-free. Most are some shade of tan, brown, or black dorsally and laterally, but a few are clad in greens, golds, and dull reds. Toads are not nimble escape artists; they rely on nocturnal activity and skin secretions to deter predators. The skin secretions are produced primarily in the parotid (shoulder) glands. Obvious parotid glands are unique to toads. Protect yourself and the toad by washing your hands both before and after handling it.

Most toads are between 2 and 4 inches (5–10 cm) in snout–vent length. A few are smaller, and some, such as the Amazonian giant toads, may reach 8 inches (20 cm) or more. Worms and insects are the preferred diet, but some of the larger species also eat small vertebrates when the opportunity arises.

Although most true toads are essentially terrestrial, most also gather near quiet waters to breed. Most exhibit the "normal" anuran mode of reproduction. Atmospheric and climatic phenomena (such as the advent of the rainy season and low barometric pressure) induce breeding. The eggs are laid by the females and fertilized by the males while the pairs amplex in streams or other water sources. The tadpoles are aquatic, and metamorphosis occurs after several weeks of growth.

Some bufos climb and may be found at night a foot to several feet above the ground, often sitting quietly on a broad, flat leaf.

10. Eyelashed Forest Toad

Bufo ceratophrys

Size: This is a toad of average size. Males attain a snout–vent length of about 2.5 inches (6.5 cm); females may reach 3 inches (7.5 cm).

Identifying features: Like most forest toads, *B. ceratophrys* is clad in a variable pattern of grays, tans, and browns dorsally, and is tan and brown ventrally. A dark line, widest on the head, begins at the tip of the snout and continues along the side to the groin. The cranial crests are not well defined. The elliptical parotid glands slope diagonally downward from the shoulder and are light above and dark below. The hind limbs are dark banded. The anterior surface of the forelimbs may be uniformly dark.

Voice: Unknown.

Reproduction: Unknown. We found about a dozen 0.5–1-inch-long (1.5–

2.5-cm) juveniles in a still-drying floodplain of a small rainforest creek in late December.

Similar species: This is the only true toad of the upper Amazon with noticeable "horns," or "eyelashes," on the upper eyelids.

Habitat/Range: As currently known, this is considered a species of primary rainforest habitats in the upper Amazon.

Comments: Those we have found have been active by day. Nighttime walks through the same area disclosed no active toads.

11. Sharp-Nosed Toad

Bufo dapsilis

Size: Females attain an SVL of about 3 inches (7.5 cm); males are about half an inch (1–1.5 cm) smaller.

Identifying features: This is a smooth-skinned toad of moderate size and variable color. The dorsum is gray, tan, or warm brown, with or without irregular darker markings. The sides may vary from pinkish orange to dark olive, shading to tan or grayish tan ventrally. A longitudinal series of contiguous (usually) white tubercles (often narrowly bordered below with darker pigment) effectively separates the dorsal color from the lateral color. There are low cranial crests and elongate parotid glands, and the nose is variably lengthened. The head is not abnormally widened posteriorly.

Voice: Unknown.

Reproduction: Unknown.

Similar species: The combination of the rather bluntly elongate nose, parotid glands, nontriangular head, cranial crests, and (often) pinkish orange sides will differentiate this species from most other anurans of Amazonian Peru. An undescribed toad popularly dubbed the "Pinocchio" toad has an elongate nasal appendage rather than just a sharp nose. The very common crested toads (*B. margaritifer* ssp.) have a flattened head and a rounded nose.

Habitat/Range: This is considered a leaf litter species of primary forests. Those we have found were in western Peru.

Comments: Little is known about the habits and habitat of this pretty toad. The species is currently thought to be uncommon. As research into the herpetofauna of the Amazon Basin continues, we may find that there are actually two or more species now contained under this species heading.

12. Peruvian Smooth-Sided Toad
Bufo glaberrimus (complex)

Size: Both males and females reach an SVL of about 3.25 inches (8 cm).
Identifying features: The dorsum is some shade of tan. The sides, from snout to groin, are dark brown. The venter is pale gray with light spots. The dorsal surfaces of the rear legs are banded. There are no ridges (cranial crests) atop the head, and the prominent parotid glands are oval.
Voice: A mewling call, which carries poorly, voiced under the cover of darkness from riverside and backwater situations.
Reproduction: Unknown.
Similar species: Size and range are the best determinants. Although more than one species occurs in northwestern Amazonia, the features that differentiate them have not yet been precisely determined.
Habitat/Range: This toad, which seems to be nocturnal, occurs in primary and secondary forest situations. The presence at different times of two sitting atop floating logs moored about 20 feet from shore indicates a willingness to swim.
Comments: The smooth-sided toad group includes a number of similarly patterned and colored species that vary in size from the small Truando toad, *B. haematiticus*, of Central America to the huge (8.5 inches, or 22 cm) Blomberg's toad of Colombia's western mountains. *Bufo glaberrimus* (actually a complex of similar-appearing but genetically different species) is the representative of this complex most often seen in the upper Amazon.

13. Eastern Smooth-Sided Toad
Bufo guttatus

Size: Both sexes reach an SVL of about 6 inches (15 cm).
Identifying features: The dorsum is some shade of tan. The sides are dark brown. The venter is pale gray with light spots. The back is often sparsely peppered with tiny red spicules. The dorsal surface of the rear legs may be banded. There are no ridges (cranial crests) atop the head, and the prominent parotid glands are oval.
Voice: A mewl, which does not carry well, given nocturnally from riverside and backwater situations.
Reproduction: The several thousand eggs are laid during the rainy season.
Similar species: See the account for *Bufo glaberrimus* of the Peruvian Amazon.

Habitat/Range: This species is quite abundant in some parts of its range. It seems to occur in primary and secondary forest situations in the eastern Amazon Basin.

Comments: *Bufo guttatus* is a species of eastern South America. It is closely allied to the smaller, and very similarly colored, *B. glaberrimus* of the Peruvian Amazon.

14. Crested Forest Toad

Bufo margaritifer complex (formerly known as *B. typhonius*)

Size: Males attain an SVL of 2.75 inches (7 cm); females reach just over 3 inches (7.5 cm).

Identifying features: The cranial crests are extremely variable. They may be very tall, nearly vertical, and almost parallel; wide and angling widely outward posteriorly; or low and rather insignificant. Males may differ strikingly from females in appearance, and both sexes of some forms are not yet known. The dorsal color varies from solid unmarked brown, through prominently spotted tan, to terra cotta. The sides may be significantly lighter than the back, and a white vertebral line may or may not be present. On some specimens (especially adult females) the neural processes of the spinal vertebrae protrude through the skin. A row of tubercles extends from the parotid gland to the groin; these may be conical papillae. The parotid glands are rather small and elliptical. The venter is as variable as the dorsum, being gray, white, or cream, and spotted or unspotted.

Voice: The breeding calls are also variable, but all seem to be short, sharp rattles.

Reproduction: The double strings of eggs are laid in pools and quiet forest streams. Clutches vary in size from 100 to more than 2000 eggs. The clutch size may be species as well as size dependent.

Similar species: None. The divergent cranial crests and row of lateral tubercles are diagnostic of the species in this complex.

Habitat/Range: This is a toad of primary and secondary forests, and, in some cases at least, forest clearings. Specimens are often found at night sitting a foot or so above the ground litter on a wide leaf or a bent sapling. Members of this species complex are widely distributed through northern South America.

Comments: The "complex" designation refers to the similar-appearing, sexually dimorphic, undescribed species (according to the current understanding, there are at least three) referred to as *B. margaritifer.* Until very recently, the toads in this Neotropical group were known taxonomically as the *Bufo typhonius* complex. The name was changed when taxonomists discovered that *B. typhonius* had already been applied to an Asian species.

15. Common Giant Toad

Bufo marinus

Size: This is the largest toad in the region. Females attain an SVL of more than 7 inches (17.8 cm); males are adult at just over 4 inches (10 cm).

Identifying features: This huge toad has a glandular gray, tan, reddish, or brown dorsal skin bearing spine-tipped tubercles. Darker markings, if present, may be more pronounced anteriorly. The cranial crests are pronounced; the parotid glands are proportionally immense and extend partially down the side. The skin toxins are virulent. The off-white belly is spotted with darker pigment. There are at least two rather well defined color variations, the more uniform of which may be related to advanced age (see photo 15B).

Voice: A loud, low-pitched, slowly pulsed, rattling trill.

Reproduction: Large females may lay clutches of up to 13,000 eggs in double strings, but they usually lay less than half that number.

Similar species: This is an abundant species throughout much of the Amazon Basin. The huge, downward-angled parotid glands are distinctive.

Habitat/Range: Cane toads are most commonly seen in cleared agricultural areas, villages, open riverbanks, and other disturbed habitats. They are a common and often ignored species of the Neotropics and are now established in Florida (USA), Australia, and other countries.

Genus *Dendrophryniscus;* Leaf Toads

As currently defined, there are only three species in this Neotropical genus. Although they are primarily diurnal in their activity patterns, these toads are also somewhat crepuscular (active at dawn and dusk), and their activity extends to nighttime during the breeding season. The dorsum is cryptically colored in browns or tans; the belly is quite brightly colored. Ants seem to make up most of the diet. Usually associated with leaf litter in rainforest habitats, these elfin amphibians are quite capable of climbing and are often seen a foot or two above the ground on the broad leaves of herbaceous plants. Strings of eggs are laid in shallow water.

16. Orange-Bellied Leaf Toad

Dendrophryniscus minutus

Size: Males attain an SVL of 0.63 inch (1.5 cm); females barely exceed 0.75 inch (2 cm).

Identifying features: This is one of the smallest frogs in the Amazon region, and is certainly the smallest member of its family here. The body and head are somewhat flattened. The head is rather narrow and tapers anteriorly to a pointed nose. The dorsal skin is covered with tiny spicules. There are neither cranial crests nor parotid glands. The dorsum is brown, and the sides may be somewhat lighter. The belly is orange with black markings. The bottoms of all four feet are orange to orange-red.

Voice: Several frequently repeated piping notes.

Reproduction: Large females may lay strings of more than 200 eggs.

Similar species: The tiny size, solid dull brown dorsum, spiculate skin, and orange palms and soles are diagnostic.

Habitat/Range: Although this tiny bufonid is often said to be diurnal, we found individuals actively climbing low plants at a pond edge in primary forest at night. One large female was sitting on a broad leaf about a foot above the ground eating foraging ants.

Glass Frogs: Family Centrolenidae

Many of the centrolenids are small, arboreal, delicate-looking frogs. Most are persistently nocturnal, dwell along streams, and call from elevated positions beside or over forest streams. The eggs are attached to vegetation above the stream, and the tadpoles drop into the water after hatching. The common name is derived from the transparent ventral skin of many species.

Genus *Cochranella;* Neotropical Glass Frogs

Only 1 of the more than 40 species in this genus occurs in the western Amazon. The pale green dorsum blends well with the underside of the leaves on which these arboreal, nocturnal frogs hunker down to spend the hours of daylight. The ventral skin is quite transparent. The toe pads are well developed. Glass frogs become active after dark and may be seen on vegetation near or above water. Ants are a sizable portion of the diet.

17. Amazonian Glass Frog

Cochranella ritae

Size: Both sexes attain a length of 1 inch (2.5 cm).

Identifying features: This glass frog is a beautiful, translucent bluish green dorsally with numerous small dark spots. The hind limbs are also spotted. The limbs and sides shade to pale yellow ventrally. The belly is translucent white. The feet bear prominent toe pads.

Voice: Unknown.

Reproduction: The breeding biology is undescribed but is probably similar to that of other members of the genus, which lay clusters of eggs on leaves overhanging the water. On hatching, the tadpoles drop into the water to complete their development.

Similar species: *Hyla granosa* lacks the dark dorsal spots. The various hatchet-faced treefrogs (*Sphaenorhynchus* spp.) have a sharp nose and either *pale* spots on the dorsum *or* dark dorsolateral lines and *dark* spots. The various phyllomedusine treefrogs have opposable thumbs. *Scarthyla ostinodactyla* has a white lateral stripe, and *Eleutherodactylus acuminatus* has a sharp nose and a dark canthal stripe.

Habitat/Range: Unknown. The few specimens found have been along forest streams at night. This appears to be an uncommon species.

Poison Frogs: Family Dendrobatidae

Although dendrobatids have long been known as dart-poison (or arrow-poison) frogs, only three species (members of the genus *Phyllobates*, extralimital to this guide) are known for their lethal skin secretions. Except for the rocket frogs of the genus *Colostethus*, all dendrobatids are now referred to merely as "poison frogs."

Representatives of three genera may be encountered in the Amazon Basin. The genera *Dendrobates* and *Epipedobates* include brightly colored frogs; *Colostethus* does not.

Although it may be difficult to believe that these colorful, diurnal frogs could be easily overlooked, that is frequently the case. They are all very alert, darting beneath fallen leaves or backing into a bromeliad axil at the *slightest* disturbance. The dark color of the sides blends remarkably well with the equally dark leaf litter, and the bright dorsum looks like a fallen flower petal.

The reproductive biology of dendrobatid frogs is complex and interesting. Courtship differs from species to species but may involve butting, nudging, or circling of the female by the male. Female poison frogs deposit their eggs in moisture-retaining terrestrial situations. There is no actual amplexus. Sometimes the eggs are fertilized while the frogs sit "rump to rump," at other times after the female has left the deposition site. One of the parents—usually the male—remains in attendance on the clutch. When the eggs hatch, the tadpoles wriggle and slide onto the back of the attending parent, who carries them to the edge of a swamp, pool, slow forest stream, or, in some cases, to the water-holding cup of an arboreal bromeliad or a tree-trunk hollow. The tadpoles then leave the back of the parent to complete their development. When bromeliad cups are used, the female parent returns occasionally to deposit one or more infertile eggs as a food source for the tadpoles.

These frogs are very territorial, and especially so at breeding time. Both males and females grapple and shove others of their kind, with the winners securing the best microhabitats.

Note: Although color and pattern are the usual criteria by which observers identify these frogs in the field, intraspecific variability and interspecies similarities can make identification difficult. For example, the color and pattern of the dyeing poison frog, *Dendrobates tinctorius,* may vary from yellow to blue to black, and from profusely spotted to nearly uniformly colored—yet all are apparently the same species. In contrast there is the *D. ventrimaculatus* complex, a half dozen or more distinct species that are all quite similar in appearance. Use range as a tool when attempting identification.

Genus *Colostethus;* Rocket Frogs

Of the 90-plus species in this genus, only a handful occur in the Amazon Basin. All are small, primarily terrestrial frogs that are occasionally seen along rainforest streams. Although they are members of a family noted for brilliant colors, the rocket frogs are quite dull, basically nontoxic, and blend well with the leaf litter in their favored forest habitats. They are agile, alert, long-distance leapers—thus their common name, "rocket frogs." They eat ants, springtails, and other tiny invertebrates found in the leaf litter. Although the rocket frogs do have toe pads, these are smaller proportionally than those borne by other dendrobatid genera.

18. Ucayali Rocket Frog

Colostethus marchesianus

Size: Both sexes reach a length of about 0.75 inch (2 cm).

Identifying features: The dorsum is dark tan to brown, often lightest anteriorly, with a lighter, broad (usually) cafe-au-lait dorsolateral stripe on each side. Below each of these is an even-edged chocolate brown stripe that extends from nose to groin. The cream-colored venter is precisely separated from the chocolate lateral stripe by a thin white stripe.

Voice: The calls, both territorial and breeding, consist of a series of double chirps.

Reproduction: Egg deposition continues through nearly the entire rainy season. The male carries the tadpoles to shallow water.

Similar species: None. The cafe-au-lait dorsolateral stripes bordered below by a wide chocolate stripe are diagnostic.

Habitat/Range: Look for this frog in moisture-retaining areas of leaf litter and other forest debris in secondary and primary forests in Amazonian Peru.

Genus *Dendrobates;* Poison Frogs

Although the poison frogs vary in color both by species and individually, some are so remarkably brilliant that no one can casually pass them by. They vary in length from about 0.6 inch to 2 inches (1.5–5 cm). At least some of the 30–plus species, most of which are eagerly sought by zoological gardens and private herpetoculturists, are now being reliably bred in captivity.

The alkaloid skin secretions of some species give the poison frogs their common name. The indigenous people of the Amazon Basin concoct a potent toxin from these compounds with which they coat darts and arrows. The presence or absence of certain of these alkaloid compounds is among the characters that define the various species. The diet determines the toxicity of the skin secretions, and an important component appears to be formic acid–containing ants of several species. When taken captive and fed the traditional herpetocultural diet of termites, tiny crickets, and fruit flies, the skin secretions of even the most poisonous frogs quickly lose toxicity.

Some poison frogs are primarily terrestrial. The lives of others center high in rainforest trees, often amid the clumps of water-retaining arboreal bromeliads in which many of these frogs breed. All the *Dendrobates* have well-developed toe pads, and many are excellent climbers.

Dendrobates quinquevittatus and its allies are currently in a state of taxonomic confusion. The patterns of the dorsal and dorsolateral stripes have been used to define new species such as *D. ventrimaculatus, D. amazonicus, D. callegarii,* and *D. duellmani.*

19. Blue Poison Frog

Dendrobates azureus

Size: This is one of the larger poison frogs. Adults are about 1.75 inches (4.5 cm) long; females are usually slightly larger than males.

Identifying features: The ground color of this spectacular frog is bright blue (somewhat paler ventrolaterally). The venter is pale blue. Typically the legs are the darkest blue. The back, sides, and belly are variably patterned with black spots. These may be tiny and discrete, large and discrete, or may adjoin into irregularly edged bars (especially dorsally). The color and pattern are observable even in tadpoles. Blue poison frogs are among the typically hunchbacked species that tend to sit with forelegs flexed, in a hunkered-down position.

Voice: Males produce easily overlooked peeps.

Reproduction: Males are aggressively territorial and attend the small clutches (3–18) of eggs. Both sexes carry tadpoles to their shallow-water development sites.

Similar species: Some dyeing poison frogs (*D. tinctorius*) are quite similar in color, but they usually sit in a more erect posture and often (but not always) have at least a little yellow on the back. The blue and black morph of the dyeing poison frog that lacks yellow and is known as the "New River morph" can be particularly confusing.

Habitat/Range: This poison frog has become quite uncommon over much of its original range and is now found in isolated pockets of pinelands and surrounding rainforest near the Brazilian border in southwestern Suriname. Of difficult access, this region is technically somewhat north of the actual delineation of the Amazon Basin but is drained by several rivers that do terminate in the Amazon.

Comments: Some herpetologists think that the blue poison frog is a divergent phase of the very widely distributed and immensely variable dyeing poison frog, *D. tinctorius*. There do seem to be some constant differences, however, posture among them.

20. Biolat Poison Frog

Dendrobates biolat

Size: This is one of the truly tiny poison frogs. Adults are only about 0.6 inch (1.5 cm) long.

Identifying features: *Dendrobates biolat* has five golden yellow stripes on the black back and sides. All four limbs are a pale but distinct blue with black spots. The legs at the insertion are unspotted and may be pale blue, cream, or yellow. The yellow vertebral stripe curves over the tip of the snout, and the two yellow dorsolateral lines angle abruptly inward just anterior to each eye. The upper lip is yellow.

Voice: Buzzing notes similar to those of many frogs in this complex.

Reproduction: This frog is thought to breed in the water-holding cups of arboreal bromeliads.

Similar species: *Dendrobates biolat* is a member of the *D. quinquevittatus* complex. It is just as tiny as *D. lamasi, D. quinquevittatus, D. ventrimaculatus*, and others, and is confusingly similar in color as well. These species are very difficult to distinguish without knowledge of the collection site. Locale is your best guide for identification.

Habitat/Range: The biolat poison frog is thought to be extensively arboreal. This species is restricted to southeastern Peru.

21. Brazil-Nut Poison Frog

Dendrobates castaneoticus

Size: This moderate-sized poison frog attains a length of about 1 inch (2.5 cm).

Identifying features: This is one of the more easily identified poison frogs. The ground color is black, but there are white to blue-white markings on the back and sides. A patch of bright yellow (to orange) is present at the insertion of each forelimb as well as on each tibia and femur. The black belly is less distinctly patterned than the dorsum.

Voice: Unknown.

Reproduction: Breeding is accomplished in traditional poison frog manner. The tadpoles are transported to, and deposited in, very small amounts of standing water in, for example, depressions in fallen trees, in curved fallen leaves, and the opened husks of Brazil nuts.

Similar species: The white dorsal spots and yellow to orange blotches on the otherwise black legs are distinctive.

Habitat/Range: This is a primarily terrestrial frog from northeastern Brazil.

22. Fantastic Poison Frog

Dendrobates fantasticus

Size: Adults attain a length of about 0.6 inch (1.5 cm).

Identifying features: Although this frog is often referred to as the red-headed poison frog, the area from the head back to the shoulders may actually be red, orange, or yellowish. A black mark in the shape of a butterfly or a star may be present on the crown, or there may be a black spot on each upper eyelid. The body is black reticulated with a light (often the very palest orange) color. The limbs are often bluish with black spots. The pale blue belly is spotted with black.

Voice: Buzzing notes like those of other members of this complex.

Reproduction: The few eggs are laid on bromeliad leaves, often high in the trees. The tadpoles develop in the water-holding cups of the bromeliads.

Similar species: Range will be an important ally in identifying this frog. Other poison frogs have more, less, or duller red on the back and lack the black spot(s) between the eyes.

Habitat/Range: These arboreal frogs are only occasionally seen on the ground. This species is found in the Putumayo watershed where the borders of Peru, Colombia, and Brazil converge.

23. Splash-Backed Poison Frog

Dendrobates galactonotus

Size: Adults are about 1.5 inches (4 cm) long.

Identifying features: This variably colored and patterned frog may be a solid dull red, pumpkin orange, or butter yellow, and either with or without black on the sides, limbs, and dorsum. If the sides are black, vertical or diagonal streaks of the dorsal color may extend diagonally downward from the back, terminating on the lower sides. The limbs, if black, may or may not be flecked with yellow or orange. The belly is usually black.

Voice: Nasal peeps.

Reproduction: The males transport the several tadpoles from the hatching site to standing water where they complete their development.

Similar species: This frog is thought to be most closely allied with the dyeing poison frog, *D. tinctorius*. Their dorsal patterns immediately separate the two.

Habitat/Range: Look for this little terrestrial frog in patches of leaf litter in the rainforests of eastern and central Brazil. As currently understood, the species occurs in three discrete populations.

24. Mimic Poison Frog

Dendrobates imitator

Size: Only about 0.75 inch (2 cm) long; this is one of the tinier poison frogs.

Identifying features: *Dendrobates imitator* is a beautiful and variably patterned little frog. The light reticulum is often orange, yellow, or olive yellow anteriorly, shading to green (sometimes blue-green, olive green, or lime) posteriorly and ventrally. The ventral coloration consists of numerous black spots on a background that is yellow(ish) anteriorly and greenish posteriorly. A pair of large black spots is usually present on the tip of the snout. The throat is yellow heavily spotted with black.

Voice: Like the others in the *D. ventrimaculatus* group, the male's territorial call is a repetitive buzz.

Reproduction: Males carry the tadpoles to arboreal water-holding bromeliads to complete their development.

Similar species: Many individuals superficially resemble *D. ventrimaculatus* but tend to have a busier pattern of dorsal black spots than that species. The pattern of prominent dorsal and lateral spots is usually diagnostic.

Habitat/Range: This remarkably colored but variable frog is apparently found in pockets of suitable habitat along many river systems. It appears to be quite arboreal.

Comments: It has been suggested, but is not yet generally accepted, that a subspecies of this frog exists. Currently identified as *D. imitator intermedius* by some researchers (and as a full species, *D. intermedius*, by others), these frogs are much more similar to *D. fantasticus* in appearance than to *D. imitator* (see photo 24B).

25. Pasco Poison Frog

Dendrobates lamasi

Size: Adults are 0.6–0.75 inch (1.5–2 cm) in length. Females are more robust than males, especially when gravid.

Identifying features: Five yellow to green stripes divide the black back and sides. On each side there is a brightly colored lateral stripe and an equally bright dorsolateral stripe. The vertebral stripe is prominent and forms a T anteriorly. The top of the T runs from upper lip to upper lip immediately anterior to the eyes. Isolated by the yellow of the upper lips and the transverse preocular band, the snout is typically a discrete black spot. A yellow stripe crosses the posterior sacral area, connecting the two dorsolateral stripes and the vertebral stripe. All four limbs are grayish white, grayish blue, or pale blue, and are prominently spotted with black polka dots. The throat and belly are often yellowish and have black spots.

Voice: The often-repeated calls of the males have a buzzing, insectlike quality.

Reproduction: Although little is known about the reproductive biology in the wild, this frog is thought to be a bromeliad breeder.

Similar species: This is one of several confusingly similar members of the *D. quinquevittatus* complex. Compare the photos and ranges of *D. biolat, D. fantasticus, D. imitator, D. quinquevittatus,* and *D. ventrimaculatus. Dendrobates lamasi* differs from other members of the group primarily in the structure of its call. Rely primarily on distribution for identification.

Habitat/Range: Although they are frequently seen on the ground, these rainforest frogs appear to be primarily arboreal inhabitants of mossy, epiphyte-laden trunks and limbs, and especially of bromeliad clusters and cups. The species is found east of the Peruvian Andes, in central Peru, near Tingo Maria.

Comments: Like other members of this species complex, the Pasco poison frog is difficult to differentiate from its closest relatives. Its location in Peru will help identify it.

26. Rio Madeira (Five-Striped) Poison Frog

Dendrobates quinquevittatus

Size: Females are adult at about 0.75 inch (2 cm) in length; males are slightly smaller.

Identifying features: This tiny frog is variably colored. The dark back has three blue, green, or yellowish stripes. The blue belly is strongly patterned with black. The orange-yellow throat is also black spotted. This is a tiny, somewhat robust poison frog.

Voice: Calling males produce a series of quiet buzzes.

Reproduction: This little frog breeds in typical fashion. A gravid female is attracted by the buzzing calls of the male, who then apparently leads her to the deposition site where she lays several eggs, which he then fertilizes. After hatching, the tadpoles are carried by the male(?) to a shallow-water site where they swim free and complete their development.

Similar species: In some of its phases, *Dendrobates ventrimaculatus* closely approaches this species in color and pattern. Use distribution as the principal identification criterion.

Habitat/Range: This is a rainforest species of the Rio Madeira drainage on the Brazilian side of the Bolivian border.

Comments: The precise delineation of species characteristics in the *D. quinquevittatus* complex remains unsettled.

27. Red-Backed Poison Frog

Dendrobates reticulatus

Size: Both sexes attain an SVL of about 0.75 inch (2 cm); females are marginally larger than males.

Identifying features: This eagerly sought frog is probably the most spectacularly colored species seen with any regularity by ecotourists in Amazonian Peru. The dorsal skin is smooth and the anterior dorsum, including the top and sides of the head, is brilliant red. Dark spots may or may not be present. The posterior dorsum, sides, legs, and belly are black with an azure blue to blue-green reticulum.

Voice: The calls of the males are insectlike buzzes.

Reproduction: The reproductive biology is not well known. Males have been seen carrying one or two tadpoles on their backs from ground level to arboreal bromeliads. Three eggs being "attended" by a frog of this species were found in an arboreal bromeliad.

Similar species: None. The other poison frogs in the region have a striped or overall spotted pattern, or the red of the dorsum is noticeably less brilliant.

Habitat/Range: Although individuals are seen in small numbers in the leaf litter, this is an arboreal poison frog of primary and secondary forests. It ascends trees by *hopping* up trunks, seemingly in absolute defiance of gravity. It is found in northeastern Peru and immediately adjacent Brazil.

28. Dyeing Poison Frog

Dendrobates tinctorius

Size: This is one of the largest of the poison frogs, commonly attaining 2 inches (5 cm) in length. Females are more robust, may be marginally larger, and supposedly have proportionally larger toe pads that are more truncate anteriorly than those of the males.

Identifying features: "Variable" is perhaps the most appropriate word to describe the color and pattern of this species. Some degree of black on the dorsum and limbs seems the only constant. The ground color of the limbs is often blue but may be black or brilliant yellow. Limbs have spots of contrasting color. The dorsum is often patterned (spotted, striped, or reticulated) with yellow or orange, and sometimes with white or blue. The sides may be predominantly yellow, blue, black, or white. If of a lighter color, the sides are spotted or reticulated with dark areas; if of a dark color, they are variably marked with light patches. Colors and patterns may be visible on large tadpoles.

Voice: A series of buzzing peeps.

Reproduction: Breeding is quite typical of the poison frogs. Females are first drawn to the calls of the males, then are led by the males to the actual deposition site. As many as 15 eggs may be laid in a clutch. Males transport the tadpoles to the shallow-water site in which development will occur. Metamorphosis takes about two months.

Similar species: See the account for the blue poison frog, *Dendrobates azureus*. In most of its myriad phases the dyeing poison frog has some yellow or white on its back; however, the recently discovered "New River morph" is blue and black and very similar to *D. azureus*. The latter usually sits with its forelimbs flexed, however, while *D. tinctorius* sits with its forelimbs almost straight.

Habitat/Range: The dyeing poison frog inhabits pockets of low-altitude rainforest in Guyana, Suriname, French Guiana, and northeastern Brazil. Although technically north of the Amazon Basin, much of the range of this species is drained by rivers that eventually terminate in the Amazon.

29. Amazonian Poison Frog

Dendrobates ventrimaculatus complex

Size: About 0.75 inch (2 cm); females *may* be marginally larger and more robust than males.

Identifying features: This beauty is the second most spectacularly colored poison frog in the Iquitos region. The dorsal color is black. There are three to five wide, brilliant yellow or orange stripes. These include a middorsal stripe (which, if present, may be single and complete or may fork into a Y anteriorly), a dorsolateral stripe on each side, and often a labial stripe that may continue along each side as a lateral stripe to the groin. The latter is often orange anterior to the forelimb and blue from the forelimb to the groin. The limbs are blue to blue-green with either a few large black spots or a reticulum of black. The belly is black with reticulations of blue (in some populations the belly is predominantly yellow). The throat is yellow to orange patterned with black.

Voice: A series of insectlike buzzes.

Reproduction: The breeding biology in the wild is unknown. In terrarium habitats this species prefers to lay its two to five eggs in a bromeliad.

Similar species: This species (actually a complex of three or four species) is the only poison frog over much of its range with three brilliant yellow to orange dorsal stripes. Where other species of the complex occur, identification can be very difficult.

Habitat/Range: Amazonian poison frogs occur in primary and secondary forests and appear from time to time near forest tourist lodges. They are most abundant in pockets of damp leaf litter. The species is widely distributed in the Iquitos region, northern Peru, adjacent Colombia, and Brazil; smaller populations occur in other areas of Brazil and French Guyana.

Comments: It is currently thought that at least four species are included in the *D. ventrimaculatus* designation. The other three are occasionally referred to as (1) the Amazon poison frog, *D. amazonicus* (variable and very poorly differentiated from the equally variable *D. ventrimaculatus*); (2) Duellman's poison frog, *D. duellmani* (no apical flash marks); and (3) Callegari's poison frog, *D. callegari* (no vertebral stripe). Acceptance of these names has been limited to date because intraspecific variability at times obscures the defining criteria.

Genus *Epipedobates;* Poison Frogs

To most observers, the approximately 25 species of little forest frogs in this genus are virtually identical with those in the sister genus *Dendrobates*. Like *Dendrobates*, the *Epipedobates* species range in length from about 0.75 to 2 inches (2–5 cm). Although they have toe pads, the *Epi*-

pedobates seem less arboreally inclined than the *Dendrobates* species. Most bear linear patterns and are less flamboyantly colored than many of the *Dendrobates*. The two genera are differentiated primarily by analysis of skin alkaloids.

30. Sky Blue Poison Frog

Epipedobates azureiventris

Size: Adults are about 1 inch (2.5 cm) long; females are marginally larger than males.

Identifying features: The common name of this frog derives from the predominant belly color. The limbs are greenish blue. Both belly and limbs are spotted with black. The dorsum is predominantly black. A yellow to bright orange dorsolateral line, beginning on the tip of the snout and continuing over the eyelid, is present on each side. An orange stripe extends forward from the groin to mid-side. A yellow(ish) stripe is present on the upper lip and usually extends well onto the forearm. These are relatively robust frogs.

Voice: Soft trilling notes.

Reproduction: The female lays 10–15 eggs in a moist terrestrial location; these are then fertilized by the attending male. After the eggs hatch, the male transports the tadpoles to a shallow-water site where they undergo development and metamorphosis.

Similar species: The presence of only two orange lines on the dorsum separates this species from *D. ventrimaculatus*.

Habitat/Range: The sky blue poison frog is a primarily terrestrial inhabitant of rainforests near the Rio Maranon and Rio Ucayali.

31. Spotted-Thighed Poison Frog

Epipedobates femoralis

Size: Females are just over 1 inch (2.5 cm) in SVL; males are seldom more than 0.9 inch (2.3 cm).

Identifying features: Both a light dorsolateral line *and* a ventrolateral line are present. The dorsolateral line separates the dark sides from the (usually) much lighter back, and the ventrolateral line bisects the dark sides. The belly is a dark-spotted cream. A yellow femoral spot (red in some populations) extends from the groin over the *rear* of the thigh.

Voice: Dual chirps.

Reproduction: The male carries the tadpoles to a water-holding log hollow, pond, or stream edge habitat.

Similar species: The very similar *E. hahneli* has a black-reticulated blue belly, a more anterior and smaller femoral spot, and lacks a ventrolateral stripe. The leptodactylid painted antnest frog, *Lithodytes lineatus,* also looks much like this species but is larger and lacks ventrolateral stripes.

Habitat/Range: Like other poison frogs, males of this territorial, primarily terrestrial species choose elevated sites from which to call. They are present in moist leaf litter in primary and secondary forests in disjunct locations in Amazonian Peru, Ecuador, Brazil, Colombia, and the Guianas.

32. Pale-Striped Poison Frog

Epipedobates hahneli

Size: Adult females are just under 1 inch (2.5 cm) in SVL; males are seldom larger than 0.75 inch (2 cm).

Identifying features: This tiny frog is a paler-striped and seemingly more common edition of *E. femoralis.* You must have the frog in hand (to check for the presence or absence of ventrolateral striping) to make a positive identification. The dorsal and lateral coloration is often the same (or nearly so) as that of *E. femoralis.* The dorsolateral stripes are pale (off-white to cream). The labial stripe extends only to the forelimb. Ventrolateral stripes are absent. The belly is blue and has black reticulations.

Voice: A short series of peeps.

Reproduction: Males carry the tadpoles to shallow-water locations to complete their development. We have found tadpoles of this species in water-holding depressions in fallen logs.

Similar species: Neither *Lithodytes lineatus* nor *Epipedobates femoralis* has a dark-reticulated blue venter.

Habitat/Range: These territorial frogs are quite commonly encountered in areas of primary and secondary forests that have leaf litter and other moisture-holding natural debris. Males often voice their peeping calls while sitting by day in elevated positions. Found in Peruvian and Brazilian Amazon.

33. Ruby Poison Frog

Epipedobates parvulus

Size: Adults are slightly less than 1 inch (2.5 cm) in length.

Identifying features: The ruby poison frog has a granular, brownish red to dull red dorsum; blue-green sides; brownish to greenish brown legs; a yellow spot at the axilla of each forelimb; and two yellow spots in the groin. It *lacks* a well-defined lateral stripe. The belly is pale blue with darker reticulations.

Voice: An often-repeated soft, two-toned whistle. Males often choose the vegetation-clad tops of fallen logs and standing stumps as calling sites, but may also call from the ground.

Reproduction: Normal clutches consist of 5–10 eggs, but up to 16 have been documented. The eggs are laid in suitably protected and moist terrestrial locations. The tadpoles wriggle onto the back of the male frog, who transports them to ephemeral pools or the quiet edges of forest streams to complete their development.

Similar species: *Epipedobates zaparo* is very similar but lacks the yellow flash marks and has a well-defined bluish lateral stripe on each side.

Habitat/Range: This diurnal, terrestrial frog is associated with the low hills and ridges and relatively steep (and often muddy) inclines of upland forests. It has been found in Ecuador and Peru.

Comments: Despite its common name, this is not one of the more colorful poison frogs.

34. Spotted-Legged Poison Frog

Epipedobates pictus

Size: Males attain a length of about 0.75 inch (2 cm). The more robust females may reach a full inch (2.5 cm).

Identifying features: Although variable, this is usually one of the least colorful members of the genus. The dorsum is predominantly dark brown. A variably contrasting dorsolateral stripe extends from the tip of the snout, over each eyelid, and terminates in the groin. Light middorsal spots are sometimes present. A bluish line is present on the upper lip. An orange spot is present on the anterior of each femur, at the insertion of the forelimb, and on the underside of each shank.

Voice: A series of buzzing peeps.

Reproduction: The female lays 4–15 eggs in a protected, moist terrestrial location, and the tadpoles are transported (apparently by the male) to a shallow-water site to complete their development.

Similar species: The orange spot on the underside of the shank differentiates this species from most others.

Habitat/Range: This frog occurs (quite probably as a species complex) in low-altitude rainforest habitats in widely scattered areas of Brazil, Bolivia, Colombia, Ecuador, all three of the Guianas, extreme northern Paraguay, Peru, and extreme eastern Venezuela.

35. Silverstone's Poison Frog

Epipedobates silverstonei

Size: Adults are 1.5–1.75 inches (4–4.5 cm) long.

Identifying features: This jewel of the rainforest is brilliant in color but variable in pattern. Many are predominantly bright yellow-orange to tangerine both dorsally and ventrally; others have profuse dark spotting and streaking on the back. On some individuals the orange is largely restricted to the head and shoulders and the rest of the back is brownish. A dark eye-to-ear stripe is often, but not invariably, present. Young specimens are less brightly colored than the adults.

Voice: A trilling peep.

Reproduction: Males transport the 15–35 tadpoles to shallow standing water to complete their development.

Similar species: The very brilliant adult coloration and the very limited range should identify this remarkable frog.

Habitat/Range: Although it can climb, this is predominantly a terrestrial frog of cool rainforest habitats at moderate elevations. Individuals are often found near villages and at the edges of newly cut agricultural plots. The species is found in the Cordillera Azul in central Peru.

36. Three-Striped Poison Frog

Epipedobates trivittatus

Size: At an adult size of more than 1.75 inches (4.5 cm), this is the largest poison frog of Amazonian Peru and one of the largest in the family. East of Peru its size may be equaled or exceeded by other species.

Identifying features: This pretty frog has either two or three *broad* bright orange-red, orange, yellow, or lime green dorsal stripes that begin on the snout and continue without interruption into the groin. A light (yellow, blue, or green) ventrolateral stripe is usually evident. The skin of the dorsum, sides, and belly is black. There are bluish spots on the venter. The limbs are dark but are usually spotted with the stripe color.

Voice: The repetitive clicking peeps of the males issue from protected terrestrial sites throughout the day.

Reproduction: The clutch size is 20–66 eggs. Males transport the tadpoles to suitable aquatic sites to complete their development.

Similar species: None. *Epipedobates trivittatus* is one of the larger poison frogs. Many sympatric species are adults at an inch or less in length. In the northwestern Amazon Basin the *broad* yellow to green stripes and yellow to green legs are definitive. Elsewhere in its range this species may be more difficult to identify.

Habitat/Range: This diurnal frog may be encountered in secondary and primary forests and near agricultural clearings and habitations. It is widely distributed from east-central to northeastern Peru, in adjacent Colombia and Brazil, in interior and eastern Brazil along the Amazon (Rio Solimoes), and in all of the Guianas.

37. Sanguine Poison Frog

Epipedobates zaparo

Size: Adults are just over 1 inch (2.5 cm) long.

Identifying features: The dorsal skin is noticeably granular. The side skin is smoother. The anterior back and top of the head are dark red. The posterior back and upper sides are black. A light blue stripe parallels the upper lip and a second blue stripe is present on the posterior upper sides. The belly, lower sides, and anterior of the tarsus are also blue.

Voice: Soft dual peeps.

Reproduction: From 3 to 15 eggs represent a normal clutch. The tadpoles are carried a few at a time by the attending male from the deposition site to shallow standing water to complete their development.

Similar species: This is the "in-between" red frog of the northwestern Amazon Basin. It is very much like a brighter than normal ruby poison frog (*E. parvulus*) but less colorful than the red-backed poison frog (*Dendrobates reticulatus*), which has strongly reticulated sides and legs and smooth dorsal skin. The sanguine poison frog has well-defined light blue labial (upper lip) and posterior dorsolateral stripes. Although both of these markings are present on *E. parvulus* as well, they are poorly defined.

Habitat/Range: This is an alert leaf litter frog of upland rainforests. Despite its bright coloration, it can vanish in a single small hop. The species ranges from south-central Ecuador to Peru's upper Amazon region.

Treefrogs and Allies: Family Hylidae

The hylids are the largest assemblage of Amazonian frog species. Three subfamilies—the Hemiphractinae, the Hylinae, and the Phyllomedusinae —are represented.

Most hylids have large, flattened toe pads that assist in climbing. Some are canopy species, but many are found in low shrubbery and herbaceous vegetation. Many (probably most) are capable of extensive color changes. Some have distinctly different daytime and nighttime colorations. Some species have two or more color phases; geographic variations of color and pattern are also known. The males of most species have distinctive voices.

Like most anurans, the treefrogs are found most easily after dark when they become active in the trees and shrubs and congregate at pools and lakes in breeding aggregations. Although large choruses may be heard calling from emergent aquatic vegetation, these frogs can be very difficult to see. Treefrogs sometimes accidentally drop into tour boats from river edge shrubbery.

Treefrogs

Subfamily Hemiphractinae; Egg-Brooding Treefrogs

Genus *Hemiphractus;* Casque-Headed Treefrogs

The hemiphractines are the most divergent of the hylids in appearance and breeding biology. There are approximately six species in this Neotropical genus, and three may be found in the areas ecotours often visit. Two of the three are strongly arboreal and have prominent digital discs. The third, *H. scutatus* (not pictured), has inconspicuous digital discs and is terrestrial. All are nocturnal.

The head is prominently triangular when viewed from above. The casque-heads are thought to prey on frogs and insects. When disturbed these frogs open the mouth wide in a defense posture and may attempt to bite. No member of this genus is known to produce advertisement calls, but some do voice distress calls when grasped.

The few (up to about 20) large, unpigmented eggs are carried on the back of the female throughout their development. The babies of the Amazonian forms emerge from the egg capsules as miniatures of the adults, a process called direct development. The incubation period seems to be in the vicinity of 60–80 days.

38. Peruvian Casque-Headed Treefrog

Hemiphractus helioi

Size: Females may attain a length of 3 inches (7.5 cm); the males are somewhat smaller.

Identifying features: The extended snout of this bizarre-looking forest treefrog is depressed rather than laterally compressed; the head is prominently triangular. Short heel spurs (calcars) are present. The dorsum is tan to grayish brown with irregular darker markings. Light vertical stripes may appear on the snout. The limbs are banded, and prominent toe pads are present on all digits. The venter is off-white to grayish.

Voice: No breeding call has yet been associated with this frog.

Reproduction: Eighteen eggs were found on the dorsum of a female. The metamorphs emerge from the egg capsules as miniatures of the adults. The incubation duration is unknown.

Similar species: Several other frog species found in Amazonia have a strongly triangular head. Of these, several lack distinct toe pads, heel spurs, or both. Others, such as the long-nosed egg-brooding treefrog, have a longer snout and heel spurs. The Peruvian casque-head is most similar to Johnson's egg-brooding treefrog (*H. johnsoni*) of Colombia.

Habitat/Range: This frog seems largely restricted to primary forests but is occasionally found in old secondary forests in the upper Amazon Basin and lower Amazon slopes of the Andes from Ecuador to Bolivia.

Comments: This is an uncommon, nocturnal species. Individuals often cling to saplings or sit on palm fronds a yard or two above the ground. They eat small vertebrates, including frogs and possibly lizards, and large invertebrates, and will bite the hand that carelessly restrains them.

39. Long-Nosed Casque-Headed Treefrog

Hemiphractus proboscideus

Size: 1.5–2.5 inches (4–6.5 cm).

Identifying features: This seems to be the most frequently encountered casque-head in the Amazon Basin. It has a bony, enlarged, triangular head;

a laterally flattened dermal process on the tip of the snout; several projections on each upper eyelid; toe pads; prominent calcars (heel spurs); and an array of dermal tubercles on the dorsum and limbs. The tubercles on the forearms are rather precisely arranged in horizontal rows (this is a diagnostic characteristic). The color is some shade of brown with a pattern of irregular diagonal stripes and spots dorsally, laterally, and on the upper surfaces of the limbs. The markings may be tan, deep brown, grayish, or greenish. The tongue and interior of the mouth are bright yellow. The body is flattened or depressed; the spinal vertebrae protrude through the dorsal muscles of adults, forming a series of skin-covered projections.

Voice: The breeding call, if any, is unknown.

Reproduction: The eggs—more than 20—adhere to the skin of the female's back and undergo direct development. The incubation duration is unknown.

Similar species: *Hemiphractus johnsoni* (no photo) and *H. helioi* have only scattered tubercles on the forearms and an overall smoother skin, and the nose process on both species is horizontally flattened (depressed); *H. scutatus* (no photo) is much heavier bodied, lacks calcars and toe pads, and has only a rudimentary nose process. Horned frogs and crested toads lack toe pads.

Habitat: Little is known about the biology of this frog. Those we have seen were found at night sitting on vegetation 3–5 feet (1–2.5 m) above the ground in primary forest. We have found this species to be active on both rainy and dry nights.

Comments: When threatened, this frog will gape and may bite. It feeds on smaller frogs, lizards, and large insects.

Subfamily Hylinae; Typical Treefrogs

Genus *Hyla*; Treefrogs

The approximately 300 *Hyla* species are distributed in both the Old (Eurasia) and New Worlds (the Americas and nearby islands). They vary in length from about 0.9 inch to about 5 inches (2–12.5 cm). The genus is abundantly represented in Amazonas.

The toe pads of most species are well developed and prominently visible. Most species are persistently arboreal. They are typically nocturnal. All are capable of swimming, and most have extensively webbed hind feet. Colors can be brilliant to dull; patterns can vary from intricate to almost nonexistent.

Breeding is usually triggered by the advent of the rainy season and is especially rampant during periods of very low barometric pressure. The males voice loud (almost raucous in some species), distinctive breeding (advertisement) calls. Eggs may number from a few dozen to several thousand and may be laid on a leaf above the water or actually in the water. A few species build streamside nests (by kicking out depressions) in which the eggs are laid. The tadpoles undergo normal development, having an aquatic stage.

Smaller hylines eat tiny invertebrates; larger species accept larger prey.

40. Gladiator Treefrog

Hyla boans

Size: This is one of the larger treefrogs of the Amazon Basin. Males, the larger sex, may attain a snout–vent length of nearly 5 inches (12.5 cm). Females are adult at about 4.25 inches (10.5 cm).

Identifying features: The dorsal color is olive fawn to tan or light brown. Cold, inactive frogs are often darker than warmer, active ones. The lateral pattern consists of gray bars that are flecked with white and separated by thin areas of white. The venter is white to off-white. The fingers and toes are webbed to the bases of the discs. A small, wedge-shaped calcar (heel spur) is present on each heel. The iris is bronzy and there are reticulations on the lower eyelid.

Voice: A series of hollow booming notes voiced while the male frog is sitting in a riverside tree or in the nesting depression.

Reproduction: This is a nest-building frog. Males hollow out a shallow depression near a river or stream where water seepage will keep the depression filled. A large female can lay up to 3000 eggs. Males actively grapple with interloping males in defense of their nesting site, hence the name "gladiator frog."

Similar species: The large size and faded flank markings are distinctive. Other sympatric treefrogs are significantly smaller when adult, have less fully webbed fingers, lack heel spurs, or have more prominently barred or spotted flanks. However, also see the accounts for *Hyla calcarata, H. fasciata, H. geographica,* and *H. microderma.*

Habitat/Range: This giant treefrog is often heard calling from the forested banks of medium to large streams and rivers throughout much of the Amazon Basin.

41. Short-Nosed Treefrog

Hyla brevifrons

Size: The SVL is just under 1 inch (2.5 cm).
Identifying features: Never brightly colored, this small treefrog can be quite variably patterned; the pattern is best determined at night. The overall dorsal coloration is olive gray to olive tan. There is often a paler dorsolateral stripe on each side; this is broad on females but may be broad or narrow on males. If present, the stripe is best defined at night and at all times along its ventral edge. A dark ocular stripe begins at the tip of the nose, angles downward at the eye, passes over the tympanum and above the axilla, and terminates on the lower side anterior to the groin. Two light marks are present on the upper lip. Although these may be difficult to see, they are usually the best field mark. A dark spot is usually present on the side above the hind leg. The thigh is dark (brownish).
Voice: The breeding call consists of many rapidly repeated peeps.
Reproduction: The 51–100 eggs are laid a short distance above the water or just at water level on emergent vegetation. On hatching, the tadpoles drop or wriggle into the water and complete their development.
Similar species: Many other small treefrogs are quite similar in appearance, including *H. rhodopepla* (dark lateral stripe), *H. minuta* (no lateral stripe), *H. riveroi* (three light labial bars), and *H. rossalleni* (thin dark or no lateral stripe).
Habitat/Range: The short-nosed treefrog is a species of small forest ponds as well as of oxbow edges. Individuals are often found where emergent grasses are dense, and, like many of their small congeners, are far more easily heard than seen. The species ranges over much of the northwestern Amazon Basin.

42. Convict Treefrog

Hyla calcarata

Size: Males are about 1.5 inches (4 cm) long; females may reach 2.25 inches (5.5 cm).
Identifying features: Although quietly colored, this is one of the prettier and more prominently marked of the moderate-sized treefrogs. The dorsal coloration may vary from tan to terra cotta, and pales during the day. The whitish sides are prominently marked with vertical bars of black. The venter is white. There are no reticulations on the lower eyelid. The iris is

cream or very pale bronze. There are very prominent heel spurs. The fingers are webbed only at their bases; the toes are from one-half to two-thirds webbed.

Voice: Males call in a low-pitched rattle at night while perched transversely on the branches of shrubs above the water of forest streams. We have found calling convict treefrogs up to 5 feet (2.5 m) above the water.

Reproduction: The 1000-plus eggs form a surface film.

Similar species: No other treefrog has such prominently barred thighs and flanks and such a pronounced tarsal spur; but see the accounts for *Hyla boans, H. fasciata, H. geographica,* and *H. microderma.*

Habitat/Range: Although you may find these wary frogs by day as they huddle on shrubs above forest streams and rivers or rest on the surface of leaves of forest plants, they are far more easily found after nightfall as they call or forage throughout much of the Amazon Basin.

43. Spotted-Thighed Treefrog

Hyla fasciata

Size: Adult females are 2 inches (5 cm) in SVL; males are adult at 1.6 inches (4 cm).

Identifying features: These frogs look like smaller, paler, less precisely marked convict treefrogs with smaller calcars and darker irises. Day–night differences in color can be pronounced. The dorsum is usually yellowish at night and brownish by day. The lower sides are lighter. Dark freckling is present posterolaterally. More prominent dark dotting appears on the rear of the thigh. A darker vertebral line is often present, and very irregular, usually very obscure transverse barring may be visible on the back. The venter is usually off-white. The lower eyelid is not reticulated. The fingers are not webbed; the toes are webbed for about one-half of their length.

Voice: During the rainy season, these forest frogs voice their bisyllabic call from positions low in the shrubs overhanging the quiet waters of pools and backwaters.

Reproduction: The more than 1510 eggs float as a surface film.

Similar species: *Hyla calcarata* has larger calcars and prominent, precise barring on the flanks and thighs. *Hyla geographica* has gray-flecked sides but no discrete lateral or thigh spotting. Also see the accounts for *H. boans, H. calcarata, H. geographica,* and *H. microderma.*

Habitat/Range: *Hyla fasciata* is primarily nocturnal but may be encountered by day as it sleeps low on shrubs and herbs, usually close to a water source. Ecotourists often see them at night during canoe trips into seasonally flooded forests in Amazonia, Ecuador, Peru, and western Brazil.

44. Map Treefrog

Hyla geographica

Size: Males seldom exceed 2.25 inches (5.5 cm) in SVL; females may slightly exceed 3 inches (7.5 cm).

Identifying features: This large treefrog is variably colored and patterned. The dorsal ground color is some shade of brown, and there are irregular darker brown to russet, cream, and white dorsal figures, spots, and bars. The barring is especially prominent on the exposed surfaces of the hind limbs. A small heel spur is present. The sides are dappled gray but lack discrete spots or bars. There are scattered black(ish) spots on the cream to white venter. The iris is reddish brown. The fingers are webbed for about one-half their length; the toes are three-quarters webbed. Horny nuptial pads are present on the thumbs of reproductively active males.

Voice: During the rainy season males give moaning calls sometimes interspersed with chuckles.

Reproduction: The female lays a surface film of more than 2000 eggs.

Similar species: *Hyla boans*, the most similar species, has fully webbed fingers and toes and is much larger than *H. geographica* when adult. *Hyla calcarata* and *H. fasciata* have either precise barring or discrete spots on the sides and thighs. *Hyla microderma* has reticulations on the eyelids that are visible when its eyes are closed.

Habitat/Range: This beautiful treefrog can be found alongside streams, rivers, and ponds. It may be heard and is most easily seen at night as it calls while sitting transversely on branches above the water. It is found in Amazonian Colombia, Brazil, Ecuador, and Peru.

45. Rough-Skinned Green Treefrog

Hyla granosa

Size: This is a moderate-sized treefrog. Males average 1.5 inches (4 cm) in SVL; females may near 2 inches (5 cm).

Identifying features: This is one of the most distinctive treefrogs of the Iquitos region. The tannish green, olive green, to leaf green dorsal and lateral skin is granular and translucent. The ventral skin is on the transparent side of translucent, and the hidden surfaces of the legs and groin are bluish green. The eyes are large and have a blue-rimmed cream iris. The snout is very bluntly rounded. Breeding males develop a thumb (nuptial) spine to assist them in holding gravid females. Only the outer finger is webbed; the toes are webbed for about two-thirds of their length.

Voice: A repeated hoot, often given while the frog is concealed between the leaves of broad-leaved, emergent, or streamside shrubs.

Reproduction: The female lays a film of more than 510 eggs in quiet or slowly flowing waters.

Similar species: *Hyla punctata* usually has red and/or yellow dorsal markings and a red dorsolateral stripe. The treefrogs of the genus *Sphaenorhynchus* have more sharply pointed snouts, cloacal dermal flaps, or dorsal spotting. Phyllomedusine treefrogs have vertical pupils.

Habitat/Range: These common to abundant forest pool and flooded backwater treefrogs are best sought at night by following their calls to the source. Since males usually call while sitting between two leaves, they can be difficult to find even then. Found in Guyana, Ecuador, Colombia, Brazil, Venezuela, and Peru.

46. Many-Striped Treefrog

Hyla haraldschultzi

Size: Females reach 1 inch (2.5 cm) in SVL; males are slightly smaller.

Identifying features: By day, this tiny tan treefrog has six variably defined, but often prominent, reddish longitudinal stripes. By night, the stripes pale and fragment, and the dorsum becomes longitudinally flecked. The body is long and proportionally slender. The fingers are basally webbed; the toes are webbed for about one-third of their length. The iris is a reddish tan similar to the dorsal ground color. The venter is cream.

Voice: A rapidly repeated multisyllabic call; the terminal note is the longest.

Reproduction: Unknown.

Similar species: None.

Habitat/Range: We have found this tiny hylid calling from the grasses along a flooded footpath through secondary forest, sitting quietly at night on the leaves of forest shrubs, and calling from oxbow-edge water lettuce.

Comments: Its comparative slenderness seems to allow this frog an unexpected flexibility. It often turns its head and arcs its body.

47. Cinnamon Treefrog

Hyla koechlini

Size: To 1 inch (2.5 cm).

Identifying features: The dorsum of this small, pudgy, attractive little treefrog is tan to yellow-brown at night and cinnamon by day. Obscure darker chevrons may be visible. Except for a light spot beneath each eye, the sides of the face, the groin, and the hidden surface of the thighs are chocolate brown to black. The light ventral skin is granular and mottled with dark pigment. The iris is reddish tan, often slightly lighter than the dorsum.

Voice: From one to several high-pitched peeps.

Reproduction: The 200–300 eggs float as a surface film.

Similar species: Several other small brownish treefrogs have reddish tan irises, but none is known to have the dark groin and thighs of *H. koechlini*.

Habitat/Range: This arboreal species descends to shrubs at night to call and breeds in ponds in seasonally flooded forests of Amazonian Peru; range poorly defined.

48. Rocket Treefrog

Hyla lanciformis

Size: Males are about 3 inches (7.5 cm) in SVL; females reach 4 inches (10 cm).

Identifying features: The dorsum of this large, streamlined treefrog is tan. The nose is sharply pointed. Crossbars are often present, especially on young specimens. There is a distinctive light labial stripe and a light-edged dark canthal stripe, which continues over the tympanum to the groin. Posteriorly the venter is white or off-white. The chest is dark with light spots, and the throat is light with dark spots. The fingers are basally webbed; the toes are about two-thirds webbed. Breeding males have a spine on each thumb. The iris is bronze to brown.

Voice: The single loud quack is quite distinctive. Breeding males can be heard throughout the year in forest edge pools.

Reproduction: The eggs, which form a surface film, can number more than 2000.

Similar species: None. It would be difficult to mistake this rocket-shaped frog for more normally proportioned blocky treefrogs.

Habitat: This common, highly arboreal treefrog may be encountered in a wide variety of habitats in most of the Amazon drainage.

49. Plain-Colored Treefrog

Hyla leali

Size: Males are about 0.75 inch (2 cm) in SVL; females are about 1 inch (2.5 cm).

Identifying features: This very nondescript treefrog is not always easy to identify. You can most reliably identify it by ruling out what it *cannot* be. The color tends to be cream, tan, or very light brown with pinkish overtones. There may be a somewhat darker X on the back. A lighter spot is present on the upper lip below the nostril, and another large one is usually visible below the eye. A third, usually poorly defined, light spot may be present below the tympanum.

Voice: The call consists of two syllables often repeated. We have found males calling while clinging to emergent vegetation at the edges and away from the shore of weed-choked oxbows.

Reproduction: The 510 or more eggs are laid directly in the water.

Similar species: Other small treefrogs tend to be grayer or richer brown, tend to have a well-defined dorsal pattern and white lines or spots of color on their hind limbs, or tend to have more than one (or no) well-defined spot on the upper lip.

Habitat/Range: We have found *H. leali* only while it was calling. Choruses consisting of large numbers of calling males were easily tracked to patches of emergent vegetation in oxbows. When not breeding, this small treefrog is associated with secondary forest habitats and clearings in Amazonian Bolivia, Peru, and Brazil.

50. Clown Treefrog, Giraffe Treefrog

Hyla leucophyllata

Size: Males average about 1.25 inches (3 cm); the larger females can attain 1.5 inches (4 cm).

Identifying features: The fingers and toes are orange-red and webbed. The axillae and groin are also reddish orange. The iris is bronzy. This frog occurs in two distinct color phases, and perhaps in intermediate ones as well.

In the apparently more common "clown" phase, the dorsum is brown to purplish brown. The top of the snout is patterned with a creamy gold to buff (sometimes white-edged) triangle, the two posterior tips of which lengthen into broad creamy gold to buff (again, sometimes white-edged) dorsolateral bars. A light enamel cream to goldish spot is often present on the posterior back, one or two light bars are present on the femur, and there is a light heel spot.

The "giraffe" color phase, with its reticulated pattern and irregular spots, is not as often seen. The back and sides are brown to purple-brown. The reticulations are light tan. The red of the toes, axillae, groin, and venter is reduced in extent and intensity.

Voice: An often-repeated series of short, harsh notes.

Reproduction: This is a "leaf frog." The 300–600 eggs are placed on over-water vegetation, and the tadpoles drop into the water at hatching to complete their development.

Similar species: The smaller but very similar *Hyla bifurca* (not pictured) lacks spots on the femur. The light dorsal markings of *H. sarayacuensis* lack boldly precise edges. In many of its phases, the confusingly similar *H. triangulum* is light with dark markings and the red is brighter on the venter.

Habitat/Range: This forest pool and forest edge species may often be heard calling in considerable numbers. We have found them on horizontal twigs above the water and on emergent grasses. Widespread throughout the Amazon Basin.

Comments: The giraffe phase was long thought to be a separate species and was given the now invalid scientific name *Hyla favosa*.

51. Neotropical Marbled Treefrog

Hyla marmorata

Size: Females reach an SVL of about 2.25 inches (5.5 cm); males are fully grown at about 1.75 inches (4.5 cm).

Identifying features: The snout is short and broadly rounded. This is a brownish gray to gray treefrog with a highly variable pattern. Many of the markings are dark, but some are lighter and resemble patchy lichens or bird droppings. The posterior one-third of the frog is often lighter than the anterior, and the color change is usually precisely delineated. The belly is yellowish with black markings. The fingers and toes are extensively webbed. The toe pads are large and rounded. The limbs are edged with a fringe of skin with scalloped edges.

Voice: A low-pitched trill voiced from the ground or low shrubs at the edges of temporary ponds.

Reproduction: Females produce a surface film of more than 1200 eggs.

Similar species: The dermal fringe on the legs will differentiate this species from all but *H. tuberculosa* and *Agalychnis craspedopus*. The former is larger, often dull green, and lacks dark spots on the belly. The latter is green and has vertically elliptical pupils.

Habitat/Range: These nocturnal treefrogs are highly arboreal but do descend during the breeding season, when they may be found on the ground or in grasses and shrubs near temporary forest ponds. This species inhabits secondary and primary forests. Widespread in the Amazon Basin.

52. Yellow-Toed Treefrog

Hyla microderma

Size: Males are just over 1 inch (2.5 cm) in SVL; females are slightly larger.

Identifying features: This small brown to reddish brown treefrog has distinctive yellow toe pads. The dark dorsum is marked with variable and irregular dark crossbars and a black vertebral line. The lower sides, belly, undersurfaces of the legs, and inner fingers are cream. The whitish irises have a dark outer ring. The lower eyelids have golden reticulations. The fingers are not webbed; the toes are webbed for about half of their length.

Voice: A short clicking trill.

Reproduction: Unknown.

Similar species: The yellow toe pads of this small treefrog and the reticulated lower eyelid are diagnostic.

Habitat/Range: Much of the life history of this primary forest species remains unknown. On a late afternoon walk along the swampy edge of a seasonal pond, we found several males and a single amplexing pair. The female was slightly larger than the male. Known from Amazonian Peru, Colombia, and Ecuador.

53. Least Treefrog

Hyla minuta

Size: Adult males are barely 0.63 inch (1.5 cm) long; females may be 0.75 inch (2 cm).

Identifying features: This tiny, slender hylid is one of the most nondescript of the Amazonian treefrogs. The ground color varies from creamy tan to light brown. A darker broad interorbital bar or triangle (apex pointing rearward) and two broad dorsal bars are usually at least vaguely visible. The interorbital mark and the first dorsal bar may be joined. There are no light marks on the upper lip. No axillary membrane (a thin flange of skin from the upper arm to the body) is present. A light stripe is often visible on the heel.

Voice: Vast congresses of these frogs gather in weed-choked *cochas;* smaller numbers assemble in temporary forest pools. The call is a series of tinkling rasps. The first is the loudest and longest and is followed by one to several shorter secondary notes.

Reproduction: Small clusters of eggs are attached to plants at or just below the water surface.

Similar species: A sympatric *Hyla* species, as yet unidentified, is usually somewhat redder in color and has narrow dorsal markings and a noticeable patagium (axillary membrane).

Habitat/Range: The least treefrog occurs in forested areas and at forest edge situations as well as in seasonally flooded *cochas.* Although small numbers may use ephemeral pools for breeding, this hylid breeds prolifically in patches of emergent grasses in large oxbows and other shallow-water areas. The species ranges widely through the northern Amazon Basin.

54. Jeweled Treefrog

Hyla miyatai

Size: The elfin males are a mere 0.75 inch (2 cm) in SVL; females attain a full inch (2.5 cm).

Identifying features: *Hyla miyatai* is a yellowish treefrog with a patchy red blush that is most prominent anteriorly. A red, rearward-directed triangle is usually visible on the head. At night, in the beam of a flashlight, this frog looks metallic red. By day the colors fade to chalky white and lime green with no metallic highlights. The venter is pinkish to very pale rose. The iris is yellowish tan with pink flecks. The toe pads are large. The fingers are partially webbed (about one-third of their length); the toes are webbed for about three-quarters of their length.

Voice: A series of high-pitched, insectlike notes often voiced while the frog sits on floating vegetation or emergent grasses.

Reproduction: Although much about the breeding biology of this treefrog remains unknown, approximately 400 eggs were found in a plastic bag in which two pairs were temporarily housed.

Similar species: None. Both day and night colors are distinctive.

Habitat/Range: We have found many of these small hylids at night at the edges of seasonally flooded depressions in secondary forest. Others were in emergent vegetation at the edge of an oxbow lake. Found in lowland Ecuador and Peru.

55. Orange-Shanked Treefrog

Hyla parviceps

Size: Males reach 0.75 inch (2 cm) in SVL; females are nearly 1 inch (2.5 cm).

Identifying features: The dorsum is reddish brown to grayish with a darker dorsal figure. A white spot is visible beneath the eye. The gray venter is darkest posteriorly. The undersurfaces of the limbs are gray. The hidden surfaces of the thighs are black with prominent white spots. The hidden surface of the calf has an elongate blotch of brilliant orange. The fingers are webbed for about half of their length; the toes are webbed for three-quarters of their length.

Voice: A series of high-pitched peeps.

Reproduction: The female lays up to 300 eggs in several clusters.

Similar species: Although the frog usually must be in hand before the orange blotch on the shank is visible, this is a diagnostic marking.

Habitat/Range: This common and widespread species occurs in a variety of habitats. We thought it particularly common in swamps bearing dense stands of the emergent alligator flag (*Thalia* sp.), where it called while sitting on the broad leaves about 18 inches (45.7 cm) above the water.

56. Common Polkadot Treefrog

Hyla punctata punctata

Size: 1–1.75 inches (2.5–4.5 cm). Adult females may be somewhat larger and more robust than males.

Identifying features: This pretty treefrog bears different colors by day than by night. The dorsum is usually terra cotta by night and bright lime green by day. Darker orange (night) to bright yellow (day) spots may be present. When yellow, the dorsal spots may be partially ringed by red pigment. A terra cotta to whitish lateral line (from snout to posterior side, but lacking in the groin) is present. All four limbs are spotted with either reddish orange or yellow. The fingers are not strongly webbed; the toes are partially webbed. The venter is white. The snout is rounded when viewed from above. The throat is greenish, and brightest in chorusing males. The iris is light with dark markings but may appear entirely dark at night.

Voice: A series of low chuckling notes.

Reproduction: Clutches of more than 400 eggs have been reported.

Similar species: *Hyla granosa* is more restricted to forest rivers and pools; calls from shrubs; is less prominently spotted (often uniform green); and has a translucent greenish venter, a light iris, and a granular dorsum. Breeding males have a prepollical spine (basically a thumb spine) that may serve to stimulate the female or to help the male retain his grip during amplexus.

Habitat: This is a widepread species of flooded oxbows; open, long-lasting ponds; and grassy river-edge situations, where it calls from either surface or emergent vegetation. Small numbers can be heard even at the boat docks in Iquitos.

57. Chaco Treefrog

Hyla raniceps

Size: Occasional females (the larger sex) reach a length of about 3 inches (7.5 cm), but a more usual size for both sexes is 2–2.5 inches (5–6.5 cm).

Identifying features: Adults are big, grayish to tan treefrogs. A thin, dark brown line extends from the back of each eye rearward over the tympanum to the shoulder. Some individuals have vertical bars or vertically elongated dark spots on the rear of the thighs. The underside of the thighs has a pale purplish cast. Juveniles are green and even more nondescript than the adults.

Voice: Males typically voice hoarse croaks while sitting in shallow water or while floating (often holding onto vegetation with the finger pads) amid patches of emergent vegetation. They may also call while sitting on a riverbank or from a riverbank shrub.

Reproduction: Each clutch contains several hundred floating eggs.

Similar species: Several treefrogs in the various Amazon drainages are similar in appearance. Many of these lack dark bars on the posterior thighs, lack the postocular dark stripe, or have barred or spotted sides. *Hyla lanciformis* is more streamlined and elongate. Juveniles of many species, including the Chaco treefrog, are very difficult to identify positively.

Habitat/Range: A lowland frog, the Chaco treefrog is not at all restricted to the drier areas suggested by its common name. Indeed, although first found in the province of Chaco, Argentina, this frog is commonly encountered in lowland drainage areas of eastern South America from Argentina to Venezuela.

Comments: Because of its variability, this frog has been described under a number of different names.

58. Red-Striped Treefrog

Hyla rhodopepla

Size: Females, the larger sex, reach an SVL of 1 inch (2.5 cm); males are adult at about 0.75 inch (2 cm).

Identifying features: At night, this is a yellowish treefrog with a reddish dorsolateral stripe on each side (this fades as it nears the groin), light upper lips, and whitish flanks. Small reddish flecks, most prominent anteriorly, are usually present between the dorsolateral stripes. This frog lightens in overall color by day. When present (they may not be!), the red dorsolateral stripes are diagnostic. The venter is yellow. The iris is tan with tiny flecks of pinkish rose. The fingers are one-third webbed; the toes are one-half webbed.

Voice: A series of high-pitched peeps, with the first being the longest and strongest. Males call while sitting on or clinging to emergent vegetation such as *Thalia* sp. (alligator flag) and grasses.

Reproduction: The clutch of 300-plus eggs is laid in a number of clusters.

Similar species: *Hyla riveroi* (not pictured) may approach *H. rhodopepla* in color, but it has white patches rather than a white stripe on its upper lip.

Habitat/Range: The red-striped treefrog is common and widespread in the Amazon Basin and can be found in considerable numbers at small, ephemeral forest ponds. Look for them at night amid pond edge vegetation.

59. Golden-Nosed Treefrog

Hyla rossalleni

Size: Females reach 1.25 inches (3 cm) in SVL; males are smaller.

Identifying features: At night, in the beam of a flashlight, the metallic golden interorbital area of this small treefrog is immediately evident. During the day, this area appears cream colored. The dorsum is brown with irregular, scattered dark and cream markings. The toes, webbing, and groin are reddish. The venter is lighter. The fingers are one-half webbed; the toes are webbed for three-quarters of their length. There are no nuptial pads.

Voice: A series of rather coarse notes, the first being the longest and loudest. Males call from twigs or emergent vegetation.

Reproduction: Two amplexing pairs were found on leaves overhanging a forest pool. Other than that, the breeding biology is unknown.

Similar species: *Hyla leucophyllata, H. bifurca,* and *H. sarayacuensis* have prominently marked dorsa. *Hyla triangulum* is often prominently marked dorsally, but if unmarked lacks the metallic nose patch.

Habitat/Range: This species occurs in primary and secondary forests, where it breeds in temporarily flooded depressions and forest edge pools. It is found in Peru, Colombia, Ecuador, and Brazil.

60. Mottled Clown Treefrog

Hyla sarayacuensis

Size: Males often measure 1 inch (2.5 cm) in SVL; females are about 1.25 inches (3 cm).

Identifying features: This is a stunningly pretty but variable treefrog. The dorsal ground color is deep purplish brown. A rather well defined golden yellow patch extends from the tip of the snout to mid-eye. The imprecisely delineated golden yellow body and leg patches are of variable size and intensity. A large patch is present behind each tympanum. The dorsal pattern may be of small golden flecks, larger spots, or indefinite lighter patches. Golden elbow and wrist marks are present on each forelimb, and golden flank and heel marks are present on each hind leg. The toes, webbing, underside of the legs, and groin are orange rather than red. The remaining ventral areas are lighter. Males lack nuptial pads.

Voice: A short series of harsh notes, the first being the loudest and longest. Males call from vegetation along the edges of forest pools.

Reproduction: The 51–151 eggs adhere to the leaves of vegetation above the water. On hatching, the tadpoles drop into the water to complete their development.

Similar species: This is the only member of the species complex (*H. bifurca, H. leucophyllata, H. rossalleni,* and *H. triangulum*) with *imprecisely* delineated golden markings.

Habitat/Range: This persistently arboreal species is found in primary and secondary forests. It is seldom seen by day. At night, it descends to relatively low shrubs and may be found chorusing from twigs, trunks, and other vegetation. Found in Amazonian Colombia, Ecuador, and Peru.

61. Variable Clown Treefrog

Hyla triangulum

Size: About 1 inch (2.5 cm).

Identifying features: Positive identification can pose a challenge. The golden brown dorsum varies from unmarked to profusely marked with dark, rounded or oval, leopardlike spots. Other markings include a single dark nape spot, dark hourglass-shaped dorsal figures, and various combinations of these. Non–profusely spotted specimens usually have brown sides, faces, and outer edges of the limbs. The inner toes and fingers, the webbing, the groin, and all but the dorsal surfaces of the thighs (which are brown) are bright red. The fingers are webbed for half their length; the toes for three-quarters of their length. Where it is not red, the venter is creamy, sometimes with a rosy blush.

Voice: A series of about seven short, harsh notes, the first being the longest and loudest.

Reproduction: The variable clown treefrog breeds in seasonally flooded ponds and oxbows. The eggs are laid above the water level on water lettuce, water hyacinths, and other emergent plants.

Similar species: Other small, variably colored treefrogs that may have similar markings have orange(ish) rather than red(dish) webbing, legs, and groin. *Phrynohyas coriacea,* another species with red webbing, is much larger, exudes copious quantities of a cloying skin irritant when disturbed, and has a dark axillary blotch.

Habitat/Range: This species is found around pools and swamp edges in clearings more often than in forests. We have found them calling in association with many other small frogs while clinging to emergent vegetation and in vast numbers amid water lettuce and water hyacinths in flooded oxbow situations. Found in Peru and Ecuador.

Genus *Osteocephalus;* Bromeliad or Broad-Headed Treefrogs

The genus name is derived from the characteristic fusion of the skin of the head to the skull beneath it.

Osteocephalus are sexually dimorphic: males are smaller and have a tuberculate—in some cases, almost spiny—dorsum while the larger females have very few tubercles. Because of ontogenetic and intraspecific color and pattern variability, the frogs in this genus can be very difficult to identify. Most of the 10 or so species are persistently arboreal; some actually utilize arboreal bromeliads for breeding. Several species may descend and forage at lower points in the trees or shrubs at night. These frogs are wary, running up tree trunks to safety at the slightest disturbance.

Unlike typical treefrogs, the broad-headed (and golden-eyed) treefrogs have paired lateral (rather than single subgular) vocal pouches. On rainy nights, the loud, high-pitched chuckles of the males of some species echo from tree to tree as they call from canopy bromeliads. Other species call while sitting in low shrubs in and around freshening forest pools.

The broad-headed treefrogs are found throughout many regions of the lowland *varzeas* (seasonally flooded forests) and rainforests of northwestern Amazonia.

62. Forest Bromeliad Treefrog

Osteocephalus cabrerai

Size: Females are about 2.5 inches (6.5 cm) in SVL; males are 2 inches (5 cm).

Identifying features: The complex combination of irregularly edged moss green and slate gray patches dorsally and laterally make this one of the prettiest of a largely nondescript treefrog genus. The venter is a uniformly colored lighter gray. All four limbs are barred (or spotted) with green and dark slate. The toe pads are usually noticeably lighter than the digits. The rear legs are proportionally long. Except for a horizontal dark central stripe, the golden iris is largely unmarked. There is a white upper lip patch immediately anterior to the tympanum.

Voice: We have not yet heard a call that we can attribute to this species.

Reproduction: It is suspected that this frog breeds in forest ponds or at the edges of slow streams, and that the eggs form a surface film like those made by others in the genus. It is possible, however, that this frog breeds in bromeliad cups.

Similar species: None.

Habitat/Range: We have found this treefrog to be an uncommon resident of primary forest. Except for a single specimen found in a bromeliad in the canopy of a newly felled tree, the few we have found were on shrubs overhanging streams on the eastern side of the Amazon in northern Peru.

63. Common Bromeliad Treefrog

Osteocephalus leprieurii

Size: Females attain an SVL of about 3 inches (7.5 cm); males are about 2 inches (5 cm).

Identifying features: The dorsal skin is tan to reddish brown, and darker markings are usually visible. Some individuals may have the back patterned with rounded spots of pinkish rose; others may be transversely barred. The sides are light and may have scattered black spots. The belly is white to pale pinkish orange. The hidden surfaces of the hind limbs may be brown(ish). All four limbs are dark banded. The fingers are webbed for about one-quarter of their length; the toes for about three-quarters. The irises are gold. A light (white to tan) labial stripe is prominent.

Voice: An often-repeated high-pitched chuckle.

Reproduction: This is a forest pond breeder; the eggs form a surface film.

Similar species: This common treefrog is very similar in appearance to *Osteocephalus planiceps* but has longer legs and lacks black radiations on the irises.

Habitat/Range: Except for the purpose of breeding, this treefrog seldom leaves the bromeliads high in the trees of its primary forest habitat. Occasional individuals may forage in low shrubs. This is an abundant species in the northwestern Amazon Basin.

64. Flat-Headed Bromeliad Treefrog

Osteocephalus planiceps

Size: Females attain an SVL of about 2 inches (5 cm); males are adult at about 1.75 inches (4.5 cm).

Identifying features: This interesting frog is quite flat in appearance. The color is variable but is generally a nondescript pasty tan to reddish tan dorsally with obscure darker or lighter markings. The color lightens laterally, but the sides may be flecked with black. The belly is white. Both front and rear limbs are barred. A thin, dark canthal stripe is present. Dark masking extends from the eye to the tympanum, and often continues to the axilla. The fingers are partially webbed; the toes about three-fourths so. A light labial stripe may be present. A pair of prominent interorbital ridges may be present. The iris, which is strongly patterned with vertical black markings, is gold above and often darker below. Juveniles are poorly patterned dorsally but have enamel white heels, knees, and elbows.

Voice: A series of rolling chuckles. Males usually call from trees near the edges of forest ponds, sometimes from well above ground level.

Reproduction: This species *may* breed in the water-holding cups of bromeliads.

Similar species: Most other species in this genus are similar to this one in appearance. The principal difference will be in the degree of dark streaking on the iris and the comparative length of the hind legs. Compare the accounts for all carefully, but don't be disappointed if you are unable to assign these frogs to a species.

Habitat/Range: Although the chuckling call of this frog is often heard emanating from arboreal bromeliads, we have seen comparatively few specimens. One of our guides secured a calling male from a canopy bromeliad to allow us to identify the sound. We have also occasionally found females of this species at night in low shrubs. They are quite wary and usually leap quickly away when approached. This species is mainly an inhabitant of primary forests in the northwestern Amazon Basin.

65. Giant Broad-Headed Treefrog

Osteocephalus taurinus

Size: Some females reach an SVL of slightly more than 4 inches (10 cm); males are adult at about 3 inches (7.5 cm).

Identifying features: The dorsum may vary from tan to deep blackish brown. When the ground color is light, darker banding or irregular blotches may be visible (especially on immature animals). A dark vertebral line may be present. The sides may be lighter than the dorsum, and if so, will have dark spots. The venter is light and is dark spotted anteriorly. The head is broad and flat between the eyes, and the skin is firmly fused to the cranium. A bony ridge is visible on the crown just central to each eye. When viewed in profile, the snout is deep. The limbs are dark barred. If present at all, the light labial line will be barely discernible.

The iris is greenish with prominent black radiations. The fingers are *not* fully webbed.

Voice: A series of hoots that may be followed by a low *churr.* Males call while floating on the surface of temporary ponds and pools.

Reproduction: The large egg mass floats as a surface film.

Similar species: The two large hylas, *H. boans* and *H. geographica,* have heel spurs (which *O. taurinus* lacks). The various species in the genus *Phrynohyas* have thick, glandular skin.

Habitat/Range: This species occurs in secondary and primary forests and is often seen in and near clearings. Widespread throughout the Amazon drainage.

Comments: As now described, this is a variable species that occurs in "small" and "large" morphs. Additional studies are needed to clarify the situation.

Genus *Phrynohyas;* Golden-Eyed Treefrogs

Because of the cloying, irritating, milk-colored glandular substance these frogs exude when bothered, they are sometimes referred to as milk frogs. The dorsal skin of both sexes is glandular and weakly to strongly tuberculate. When alarmed, all *Phrynohyas* exude copious quantities of viscous secretions from the skin that are very irritating to some people. Carefully wash your hands after handling these frogs. Females are the larger sex.

Like the broad-headed treefrogs of the genus *Osteocephalus,* the golden-eyed treefrogs have paired (bilateral) vocal sacs. All species are strongly arboreal. *Phrynohyas resinifictrix* is a tree hole dweller *and* breeder. Others in this genus of about five species breed in a more traditional manner; although they spend much time in the canopy, they descend at night to feed and, if conditions are right, to breed.

66. Amazonian Milk Treefrog

Phrynohyas resinifictrix

Size: This large treefrog attains a length of about 3 inches (7.5 cm).

Identifying features: The dorsal ground color is olive tan to pale brick red (more rarely with a grayish overcast). A busy pattern of brown to reddish markings is present. The venter is off-white to cream. The fingers and toes are pale green and strongly webbed, and bear large toe pads. All four limbs are strongly barred. The dorsum is very tuberculate. Suriname and eastern Brazilian examples are pale gray with darker markings. The golden iris has an interesting pattern of black lines. This frog exudes a toxic skin secretion when handled or injured.

Voice: The male's loud bark is made even more resonant by the acoustics of the frog's cavity home. The frogs begin calling soon after darkness falls in both dry and wet weather.

Reproduction: Females lay as many as 1000 eggs. The tadpoles feed on decaying plant and animal matter in the murky water of their restricted home and probably consume the eggs of their own species as well.

Similar species: The very strongly tuberculate dorsum will differentiate this treefrog from all other Amazonian species.

Habitat/Range: Amazonian milk treefrogs live and breed in water-containing tree holes in primary forest trees and are seldom seen away from this microhabitat. It is thought that they travel the highways of interlacing tree limbs and seldom descend to the ground. This is a common but seldom seen frog of the northwestern and eastern Amazon Basin.

Comments: The milky glandular secretions are viscid, clinging, and toxic. Wash your hands both before (for the frog's benefit) and after (for your own benefit) handling this frog.

67. Common Milk Treefrog

Phrynohyas venulosa

Size: Although most are smaller, females can reach 4 inches (10 cm) in SVL; males are about 3.5 inches (9 cm).

Identifying features: This is a variably patterned frog. Some individuals are unmarked tan to brown dorsally; others have extensive dark dorsal markings. There may or may not be small tubercles. The venter is creamy white. The head is wide and the snout is broadly rounded. The hind limbs are prominently barred. A dark blotch often covers the tympanum and may extend onto the upper arm. The lower jaw edge is white.

Voice: Males produce a loud, often-repeated snore either while floating on the surface or while sitting on vegetation.

Reproduction: Females produce well over 1000 eggs per clutch.

Similar species: Males of the genus *Osteocephalus* have low spines on the dorsum. *Phrynohyas coriacea* (not pictured) has a purple-black shoulder spot, and *P. resinifictrix* has a strongly tuberculate dorsum.

Habitat/Range: *Phrynohyas venulosa* is a habitat generalist that can be found in primary and secondary forests, clearings, and villages. It breeds in all manner of water holes from small potholes to swamp edges. Widespread throughout much of Latin America.

Comments: This frog exudes glandular secretions from the dorsum in copious amounts. The secretions are thick, clinging, and apparently quite virulent. Wash your hands carefully after handling this frog!

Genus *Scarthyla;* Slender Treefrog

As currently understood, this genus is monotypic. The single species ranges widely in the northwestern Amazon Basin.

68. Slender Treefrog

Scarthyla ostinodactyla

Size: The size range is 0.75–1 inch (2–2.5 cm); females are marginally larger and more robust than males.

Identifying features: This tiny, greenish (night) to green-brown (day), sharp-nosed treefrog is alert, fast, and agile. A prominent broad light line on the lip and side separates the dark dorsum from the whitish venter. Obscure darker markings are present dorsally. The throat is green, darker on males. The toe pads are small but functional. The fingers are unwebbed; the toes are nearly fully webbed. The iris is gold.

Voice: The whistles of chorusing males may be heard by day or night. Calling males are easily approached after dark.

Reproduction: The female of an amplexing pair, held overnight for photographic purposes, laid about 100 eggs in the bag.

Similar species: Since there are many small treefrogs of somewhat similar appearance and various arrow poison frogs with *two* light *side* stripes or with a dorsolateral rather than a lateral stripe, we reemphasize the slenderness and color of this frog and the position of its light side stripe.

Habitat/Range: Occasionally encountered while resting on forest vegetation, *Scarthyla* breeds in flooded forests, sometimes in pools of considerable depth. We found them while wading after another treefrog species in water considerably deeper than waist level. This is a common species in the northwestern Amazon Basin.

Genus *Scinax;* Snouted or Narrow-Headed Treefrogs

At least 5 of the 90 or so species in this genus occur in the northwestern Amazon Basin. One Amazonian species, *S. garbei,* has at least three distinct morphs. For the most part the *Scinax* are small treefrogs of rather dull dorsal coloration. Tans, grays, and moss greens, either alone or in combination, are typical. Some species have brilliant flash marks on the hidden surfaces of the hind legs. Two such are *Scinax rubra* and *S. garbei*. The ventral skin of all is visibly granular. The toe pads of many members of the genus are round when viewed from above; those of others appear more oval, being more truncated anteriorly. The fingers are unwebbed. The webbing of the toes is rather extensive except for the innermost two, which are webbed only basally.

These frogs rest quietly on limbs and foliage during the hours of daylight and become active at nightfall, when they actively forage for the small insects that form their diet.

As is the case with most frogs, the urge to reproduce is instigated by the advent of the rainy season, and immense choruses can be heard on cloudy or rainy nights when the barometric pressure is low. The eggs are laid in water and development of the tadpole is typical.

69. Plain Narrow-Headed Treefrog

Scinax cruentomma

Size: The size range is 1–1.25 inches (2.5–3 cm); females are only marginally larger than males.

Identifying features: This small treefrog is one of the more nondescript members of the genus. Dorsally it is a variable tan or light brown. A vaguely defined, posterior-directed triangle is usually visible between the eyes, and an equally vague darker figure, which may be in contact with the interorbital triangle, is often discernible on the shoulders and back. The lower sides are cream to light tan and may bear discrete darker markings. There are no bright colors on the hidden surfaces of the thighs. A variably distinct deep reddish mark runs horizontally through the otherwise silvery iris. The snout is gently rounded and of normal length.

Voice: A single low note, usually voiced while the male is angled head-downward on a leaf or stem of an emergent or pondside plant.

Reproduction: Females lay more than 1000 eggs that form a surface film.

Similar species: There are many tan to light brown treefrogs in Amazonian Peru. Most have some distinctive marking: a lighter or darker lateral line or concealed flash marks in the groin or on the thighs. If after ruling out these possibilities you have a treefrog with no bright colors and a reddish bar through the eye, it is probably this species.

Habitat/Range: This frog is more of a habitat generalist than many other species. It occurs in forested areas but is also common in clearings and near tree falls. It may be seen high in the trees as well as on low shrubbery. It breeds in ephemeral ponds but during the dry season may be found well away from standing water. The species occurs over much of the northwestern Amazon Basin.

70. Brown-Thighed Treefrog

Scinax funerea

Size: To 1.5 inches (4 cm); the sexes are similar in size.

Identifying features: This is another drab treefrog that can be difficult to identify. It is much like *S. cruentomma* in appearance, but is slightly larger and has a better-defined interorbital triangle and dark dorsal markings. The hidden surfaces of the thighs are yellowish or off-white with variable brown bars. The dorsum is usually grayish to greenish gray with elongate brownish markings above the hips. The iris is greenish gray with dark flecks.

Voice: The single call note is louder and higher pitched than that of *S. cruentomma*, but it is similarly voiced from low vegetation.

Reproduction: The normal clutch is a surface film containing several hundred eggs.

Similar species: See the descriptions in the species accounts of other treefrogs in this genus. The most similar species, *S. cruentomma*, is usually tan to brown.

Habitat/Range: *Scinax funerea* occurs in most forest types and is agile and wary. Except when breeding, this frog seems most at home in the canopy. The species is common in the northwestern Amazon Basin, but the extremes of the range remain poorly delineated.

71. Fringe-Lipped Treefrog

Scinax garbei

Size: To 1.75 inches (4.5 cm); females are slightly larger than males.

Identifying features: The large oval toe pads, pointed nose, and tuberculate skin make this the most distinctive member of the genus. Tuberculate protuberances outline the jaw and outer edges of the legs and are present on the heels. The dorsal color is variable but is often grayish brown or deep gray, or may be mottled with light to dark green.

There are at least three morphs (or perhaps two morphs plus a miniaturized sibling species) of this interesting frog. Morph 1 is large with black-barred orange thighs; morph 2 is large with black-barred yellow thighs; and morph 3 (or perhaps, as recently suggested, a different species, *S. pedromedinai*) is small with black-barred yellow thighs.

An interorbital triangle is present but may be obscured when the frog assumes a dark dorsal color. The lips are strongly barred, and dark markings are present on the dorsum. Except for a horizontal reddish bar through the eye, the iris is silvery.

Voice: The single call note is a drawn-out quack.

Reproduction: Each clutch may consist of a surface film of more than 600 eggs.

Similar species: The long, pointed nose and prominently barred thighs are distinctive. See also the description for *Scinax rubra*.

Habitat/Range: Except for descending to low emergent and overhanging vegetation to call and breed, this is a strongly arboreal, alert, and agile frog that is not easily approached. Chorusing males usually assume a head-down stance. This species is widespread in the northwestern Amazon Basin.

72. Two-Striped Treefrog

Scinax rubra

Size: 1.5–1.75 inches (4–4.5 cm).

Identifying features: This species is gray to gray-green dorsally with well-defined light dorsolateral stripes that are boldest anteriorly. Light dorsal spots may be present. Black-edged yellow spots may be present on the lower sides and *are* present on the hidden surfaces of the thigh. The iris is silvery with dark flecks or vermiculations; these are most prominent on the upper half.

Voice: Males call their multiple *wah*s from the edges of small pools and temporary ponds, where they assume a head-down position in emergent vegetation.

Reproduction: Each clutch consists of a surface film of 500 or more eggs.

Similar species: The rounded snout, granular ventral skin, black-edged yellow spots on the thighs, and lack of labial and limb tubercles are distinctive.

Habitat/Range: Although well able to climb, *S. rubra* is less arboreal than many other members of the genus. It is commonly encountered in villages and forest clearings and may be found beneath ground debris. We have found it calling from very low on poolside shrubs as well as while hunkered down in grass clumps. Even when calling boisterously, the frogs are quick to take fright and become silent when approached. The species ranges widely from Peru to eastern Brazil.

Genus *Sphaenorhynchus;* Hatchet-Faced Treefrogs

The pretty treefrogs of this small genus (11 species) feed largely on ants. Several of the species are found outside the Amazon Basin.

Three species of *Sphaenorhynchus* occur in the northwestern Amazon Basin: tiny *S. carneus,* medium-sized *S. dorisae,* and *S. lacteus,* the largest. All are some shade of green. Day–night color changes occur. The three may be encountered in mixed choruses in grassy flooded flats along the edges of oxbow lakes and other such water sources. All seem particularly common where rafts of water lettuce (*Pistia*) are abundant. Besides body size, the comparative shape of the nose when viewed from both above and in profile is important in species identification. When viewed in profile, the snouts of all three species are sharply angled and hatchetlike. *Sphaenorhynchus dorisae* and *S. lacteus* have a dermal flap on each side of the vent.

As you canoe quietly through vegetation-choked oxbow lakes, *S. carneus* and *S. dorisae* will often jump into your boat.

73. Pygmy Hatchet-Faced Treefrog

Sphaenorhynchus carneus

Size: 0.63–0.88 inch (1.6–2.2 cm); females are somewhat the larger sex.
Identifying features: This is a tiny, rather slender, *short-nosed* treefrog with partially webbed fingers and toes. The nose appears truncate (squared) when viewed from above. By night, this frog is usually uniform pale green dorsally, greenish ventrally (except at mid-venter, where it is white), and pale blue in the axillae and groin. Males have a green vocal sac. Cream-colored canthal and dorsolateral lines are present. By day, *S. carneus* develops scattered reddish spots on the dorsum and the upper surfaces of the legs, reddish upper eyelids, and very pale reddish sides. The canthal and dorsolateral stripes are usually red by day. The iris is silver.
Voice: Strident clicks.

Reproduction: The female may lay more than 100 very adhesive, pale green eggs. We have found egg clusters between the leaves and in the central cups of water lettuce.

Similar species: Both *Hyla punctata* and *H. granosa* are larger and have long, broadly rounded noses. See also the accounts for the larger *Sphaenorhynchus dorisae* and *S. lacteus*.

Habitat/Range: Although they may be found in other types of vegetation, pygmy hatchet-faced treefrogs seem most abundant in rafts of water lettuce near the edges of oxbow and forest lakes and ponds. The species occurs on both sides of the Peruvian upper Amazon and may also occur in adjacent Brazil.

74. Spotted Hatchet-Faced Treefrog

Sphaenorhynchus dorisae

Size: The range is 0.75–1.5 inches (2–4 cm).

Identifying features: *Sphaenorhynchus dorisae* is the only one of the three *Sphaenorhynchus* species found in Peruvian Amazonia to *lack* a canthal stripe. The short nose is rounded when viewed from above. By night this frog is bluish green to jade green above. The dorsum may have scattered white spots and/or a sparse to liberal peppering of darker flecks. The throat is green. The axillae may be pale blue, but the venter and groin are mostly white. The fingers are partially webbed; the toes are fully webbed. By day, the green of the dorsum may be duller and the dark flecks more accentuated. Small, white-edged calcars are present. The iris is silver with gold flecks.

Voice: Males utter sharp *pings* in often-repeated short series while sitting on floating vegetation.

Reproduction: We found numerous blue-green egg clutches (some with more than 200 eggs) of this species between the leaves of water lettuce.

Similar species: While the smallest males of this intermediate-sized species may not be much larger than the largest female *S. carneus*, the largest female *S. dorisae* may exceed some of the nominally larger *S. lacteus* in length. Both of the other two species of *Sphaenorhynchus* have canthal stripes. *Hyla punctata* has a dorsolateral stripe; and *H. granosa* has a long, rounded snout.

Habitat/Range: All of the many *S. dorisae* we have found were in or very close to water lettuce rafts. A few were clinging a few inches above the water level on emergent grasses. This is a common species in suitable habitats in the northwestern Amazon Basin.

75. Greater Hatchet-Faced Treefrog

Sphaenorhynchus lacteus

Size: Marginally the largest of the three *Sphaenorhynchus,* this species occasionally attains 1.75 inches (4.5 cm) in length; most are somewhat smaller. Females are the larger sex.

Identifying features: The snout is rather long and pointed when viewed from above. By night, this frog is a pleasing yellowish to bright green. The charcoal canthal stripe is edged in white on the top. There are no darker or lighter dorsal spots. A white dorsolateral stripe may extend from the eye to a point posterior to the foreleg. Axillae and groin are both bright blue. This frog darkens its dorsal coloration by day. Small calcars are present. The iris is gold. The fingers are webbed for about one-half of their length; the toes for about four-fifths.

Voice: An often-repeated single metallic *ping.* The males we observed calling were sitting atop rafts of *Azolla* (a floating aquatic fern) near water lettuce and emergent grasses. Several noncalling males clung to the grasses.

Reproduction: The clutch size reportedly varies from 151 to 351 eggs, which are laid in the water.

Similar species: See the species accounts for *S. carneus* and *S. dorisae. Hyla punctata* has a reddish dorsolateral stripe, and *H. granosa* lacks a canthal stripe.

Habitat/Range: Although it may retreat to the forest edge by day, this is an abundant species in grassy or water lettuce–choked oxbow lakes and other such open areas at night. The species is common over much of the Peruvian upper Amazon, but the range is not yet precisely delimited.

Genus *Trachycephalus;* Casque-Headed Treefrogs

This genus (three species) of bony-headed treefrogs occurs in northern South America. The skin of the head is co-ossified with the heavy, angular skull.

Although it is not a good field characteristic, *Trachycephalus* differs from other South American genera in lacking both mandibular teeth and odontoid processes. These frogs are strongly nocturnal.

76. Jordan's Casque-Headed Treefrog

Trachycephalus jordani

Size: This moderately robust frog attains a length of about 3 inches (7.5 cm).

Identifying features: The dorsum is olive tan, tan, olive gray, gray, or brown. The head is wide with strong canthal and orbital ridges. The eyes appear to be directed more forward than those of many more narrow-headed frog species. The skin on the top of the head is firmly attached to the skull. The venter is off-white to white. Males have large bilateral vocal sacs.

Voice: On rainy nights the raucous *baw*s of this frog can first be heard from arboreal bromeliads high in the trees. As the evening progresses, especially if the rain continues, the frogs may descend to perches only a few feet above the ground to vocalize or forage.

Reproduction: Although a bromeliad dweller, this frog is thought to breed in shallow forest ponds in the manner typical of treefrogs. The clutch consists of several hundred eggs.

Similar species: None. The heavy skull, co-ossified skin, and forward-directed eyes are characteristic.

Habitat/Range: This persistently arboreal nocturnal frog is a seldom-seen resident of the northwestern Amazon Basin.

Leaf Frogs

Subfamily Phyllomedusinae

With a single exception, frogs belonging to the three genera of this subfamily (*Agalychnis*, *Pachymedusa*, and *Phyllomedusa*) are persistently arboreal and rather slow moving. The first finger and toe are opposable to the other digits, allowing these frogs a skid-free grasp in their treetop retreats. They are far more likely to move about in a methodical, hand-over-hand fashion than to hop. All have large, interestingly veined eyes with either gold or pale silver white irises and vertically elliptical pupils. These frogs have prominent parotid glands, and many produce a waxy skin secretion in dry weather to inhibit desiccation. Although the dorsal color of most is leaf green, the leaf frogs derive their common name from the fact that most of the species deposit their egg clutches on leaves (or attach them to a limb) above their breeding pools.

Genus *Agalychnis;* Leaf Frogs

There are about eight species in this genus of Neotropical hylids. Among them are several species of gliding ("flying") frogs, which launch themselves from a high perch, flatten the body, extend the feet and limbs, and sail to another distant perch.

The only member of the genus found in the Amazon Basin just happens to be the most spectacular. Its habits and lifestyle are only superficially known, and more study is needed to iron out unanswered questions.

77. Amazon Leaf Frog

Agalychnis craspedopus

Size: Males attain an SVL of about 2.5 inches (6.5 cm); females may be almost double that size.

Identifying features: The Amazon leaf frog, perhaps the most spectacular frog in the Amazon Basin, is unmistakable. The dark green dorsum is variably spangled with silver flecks or lichenlike markings. The lip and the limbs (especially the tarsus) bear prominent scalloped dermal flanges. The large eyes have silver irises and vertically elliptical pupils. The venter (including the ventral side of the limb and lip flanges), the inner toes, the sides, and both anterior and posterior surfaces of the flanks are bright orange. The sides and flanks are narrowly but prominently barred with dark pigment. The toes are partially webbed.

Voice: A single low cluck with comparatively little carrying power.

Reproduction: The advent of the seasonal rains induces these frogs to leave their canopy homes to breed. The female of an amplexing pair deposits her clutch of up to two dozen eggs on foliage (or occasionally on the trunk or a limb) above the water-holding depression or cavity chosen for the nest site. Jan Caldwell observed the sister taxon, *A. calcarifer,* from Central America, depositing eggs soon after daybreak; the Amazon species may do the same. As they hatch, the tadpoles drop from the deteriorating jelly cluster into the water below to complete their development.

Similar species: *Phyllomedusa tomopterna* also has barred thighs but has unwebbed feet. *Hyla tuberculosa* (not pictured) has flanged limbs but lacks the orange sides and venter and has horizontal pupils.

Habitat/Range: This medium-sized to large treefrog is considered a canopy dweller. Its clucks can be heard originating from canopy epiphytes or tree holes in the northwestern Amazon Basin. The species is known to occur only in Colombia, Ecuador, and Peru. It seems most common in Peru along the Rio Ucayali.

Genus *Phyllomedusa*; Monkey Frogs

This genus encompasses about 30 species of small to large (1.25–4.5 inches; 3–11.5 cm) frogs that are, save for a single species, persistently arboreal. These are slow-moving frogs that rely more on camouflage than evasive maneuvers to avoid detection. Although fully capable of leaping, the monkey frogs more often move along branches in a methodical hand-over-hand progression. Species from seasonally arid areas produce a waxy skin secretion that retards desiccation. They distribute the secretions all over the body using their front feet. All of these frogs are insectivorous, and many are now bred in considerable numbers by herpetoculturists. The eggs are laid on leaves overhanging the water, and after hatching, the tadpoles drop into the water to complete their development.

The large eyes have vertically elliptical pupils. The first finger and the first toe are opposable to the other digits, providing a sure and strong grasp. The toe pads are well developed. These canopy treefrogs descend to breed in ponds, pools, or even water-filled depressions in fallen trees. The call of most is a single rather soft cluck that is infrequently repeated.

78. Giant Monkey Frog

Phyllomedusa bicolor

Size: Females may reach 4.5 inches (11.5 cm) in SVL; males reach 3.75 inches (9.5 cm).

Identifying features: This is a hulking, big-headed, silver-eyed treefrog. The parotid glands are enormous, extending from behind the eye to past the shoulders. Although the dorsum is most often bright leaf green, a cold or stressed individual may turn dull olive. The venter is gray. The flanks and both the anterior and posterior surfaces of the thighs are reddish gray with dark-edged light ocelli. Ocelli are also usually present on the chest. The toes are not webbed.

Voice: The call, sometimes given from 25 or more feet up in a tree, consists of a loud cluck with little carrying power followed by several additional clucks descending in volume.

Reproduction: The clutch size, 151–300 eggs, is small for such a large frog. The eggs are deposited on vegetation near water.

Similar species: The more infrequently seen but almost as large *Phyllomedusa tarsius* has gold eyes with reddish venation.

Habitat/Range: This giant treefrog lives in canopy situations in primary and secondary forests of the northern Amazon Basin. Because of their habitat, camouflaging color, and seemingly low population densities, they are not frequently seen.

Comments: The skin secretions of this species are virulent. Wash your hands after handling them.

79. Orange-Legged Monkey Frog

Phyllomedusa hypocondrialis hypocondrialis

Size: This is one of the smallest members of the genus. Both sexes are adult at about 1.5 inches (4 cm) in SVL but occasionally get slightly larger.

Identifying features: Although the dorsal color may vary from bluish through olive to bright green, the black-barred orange of the sides, flanks, and upper arms is constant. The dull dorsal colors are often associated with stressful conditions—cool temperatures, fright, etc.—or quiescence. The bright green dorsum is usually seen at night, when this little frog is normally active. The black pattern on the sides and upper forearms is usually of simple bars, while that on the rear of the thighs is often a series of inverted Vs. The belly is white. The pupils are vertically elliptical. The upper lip is very light green to white. This slender frog is less angular than many of its conspecifics.

Voice: A single harsh, infrequently repeated *wrak*.

Reproduction: Females attach small clutches of large eggs to grasses at pond edges. After hatching, the tadpoles drop or wriggle into the water to complete their development.

Similar species: None. This is the only *small* monkey frog in the area with prominently barred orange flanks, forearms, and thighs.

Habitat/Range: Like most *Phyllomedusa* species, this monkey frog remains high in the trees during the day and on dry nights, but descends to forage and breed at the advent of the rainy season. Look for it among low shrubs and tall grasses at the edges of ephemeral forest ponds in the eastern Amazon Basin.

80. Warty (Tarsier) Monkey Frog

Phyllomedusa tarsius

Size: Exceeded in size (and then not greatly) only by *P. bicolor,* female *P. tarsius* may reach 4 inches (11.2 cm) in SVL; males reach 3.75 inches (9.5 cm).

Identifying features: This canopy-dwelling treefrog is big, heavy bodied, slow moving, and seldom seen. The skin is strongly tuberculate. The coppery red eyes are strongly veined. The parotid glands are enormous, extending from behind the eye to midbody or beyond. Although the dorsum is most often forest green, a cold or stressed individual may turn dull olive. The throat, chest, and undersurfaces of the legs are brown. The belly is gray to orange-gray. The transition from the green dorsum to the lighter ventrum is precise but irregular. Light spots are often present on the sides. The toes are not webbed.

Voice: The call, often voiced from canopy level, is a loud cluck audible for only a short distance.

Reproduction: The advent of the rainy season induces this frog to descend from the canopy to vocalize and breed. The female lays more than 510 eggs on a leaf overhanging water and usually rolls the leaf around the clutch. After hatching, the tadpoles slide into the water to complete their development.

Similar species: This leaf frog is almost as large as *Phyllomedusa bicolor* but is distinguished from that species by its silvery white iris and *prominent* flank spots.

Habitat/Range: Low population densities occur in canopy situations in primary and secondary forests pretty much throughout the northern Amazon Basin.

Comments: The skin secretions of this species are virulent. Wash your hands after handling them!

81. Barred (Tiger-Striped) Monkey Frog

Phyllomedusa tomopterna

Size: Males are only about 1.75 inches (4.5 cm) in SVL; females are about 2.25 inches (5.5 cm).

Identifying features: This leaf frog has prominent heel spurs. The dorsum is usually leaf green; the sides and hidden surfaces of the hind limbs are orange with broad, vertical purplish black bars. The venter is white anteriorly, shading to very pale orange posteriorly. The irises are silver. The toes are not webbed.

Voice: A single low cluck with comparatively little carrying power.

Reproduction: The female lays 25–70 eggs per clutch.

Similar species: *Agalychnis craspedopus* also has barred thighs but has webbed feet as well.

Habitat/Range: This medium-sized treefrog utilizes a wide range of habitats. It may call from pools deep in the forest, from swamp edges, or from puddles in agricultural clearings. The species is found over much of the northern Amazon Basin.

82. White-Lined Monkey Frog

Phyllomedusa vaillanti

Size: Males reach a length of 2 inches (5 cm); females are about 3 inches (7.5 cm) in SVL.

Identifying features: The skin of the dorsum is rough, and that of the hind limbs is tuberculate. Individual frogs may vary from pale to dark green dorsally, with light forest green being a common hue. The belly is grayish, but a green spot is present on the chest and a pair of cream spots is present on the throat. The undersurface of the rear limbs is reddish, and each leg bears a row of cream, yellow, or orange spots. An elongate parotid gland is present along each side of the body. The toes lack webbing.

Voice: The breeding call is a single, raspy chucking note repeated about 12 times per minute.

Reproduction: Eggs, more than 510 per clutch, are placed on foliage overhanging ephemeral forest ponds.

Similar species: None; the very elongate parotid glands, linear white tubercles, and reddish underlegs are diagnostic.

Habitat/Range: These treefrogs may spend considerable time in the canopy but descend to call from low shrubs near ponds on rainy or otherwise suitable nights. The species occurs in secondary and primary forests and is widespread over much of the northern Amazon Basin.

Tropical Frogs: Family Leptodactylidae

The members of this tropical family can be informally divided into two groups: the few that can be easily identified and all the others. On a more formal basis, the family comprises three subfamilies: the horned frogs, subfamily Ceratophryninae; the jungle frogs, subfamily Leptodactylinae; and the rain frogs or eleutherodactyline frogs, subfamily Telmatobiinae. The latter are the most difficult to identify to species.

The eleutherodactylines look much like one another. The difficulty in telling them apart is compounded by their poorly delineated ranges. Species not previously suspected to occur in a given area may suddenly crop up, sometimes in fair numbers, on any nighttime walk.

Subfamily Ceratophryninae

Genus *Ceratophrys;* Horned Frogs

These medium-sized to large frogs are secretive and predaceous. One or another of the approximately eight species is found from Colombia and Venezuela to Argentina, in habitats as diverse as rainforest and seasonally inundated forest, or *chaco*.

The two species that we discuss are fairly common but so cryptically colored and secretive that they are seldom seen. They are short-legged and squatty in appearance. The females are noticeably larger than the males. The head is huge, and the jaws are trapdoor strong. Once a horned frog grasps a prey item, it seldom escapes. Prey consists of large insects, lizards, and other frogs. The eyes are comparatively small, and over each is a short, fleshy, upward-projecting horn.

Except when drawn by the rains to shallow ponds to breed, these are solitary frogs. They spend their time hunkered down in the leaf litter in wait-and-ambush repose. If a suitable prey item comes close enough, the frog explodes from the litter and grabs it.

The loud advertisement call is similar to the *baa* of a sheep. Clutches contain 300–600 eggs.

Tales of the supposed danger of the bite of the ornate horned frog, a large Chacoan species of southern South America, are rampant in local folklore. Legend has it that the bite of the horned frog—the *escuerzo*—is both poisonous and persistent. If a person is bitten, the story says, the frog will not release its grip until sundown. If a cow happens to graze too close, the frog will bite the lip of the cow and not release its grip until the cow starves to death. These are grandiose accomplishments indeed for an aggressive but harmless amphibian!

83. Colombian Horned Frog

Ceratophrys calcarata

Size: The 2.5-inch-long (6.5-cm) males are much smaller than the more robust 3.5-inch (9-cm) females.

Identifying features: Females tend to have a ground color of brown (occasionally with some light to forest green middorsally) that is separated into evenly outlined, elongate patches by a narrow tan reticulum. Males are similar but noticeably smaller. There is a "horn" on each upper eyelid. The immense head makes the golden-irised eyes look proportionally small. There are no rearward projections from the back of the head. The snout is rounded when viewed from above, with no anterior projection. The snout and sides of the head are strongly patterned with vertical dark and light bars. The limbs are barred, and the toes are partially webbed.

Voice: The call has been likened to the bleating of a sheep. Males begin calling during or soon after the first pond-replenishing rains of the rainy season.

Reproduction: Egg clusters, laid in quiet water, contain from 200 to more than 550 eggs. The tadpoles are carnivorous and cannibalistic.

Similar species: The Amazon horned frog, *Ceratophrys cornuta*, lacks the light dorsal reticulum and has much longer hind legs. The treefrogs of the genus *Hemiphractus* have a pointed anterior snout process and rearward projections from the sides and back of the head. *Eleutherodactylus sulcata* is smaller, has rugose skin, and lacks webbing between the toes.

Habitat/Range: Found both in seasonally dry habitats and in rainforests, this robust frog is retiring and, unless surface active, very easily overlooked. Most of its time is spent burrowed into litter. This species is found in Colombia, Venezuela, Ecuador, and possibly the Putumayo region of northern Peru.

Comments: This frog is capable of biting *hard*. Handle it carefully.

84. Amazon Horned Frog

Ceratophrys cornuta

Size: Males reach an SVL of about 2.5 inches (6.5 cm); females reach just over 4 inches (10 cm).

Identifying features: This stubby, big-headed, short-legged frog is one of the most distinctive of the leptodactyloids and the only ceratophrynine likely to be encountered in the lower Amazon Basin. Males may vary from tan to lime or darker green, or may be a combination of these colors. If green occurs on a tan frog, the color most often appears on the head and dorsal area. Females are most often tan. Darker barring, especially prominent on the rear legs, is present on both sexes. The fleshy horn above each eye and big head are distinctive.

Voice: Chorusing males produce a loud bleating.

Reproduction: Horned frogs breed in temporary forest pools. The clutch of 300–600 eggs is small for such a large frog.

Similar species: The egg-brooding treefrogs of the genus *Hemiphractus* also have horns above the eyes but are leaf litter brown in color and have a strongly triangular head. The very uncommon forest toad, *Bufo ceratophrys*, has prominent parotid glands that the Amazon horned frog lacks. The 0.5-inch-long (1.5-cm) leptodactylid species *Pseudopaludicola ceratophryes* has tiny spinelike processes rather than fleshy horns above the eyes.

Habitat/Range: This voracious frog is a wait-and-ambush hunter that conceals itself in the loose litter on the forest floor. It is found from Peru to Suriname and Brazil.

Comments: Beware. These frogs can bite *hard*! They have elongate teeth that enable them to hold struggling prey. If you handle one of these frogs, do so carefully.

Subfamily Telmatobiinae

For the most part, these are "little brown frogs" of the forest litter. A few possess rather bold markings or physical characteristics that make them relatively easy to identify. Most are small. Many species are abundant, and by virtue of biomass they are important predators. The feet are usually unwebbed. Most have small to large toe pads, the size varying by species. Some species have cutaneous flanges along their toes. Many species sit on broad leaves at night at ankle or knee height where they are easily observed in the beam of a flashlight. Most are not particularly skittish under these circumstances and will allow close approach.

The dorsal colorations mentioned are intended only as examples. These are among the most variably colored of all frogs. The presence or lack of a tympanum and the color of various body parts figure in possible identifications. Positive identification often requires having the frog in hand—and luck.

The diet consists of tiny insects.

Genus *Eleutherodactylus;* Rain Frogs

This is a huge genus (more than 500 species) of confusingly similar frogs. Although most are of Neotropical distribution, they also occur in the West Indies and other Caribbean islands; 5 species occur in the United States.

For the most part these are terrestrial frogs, but a few species are adapted to arboreal habitats. Even the terrestrial species may ascend low herbs to forage for insects on the broad leaves. All the members of this genus are small, and some are tiny. Many species are adult at an inch or slightly less (2.5 cm); others may be double that size.

The females lay only a few (usually fewer than 50, and often no more than 6–10) large eggs in moisture-retaining terrestrial sites. Complete larval development occurs within the egg capsule, and the fully metamorphosed babies emerge from the deteriorating jelly covering as miniatures of the adults.

85. Green Rain Frog

Eleutherodactylus acuminatus

Size: Males barely exceed 0.75 inch (2 cm) in SVL; females near 1 inch (2.5 cm).

Identifying features: The dorsum varies from yellow-green to tannish green, olive, or even bright green. Some degree of dark dorsal flecking is usually apparent. A dark stripe beginning at the tip of the snout and continuing through the eye to the groin is present. The limbs, lips, and sides may be peppered with minuscule light spots. A dark interorbital bar is often present. The venter is cream. The snout is rather sharply pointed, and the tympanum is not conspicuous. The irises are bronzy. The toe pads are prominent and rounded.

Voice: The single note of the male, voiced at infrequent intervals, may be likened to a whistle.

Reproduction: This elfin frog is a bromeliad breeder. Females lay up to 18 eggs.

Similar species: The green rain frog may be easily mistaken for a treefrog, but the lack of toe webbing will allow a quick differentiation. The more commonly seen *Eleutherodactylus lacrimosus* is greenish, has a rounded nose, and is some shade of light brown.

Habitat/Range: We are rarely fortunate enough to see this attractive but persistently arboreal frog. The few we have found were active at night on the branches and foliage of shrubs. The species occurs in rainforests in Ecuador, Peru, and adjacent countries.

86. Amazonian Rain Frog

Eleutherodactylus altamazonicus

Size: The males are the smaller sex. Most of those seen are about 0.6 inch (1.8 cm), but they do get slightly larger. Adult females vary in length from about 0.9 inch (2.3 cm) to nearly 1.25 inches (3 cm).

Identifying features: This can be a difficult frog to identify. As a beginning, let us note three negatives: the tympanum (external eardrum) is not at all prominent; if present, the postorbital stripe is weak; and there is no projection of the upper eyelid.

Now the positives: the tan to brown dorsum is rough (tuberculate) and prominently, but variably, patterned with lighter and darker flecks and splotches; the white speckled venter is dark tan. A **W** outlined in dark pigment and with the closed ends directed posteriorly is usually present on the shoulders. The snout is narrow but somewhat truncated. The groin is patterned with a series of orange and black bars, and the posterior surface of the thigh is barred with black. The irises may be reddish or grayish and have some darker reticulations or marblings; the toe pads are large and truncate anteriorly; the lips are usually prominently banded.

Voice: Single or double soft clicks.

Reproduction: Up to about two dozen eggs are deposited in a moist protected pocket, usually beneath surface litter.

Similar species: Conspicuous tympani and brilliant orange anterior thigh spots will differentiate otherwise look-alike species.

Habitat/Range: By day, this is a very secretive and seldom seen terrestrial frog of old secondary and primary forests. It ascends herbaceous plants, hunkering down atop the flat leaves after darkness has fallen. Expect to find this species in Ecuador, Peru, and the Brazilian Amazon.

Comments: The large number of juvenile specimens we find indicates that this is not an uncommon frog species. Yet even on nights when juvenile Amazonian rain frogs and other species are active, we see few adult *E. altamazonicus*.

87. Long-Nosed Rain Frog

Eleutherodactylus carvalhoi

Size: Males are 0.75 inch (2 cm) in SVL; females are 1 inch (2.5 cm).
Identifying features: Very little is known about this long-nosed Lilliputian. The tympanum (external eardrum) is difficult to see. The granular (coarse) belly skin is off-white and peppered with tiny brown dots. The snout is long and rather pointed. The dorsal color may vary from charcoal to pale grayish brown and may bear a narrow stripe. A light W may be present immediately behind the head. There is a *yellow* spot in the groin. The toe pads are large and rounded anteriorly.
Voice: Unknown.
Reproduction: Unknown.
Similar species: *Eleutherodactylus altamazonicus* has red-orange bars on the thigh; a short, truncated snout; and toe pads that are flattened anteriorly. *E. diadematus* has a well-defined tympanum. The yellow groin spots of *E. variabilis* usually meet midventrally.
Habitat/Range: We have found this tiny frog at night amid the ground litter in primary forests and sitting on broad leaves of low herbaceous plants and shrubs. We have found this animal in Peru, and its range may extend into surrounding countries.

88. Diadem Rain Frog

Eleutherodactylus diadematus

Size: Males attain a length of about 1 inch (2.5 cm); females are up to 1.4 inches (3.5 cm) long.
Identifying features: Perhaps the most distinctive features of this frog are the variably distinct, broad black and white diagonal bars on the posterior of each side. The dorsum may vary from brown to gray but is often very dark. Darker markings *may* be visible radiating rearward from the eyes to the shoulders. Except for scattered tubercles, the dorsal skin is smooth. The belly skin is granular, white, and has variable brown markings. Anteriorly the thighs are gray to pale tan and bear darker bars. Posteriorly the thighs are dark, either with or without darker bands. The upper lip is weakly banded. The snout is rounded, and tympani are evident. The irises may vary from deep gold to dark red above and are paler below.
Voice: We have not been able to identify the vocalizations of this arboreal frog.

Reproduction: The usual clutch consists of 5–18 eggs, but the preferred deposition site is not known.

Similar species: See the account for *E. altamazonicus,* a variable species that can be somewhat similar but usually has bright orange on the anterior thigh, an inconspicuous tympanum, and, when viewed from above, a somewhat flattened snout. Other similar species have smooth belly skin.

Habitat/Range: This is considered an arboreal species of upland primary forests. We have seen it in Amazonian Peru, and it probably occurs in adjacent areas of surrounding countries.

89. Peeping Rain Frog

Eleutherodactylus lacrimosus

Size: Males of this tiny arboreal eleutherodactyline barely exceed 0.75 inch (2 cm) in SVL; females near 1 inch (2.5 cm).

Identifying features: The dorsum may vary from yellow to olive or light brown. Darker markings, most numerous anteriorly, are often present; these may take the form of bars between the eyes. The venter is cream. The snout is bluntly rounded and the top of the head is flat. A tympanum is present; the toe pads are prominent and rounded.

Voice: A single peeping note voiced at infrequent intervals.

Reproduction: Gravid females contain about a dozen eggs, but the preferred deposition site remains unknown.

Similar species: This little frog may be more easily mistaken for a treefrog than for one of its congeners, but the lack of toe webbing will allow a quick differentiation. The more infrequently seen *E. acuminatus* is greenish, has a sharp nose, and lacks a tympanum.

Habitat/Range: We have found this attractive, persistently arboreal frog active at night on the branches and foliage of low trees and shrubs. The species ranges widely in the northwestern Amazon Basin.

90. Striped-Throated Rain Frog

Eleutherodactylus lanthanites

Size: Males are about 1 inch (2.5 cm) long; females are about 1.5 inches (4 cm).

Identifying features: This frog is some shade of brown or gray dorsally, with a busy pattern of darker pigment. The cream-colored ventral skin is smooth. The throat is gray to black with a white median stripe. The side of the face anterior to the eye is dark. A dorsolateral fold is present. A conical calcar tubercle is present. The toe pads are large and truncated anteriorly.

Voice: The mating call has not been described.

Reproduction: Gravid females carrying 30–50 eggs have been found, but the preferred deposition site remains unknown. As this is a terrestrial species, it is likely that the eggs are placed in damp leaf litter.

Similar species: Many other frogs are similar in general appearance, but the boldly striped throat of this species is usually diagnostic.

Habitat/Range: This frog is often seen at night as it sits on the foliage of shrubs and tall herbaceous plants. It may also be found in the ground litter of primary and secondary forests at night. Its range includes Amazonian Ecuador, Colombia, Peru, and probably western Brazil.

91. Luscombe's Rain Frog

Eleutherodactylus luscombei

Size: Females reach an adult size of about 1.25 inches (3 cm); males are seldom longer than 1 inch (2.5 cm).

Identifying features: The rough dorsal skin is gray, often with a brownish suffusion. A pattern, if present, is only weakly defined. The belly is off-white to cream with (sometimes obscure) darker reticulations. The rear of the thighs and underside of the tibia are dark brown. A dark stripe parallels the top and rear of the tympanum. Although two dark bars were visible on the upper lip of most of the individuals we saw, these were barely visible on a few specimens.

Voice: Unknown.

Reproduction: Unknown.

Similar species: The Colonia rain frog, *Eleutherodactylus aaptus* (not shown), is very similar but usually has black thighs.

Habitat/Range: We have found this secretive frog at the edges of agricultural clearings and on trail edge vegetation in old secondary forest. One sat midway along a mossy fallen tree that spanned a sizable creek. Luscombe's rain frog is a seldom seen species in Peru's Loreto Province. It seems localized, and its exact range has not yet been delineated.

92. Red-Bellied Rain Frog

Eleutherodactylus lythrodes

Size: Males are about 1.25 inches (3 cm) long; females are somewhat longer and more robust.

Identifying features: Some specimens may be so dark that no dorsal patterning is visible (but these may lighten); others are olive tan dorsally and somewhat darker on the sides. There may be from one (middorsal) to three thin, dark dorsal lines beginning at the shoulders and terminating above the vent. A dark canthal stripe is present; the tympanum is well defined. There are two white lip spots beneath each eye. The toe pads are relatively large. The throat is black, often with tiny white spots, and the lower lip is patterned (or even outlined) with white. The chest is dark, but lighter than the throat; the mid-ventral area is lighter still. The posterior third of the venter and most of the underside of the femur and tibia are bright red, as are the anterior and posterior surfaces of the femur. The underside of the knee and dorsal surface of the hind leg dark are barred olive tan. The snout is long and acutely rounded.

Voice: Unknown.

Reproduction: Unknown.

Similar species: None.

Habitat/Range: We found red-bellied rain frogs sitting at night on the surfaces of flat leaves of low herbaceous plants at the edge of a primary forest clearing. They have also been found in secondary forest. This species occurs in Loreto Province, Peru, but the actual limits of its range are not known.

93. Marti's Rain Frog

Eleutherodactylus martiae

Size: Males are 0.75 inch (2 cm) in SVL; females are 1 inch (2.5 cm).

Identifying features: This is a remarkably variable species even in a genus known for variability. Many specimens have a pale brown back with deeper brown markings and coppery sides. The dorsa of others may be such a deep brown that no markings are visible. Others have orange to terra cotta dorsa with sides of deep brown. The venter is gray to light brown and may be flecked with white. There is no external tympanum. The digital discs are rounded.

Voice: A series of clicks.

Reproduction: The 4–10 eggs are placed in suitably moist leaf litter, often against a fallen and decomposing log.

Similar species: *Eleutherodactylus ventrimarmoratus* has black spots on a white venter. The lack of red or yellow on the thighs and groin will separate *E. martiae* from other small species that share its habitat.

Habitat/Range: This mite of a frog is seen at night on vegetation and on top of fallen trunks and other prominences. It ranges widely in the northwestern Amazon Basin.

94. Carabaya Rain Frog

Eleutherodactylus ockendeni

Size: Males are up to 0.9 inch (2.3 cm) in SVL; females to 1.25 inches (3 cm).

Identifying features: This tiny eleutherodactyline has one or more easily visible tubercles on the upper eyelids. The dorsal ground coloration varies from tan to dark gray, usually with transverse bars and stripes. Some individuals have a brilliant orange crown. The posterior bars are often the most visible. A light W may be present immediately in back of the head. The sides are lighter than the dorsal ground color and may be spotted with brown. The venter is gray, but the hidden surfaces of the rear legs may vary from brown to pinkish. The toe pads are round.

Voice: A two-syllable *baa-aa*.

Reproduction: Gravid females have contained 12–25 eggs, but the egg deposition site is not known.

Similar species: No other similarly colored member of the genus has tubercle(s) on the upper eyelid.

Habitat/Range: The Carabaya rain frog is considered an arboreal species. It generally calls from just above head height in shrubs and trees and is seldom seen except after nightfall. This species is common in the vicinity of the Peruvian upper Amazon and also occurs in Ecuador, Colombia, and probably western Brazil.

95. Peruvian Rain Frog

Eleutherodactylus peruvianus

Size: Males, the smaller sex, attain a length of 1.25 inches (3 cm); females reach 1.75 inches (4.5 cm).

Identifying features: The smooth dorsal skin may vary from tan to olive to brown. Darker markings may or may not be visible. Dorsolateral ridges are present. The limbs *may* be prominently barred. The sides are often darker than the back, the colors being separated by the dorsolateral ridges. The belly is cream with spots of brown that vary in both intensity and quantity. There are cream spots on the rear of the calf and red to yellow spots on the hidden surface of the thighs. The large toe pads are truncated anteriorly.

Voice: Undescribed.

Reproduction: Unknown. Since this is a terrestrial frog, we surmise that the egg clutch is placed in damp leaf litter. A gravid female temporarily held for photography laid 27 eggs amid the leaves in a plastic bag.

Similar species: *Eleutherodactylus conspicillatus* may be confusingly similar but has an unspotted white belly. The other species lack prominent dorsolateral ridges.

Habitat/Range: This moderate-sized "eleuth" is often encountered in leaf litter on the primary forest floor by both day and night. This species is not as prone to climb as most others. We have found it in the Peruvian upper Amazon.

96. Broad-Headed Rain Frog

Eleutherodactylus sulcatus

Size: Males reach 1.25 inches (3 cm) in length; females, 2 inches (5 cm).

Identifying features: This stocky forest frog is often mistaken for a toad. The head is big—almost 50 percent of the snout-to-vent length—and broad but flattened. The snout is short and bluntly rounded. The dorsum and sides have both dermal tubercles and ridges. The color is generally some shade of gray but may occasionally shade to tan. The groin and concealed surfaces of the hind limbs are dark with cream spots. The belly is light gray to cream. The undersides of all feet are pale orange(ish).

Voice: Undescribed.

Reproduction: Up to 35 eggs are placed in damp forest floor leaf litter.

Similar species: The somewhat similar *Ischnocnema quixensis* tends to have proportionally larger tubercles, lacks dermal ridges, and has a less flattened head.

Habitat/Range: Knowledge of the life history of this species is scanty. We have found it in ground litter in high forest. Although seemingly not common, this frog ranges widely in the northwestern Amazon Basin.

97. Variable Rain Frog

Eleutherodactylus variabilis

Size: Males are somewhat less than 0.75 inch (2 cm) in SVL; females attain a length of about 1 inch (2.5 cm).

Identifying features: Unless adult and in hand, this small frog often poses an identification dilemma. The dorsum can be tan, brown, red-brown, or olive. Some individuals are heavily patterned with dark transverse and longitudinal markings; others may be unpatterned except for a light vertebral stripe. The tympanum is evident. The toes are basally webbed. The belly is light but has a variable amount of dark flecking. A large, *dark-edged*, yellowish to orange spot extends from the anterior of each thigh onto the groin. These spots often meet midventrally. The posterior surface of each thigh may vary from gray to pink. The toe pads are broad but truncated anteriorly.

Voice: A series of low clicks, usually voiced while the frog is sitting on low shrubs or herbs.

Reproduction: Clutches usually consist of fewer than a dozen eggs and are placed in moisture-holding forest floor leaf litter.

Similar species: Although other Iquitos region eleutherodactylines have yellow to orange groin spots, only the spots of *E. variabilis* are narrowly edged with dark pigment.

Habitat/Range: The variable rain frog occurs in a wide variety of habitats. It may be encountered during the day in ground litter in primary and secondary forests as well as in clearings and near habitations. It is one of the more common eleuths, and occurs in much of the northwestern Amazon Basin.

98. Spotted-Bellied Rain Frog

Eleutherodactylus ventrimarmoratus

Size: Males are 1 inch (2.5 cm) in SVL; females may reach 1.5 inches (4 cm).

Identifying features: This is a stout, somewhat big-headed, grayish brown to brown rain frog with a scapular W. The dorsal skin is rough and obscurely peppered with black and lighter gray. The tympanum is obscure to lacking. A dark brown mark outlines the top and rear of the spot where the tympanum would normally be. The belly and posterior thighs are off-white and prominently streaked with precisely delineated black markings.

Voice: Soft, irregularly repeated *tsks* with little carrying power.

Reproduction: Unknown.

Similar species: Other rain frogs with an obscure tympanum do not have black-streaked white thighs and belly.

Habitat/Range: This frog is often seen sitting quietly on leaves several feet above the ground along trails in old secondary and primary rainforests. The species is widespread, being found in suitable habitats in much of the Peruvian Amazon.

99. Tan-Legged Rain Frog

Eleutherodactylus species

Size: Adult males reach 1 inch (2.5 cm) in length; females are about 1.5 inches (4 cm).

Identifying features: This is another of the several rain frog species that look superficially like "typical" brown North American or European masked frogs. The rough-skinned dorsum varies from tan to brown. A narrow, darker brown mask (the canthal and supratympanal marking) begins at each nostril, passes through each eye, and terminates after wrapping around the rear of the prominent tympanum. A series of darker chevrons may be visible on the dorsum. There are no glandular dorsolateral folds. The forelimbs are often lighter in color than the body. The limbs may be strongly to vaguely marked with darker bars. The sides are usually lighter than the back. The belly is pale gray, and the hidden surfaces of the femurs are light (usually unmarked) brown. The eyes are golden. Toe pads are present.

Voice: Unknown.

Reproduction: Unknown, but other terrestrial eleutherodactylines typically lay a small number of fairly large eggs in a moist terrestrial habitat protected from desiccation by surface litter.

Similar species: *Eleutherodactylus peruvianus* has red, orange, or yellow spots on the rear of the thighs.

Habitat/Range: The specific habitat of this rainforest frog remains imperfectly delineated. The few specimens we have seen were surface active at night in Loreto Province, Peru.

Genus *Ischnocnema;* Big-Headed Rain Frogs

This Neotropical genus contains only four species, and only one, *I. quixensis,* is seen with any regularity. In fact, it is one of the most commonly encountered nocturnal anurans along trails in secondary and primary rainforests. Superficially, these frogs look much like toads, but they lack parotid glands. Like the rain frogs, to which they are related, *Ischnocnema* females lay their clutches of eggs in terrestrial sites and the babies emerge after undergoing complete development. Insects and other invertebrates are the favored dietary items.

100. Common Big-Headed Rain Frog

Ischnocnema quixensis

Size: Males of this toadlike species often attain 1.75 inches (4 cm) in SVL; females may reach 2.25 inches (5.5 cm).

Identifying features: This is a robust and, as indicated by its common name, big-headed frog. The dorsum is tuberculate but lacks elongate ridges. The color is usually some shade of tan or brown, at times with grayish overtones. Darker markings of irregular outline are usually visible. The venter is grayish tan to grayish brown with white markings. There are no toe pads.

Voice: A series of low-pitched croaks. The adults we have seen vocalizing were calling from the ground beneath buildings.

Reproduction: A clutch contains 15–50 eggs. A female being held temporarily in a plastic bag for photography laid 27 eggs. It is thought that these frogs normally deposit their eggs in protected terrestrial sites.

Similar species: The broad-headed rain frog, *Eleutherodactylus sulcatus,* has ridges as well as tubercles on its dorsum and is less robust.

Habitat/Range: This common species may be encountered at night in primary and secondary forests, at the edges of clearings, and near most of the forest tourist facilities. The species ranges widely in the northwestern Amazon Basin.

Subfamily Leptodactylinae

In Amazonas, the members of this subfamily of primarily terrestrial leptodactylids run the gamut from species such as the tiny (0.5 inch) and infrequently seen eyelashed toadlet, *Pseudopaludicola ceratophyes,* to the abundant *Adenomera hylaedactyla,* which is fully grown at barely an inch, to the bullfrog-sized *Leptodactylus pentadactylus.*

Adenomera males call both day and night. The two tiny frogs in this genus in the Iquitos region are virtually indistinguishable in the field except by call. One chirps from clearings, village edges, and other disturbed areas; the other mews from forested situations. Most other members of this subfamily are primarily nocturnal. Most leptodactylids live in burrows during the hours of daylight and call from the edges of these at night. If frightened during periods of activity, the frogs quickly retire into their burrows.

Frothy foam nests consisting of water, the gelatinous outer covering of the eggs, and sperm are built at water's edge by the kicking of spawning frogs. All of the species discussed here have a free-swimming tadpole stage. In all but *Adenomera* (whose tadpoles undergo full development in the nest) the tadpoles eventually work their way from the nest to the water to complete their development.

When caught in the beam of a flashlight held at shoulder level, the eyes of many members of this genus reflect bright red.

Genus *Adenomera;* Chirping Frogs

At least one species of this group of Neotropical burrowing frogs serves as the anuran welcoming committee for ecotourists. *Adenomera andreae* favors grassy slopes like those present in front of nearly every river edge village. Since these frogs chorus both day and night, ecotourists frequently hear the piping chirps of dozens of frogs as they board their boats and at almost every stop along the way.

Quite unlike the other species in this subfamily, *Adenomera* tadpoles develop in the nest and emerge as miniatures of the adults.

The food consists of small invertebrates.

101. Cocha Chirping Frog

Adenomera andreae

Size: Both sexes attain an SVL of about 1 inch (2.5 cm); males may be slightly smaller than females.

Identifying features: Fawn brown to grayish tan is the dorsal coloration of this tiny, plump frog. Obscure darker dorsal markings are present. Dorsal tubercles are arranged in longitudinal rows. A triangle, V, or X is usually present between the eyes and extending onto the scapular area. The belly is white.

Voice: The clear, whistled chirps of this frog emanate from grassy banks in front of nearly every riverside village.

Reproduction: The female lays 5–15 eggs in a frothy nest. The tadpoles undergo full development within the confines of the nest.

Similar species: *Adenomera hylaedactyla* is a forest species that mewls rather than whistles. Both *Adenomera* species you are likely to encounter have first and second fingers of equal length. This differentiates them from other smaller leptodactylines, which have the first finger longer than the second.

Habitat/Range: Look and listen for this frog along riverbanks, in village clearings, and in other such habitats; they often call while partially concealed. The range of this species is poorly understood. It is well known in Peru and Colombia and western Brazil, and is thought to occur in eastern Brazil as well.

102. Forest Chirping Frog

Adenomera hylaedactyla

Size: Both sexes attain an SVL of about 1 inch (2.5 cm); males may be slightly smaller than females.

Identifying features: This sharp-nosed, plump little frog varies from fawn to grayish tan in dorsal coloration and has obscure darker markings. Dorsal tubercles are arranged in longitudinal rows. A triangle, V, or X is usually present between the eyes and extending onto the shoulders. The belly is white.

Voice: The mewling notes of this tiny frog can often be heard, day or night, from moist forested areas. Individuals often call while sitting partially concealed in the burrow or beneath a fallen trunk or leaf litter.

Reproduction: The female lays her 5–15 eggs in a frothy nest. The tadpoles develop within the confines of the nest and emerge as miniatures of the adults.

Similar species: Both Peruvian *Adenomera* species have first and second fingers of equal length. *Adenomera hylaedactyla* can be distinguished from *A. andreae* by its habitat (forest) and call (a mew). The smaller species in the *Leptodactylus wagneri* complex and *Vanzolinius discodactylus* have the first finger longer than the second.

Habitat/Range: Listen for the mews of this tiny frog issuing from the leaf litter of primary and old secondary forests. This species is abundant along most of the Peruvian Amazon as well as in Ecuador, Colombia, and Brazil. Because it has long been confused with other species, its exact range is not known.

Genus *Edalorhina;* Forest Frogs

Although they are clad in quiet colors, the two species in this genus are startlingly beautiful little frogs with brilliant flash marks on the venter and a depressed countenance. They are so effectively camouflaged when sitting among the leaf litter that they are virtually invisible unless they have reason to show their flash marks.

At the advent of the rainy season, females deposit small clutches (usually 30–60 eggs) in foam nests that float in shallow, water-filled depressions in fallen logs. The almost daily rains replenish and freshen the water in these small hollows as the tadpoles develop.

The forest frogs eat all types of tiny invertebrates, including ants and fruit flies.

103. Eyelashed Forest Frog

Edalorhina perezi

Size: Females may be 1.5 inches (4 cm) in SVL; males are somewhat smaller.

Identifying features: The brown dorsum is often adorned with five to seven longitudinal, tuberculate ridges, the outermost of which forms a prominent curved dorsolateral ridge on each side. Darker dorsal markings may be present. Each upper eyelid bears several easily discernible tubercles, hence the name "eyelashed." The limbs are sparsely banded. The brown of the forelimbs is separated from the brown dorsum by a wide band of black that extends along the side and then curves downward onto the sides of the belly, which is otherwise white. An orange field containing a black spot is present in the groin. Darker bars are present on the snout. The body is somewhat flattened.

Voice: Four or five short whistled notes are voiced from calling stations along the edges of ephemeral ponds or water-holding log cavities.

Reproduction: The female lays approximately 50–100 small eggs in a floating foam nest.

Similar species: The painted forest toadlet, *Physalaemus petersi,* has an orange groin with a black spot uppermost in the orange field, lacks eyelid tubercles, and has a black and white–mottled belly. *Colostethus marchesianus* has finely granular, nontuberculate dorsal skin. Toads have parotid glands. These all lack eyelash tubercles as well.

Habitat/Range: This well-camouflaged frog may be encountered in secondary and primary forests where it is typically associated with areas rich in leaf litter. It seems primarily diurnal and is terrestrial. Widespread in the Amazon Basin.

Genus *Hydrolaetare;* River Frog

The single species in this genus is a chunky frog with dorsolaterally oriented eyes and a dorsal coloration that blends well with the mud and dead vegetation of its aquatic habitat. The fully webbed hind feet propel it easily and rapidly through the water. Nothing is known with certainty about the reproductive biology of this frog. *Hydrolaetare* is thought to eat all sorts of invertebrates, and possibly small fish and amphibians as well.

River frogs can be found along watercourses, including oxbows, in the northwestern Amazon Basin.

104. Moaning River Frog

Hydrolaetare schmidtii

Size: Although the males may be marginally smaller, both sexes near a length of 4 inches (10 cm).

Identifying features: The dorsal coloration and pattern are variable. The ventral color and pattern are diagnostic. This big frog has dorsolaterally situated eyes and a well-defined tympanum. The dorsal ground color may be mud brown (with or without a broad, darker middorsal area and spotted sides or with discrete but variable moss green spots), moss green anteriorly shading to mud brown posteriorly, or nearly entirely moss green. There are no dorsolateral folds. The belly is yellow with prominent dark (deep brown to black) dots and dashes. A pair of bars may extend from the tip of the snout, over the nostrils, and terminate in front of and between the eyes. The feet are fully webbed.

Voice: A long, moaning bleat with a rising inflection. Large choruses can be deafening.

Reproduction: Virtually nothing is known about the reproductive biology. Other burrowing leptodactylines spawn in burrows, and this species may do that as well.

Similar species: The Neotropical green frog, *Rana palmipes,* is somewhat similar but has a more erect posture, dorsolateral folds, less dorsally directed and proportionally larger eyes, and a proportionally larger tympanum.

Habitat/Range: This large and interesting frog apparently dwells in and calls from long burrows extending into the bank from the river's edge. We found large numbers of males calling in June near Iquitos, Peru. This species has been found over much of the lower Amazon.

Comment: Despite its relatively streamlined appearance, *Hydrolaetare* does not seem to be a nervous jumper. To the contrary, those few we have seen have been easily approached. The fully webbed feet must certainly provide a reasonable degree of agility and proficiency in swimming.

Genus *Leptodactylus;* Jungle Frogs

With more than 55 species, this genus is the second largest in the family Leptodactylidae. It encompasses species diverse in both size and habits. In size, the jungle frogs vary from 2 to 7 inches (5–17.5 cm). Some of the smaller Amazonian forms, such as *L. wagneri,* are very aquatic, and some of the largest species, such as *L. pentadactylus,* are primarily terrestrial. The skin secretions of some species are virulent enough to "burn" the hand that grasps them.

The smaller species eat small invertebrates; the diet of the larger types is far more diverse. *Leptodactylus pentadactylus* eats invertebrates and small vertebrates.

Some species construct a foam nest for their eggs that floats on the surface of the shallow water in which they breed. Many of the larger species construct upper stream-bank burrows that extend down to the water table. At night, males emerge and emit whooping calls, either singly or in series, to entice receptive mates. Females enter the burrows with the males and lay their egg clutches in foam nests produced by kicking air into mucous, albumin, and sperm-laced water. The tadpoles develop and undergo metamorphosis in the burrow nest.

105. Sharp-Nosed Jungle Frog

Leptodactylus bolivianus

Size: Unusual among frogs, the male of this species is the larger sex. Males attain a length of about 4 inches (10 cm) in SVL; females are about 3.5 inches (9 cm).

Identifying features: This rocket-shaped frog has long hind legs and a long, sharp nose. Breeding males have very stout forelimbs. The long toes are webbed only at the base. The dorsal color varies from brown to grayish brown, and poorly defined darker markings are usually present. The dorsolateral folds extend to the groin and are crisp and well developed. Although conspicuous, the tympanum is proportionally small. The belly is off-white, and the white throat may have darker mottlings. The hidden surfaces of the thighs are dark and light mottled.

Voice: The vocalization of the male, a single, flat *whop*, lacks the musicality of other large leptos' calls.

Reproduction: Foam nests are built in the shallows of ponds and oxbows. A nest that we examined one rainy night seemed to contain several hundred eggs.

Similar species: The dark dorsal coloration, sharp nose, very prominent dorsolateral folds, and virtually unwebbed toes will separate this species from other large leptodactylids of the region. *Rana palmipes* has dark mottling in the groin, a large tympanum, and webbed toes.

Habitat/Range: This is a frog of clearings, village edges, secondary forest, and pond edges. We have found them on pond edges along the Peruvian upper Amazon, but not in great numbers. The species ranges southward to Bolivia.

106. Smooth Jungle Frog

Leptodactylus diedrus

This small, highly aquatic frog is discussed under the *Leptodactylus wagneri* complex on page 117.

107. Rose-Sided Jungle Frog

Leptodactylus knudseni

Size: Males may near 6.5 inches (16.5 cm) in length; females are about an inch (2.5 cm) shorter.

Identifying features: This is a huge, often prettily colored frog of robust build and wary demeanor. Dorsally, adults may vary from rich creamy tan to greenish tan. The lighter specimens may be washed with a rosy blush. Darker dorsal cross bands are usually visible. The dorsolateral folds are well developed but terminate at the sacrum. The sides are often rosy or pink, but may be black. The hind limbs are prominently barred, the forelimbs more weakly so. The hidden surfaces of the femurs are dark brown to black. The belly is gray.

Immatures are olive to tan with prominent dark bands on the dorsum and legs. The sides below the dorsolateral folds are black.

Voice: Calling males produce periodic whooping notes with a rising inflection.

Reproduction: The foam nests are built at pond edges where rains can wash the tadpoles into shallow water.

Similar species: *Leptodactylus pentadactylus* is quite similar in appearance but has a darker dorsum, vertical bars or incomplete triangles rather than dark full triangles on the upper lips, and a *full* dorsolateral fold along each side.

Habitat/Range: These upland rainforest frogs are often found at night sitting near or in the mouths of their burrows along forest trails. They are wary and retire quickly if approached. Often, just the illumination of a flashlight will cause them to retreat. This species is found in the northwestern Amazon Basin.

Comments: The strongly irritating skin secretions of this and other large leptodactylids should be washed from your hands as soon as possible.

108. Common Jungle Frog

Leptodactylus leptodactyloides

This species is discussed under the *Leptodactylus wagneri* complex on page 117.

109. Smoky Jungle Frog

Leptodactylus pentadactylus

Size: Females reach an SVL of 7 inches (18 cm); males are somewhat smaller.

Identifying features: This big, stocky, tan to olive tan to brown frog may have extensive patches of red on each side. At first sight there is a tendency to think of the smoky jungle frog as a dead leaf–colored bullfrog. There are black markings on the lips, and a broken black line begins on the snout and extends through the eye to the tympanum. From that point the black markings parallel a supratympanic ridge to the groin. Prominent dorsolateral ridges are present and run to the groin. The light belly is heavily marbled with dark pigment. Juveniles tend to be more olive tan than adults and have very prominent transverse barring. The dorsal barring may be retained into adulthood. Reproductively active males have very heavy forelimbs and spiny processes on the chest and thumbs.

Voice: A single, loud, often-repeated whistled hoot (with an upward inflection). Males call while sitting in or next to their burrows or from relatively exposed areas near water.

Reproduction: The nesting depression is formed on the forest floor and may not be near standing water. Clutches range in size from several hundred to about a thousand eggs. The tadpoles, which probably are cannibalistic, are thought to be dispersed by heavy rains to nearby swamps and pools.

Similar species: The dorsolateral fold of the similar *L. knudseni* (not pictured) reaches only to the sacrum. The smaller *L. rhodomystax* has an even more prominent full-length dorsolateral fold and an even-edged light (often reddish) labial stripe.

Habitat/Range: This is a nocturnal frog of primary forests, but it may also be found in clearings near forested areas and near canal edges. The burrows are often located a few feet from a relatively permanent water source. The species ranges southward from central Middle America to northern South America.

110. Peter's Jungle Frog

Leptodactylus petersii

This species is discussed under the *Leptodactylus wagneri* complex on page 117.

111. Moustached Jungle Frog

Leptodactylus rhodomystax

Size: Males have an SVL of 3.5 inches (9 cm); females are 3 inches (7.5 cm) long.

Identifying features: The dorsal color of adults varies from tan through reddish brown to gray-brown. The dorsum of juveniles is red to maroon. The dorsolateral folds tend to be darker than the dorsum. The venter is brown-suffused cream. The posterior surface of the thighs is olive black to black and heavily speckled with oval white to yellowish spots. The broad, even-edged labial stripe may be white (juveniles) to pinkish (adults) and is bordered beneath (along the upper lip) by dark pigment.

Voice: Unknown.

Reproduction: Rodriguez and Duellman (1994) report finding clutches of up to 250 eggs in foam nests in natural depressions on the forest floor.

Similar species: This is the only large jungle frog with both a broad, even-edged labial stripe and a light-spotted dark thigh posterior.

Habitat/Range: This is a species of primary forests. Look for it throughout the northwestern Amazon Basin.

112. Warty Jungle Frog

Leptodactylus rhodonotus

Size: Males attain an SVL of just over 3 inches (7.5 cm); females are slightly larger.

Identifying features: The dorsal skin is smooth except for numerous rough tubercles. Rough dorsolateral ridges are present. The sides and limbs are also tuberculate. The dorsal coloration may vary from olive brown to olive gray. The sides beneath the dorsolateral ridges are often slightly greener or lighter than the dorsum. The throat, chest, and belly are off-white to gray with lighter spots. The thighs are off-white to light gray with darker spots or a darker reticulum. The forelimbs are dark spotted and the hind limbs are dark banded. A dark stripe is present on the snout and continues rearward on each side to a point above the axilla. The upper lip is dark. Neither fingers nor toes are webbed.

Voice: A series of five to seven rapidly repeated whistled whooping notes, each with a rising inflection.

Reproduction: Eggs are laid in a foam nest, which may (apparently) be constructed either near a forest stream or at the terminus of a water-holding burrow. The tadpoles are aquatic.

Similar species: Other species of this genus tend to be redder or browner and far less tuberculate.

Habitat/Range: This jungle frog is thought to be restricted to stretches of primary forest. Those we have heard and found were calling from the mouths of damp burrows a few feet above an intermittent stream on Peru's Rio Orosa. The species probably ranges in suitable habitat throughout much of the northwestern Amazon Basin.

Comments: Although the specific name refers to a red or rose back, this large jungle frog is actually one of the more quietly colored species, tending more toward olives than reds. Reproductively active males develop a pair of keratinized (horny) spines on the chest and two on each thumb.

113. Black-Thighed Jungle Frog

Leptodactylus stenodema

Size: Both sexes of this relatively large frog are about 4 inches (10 cm) long.

Identifying features: *Leptodactylus stenodema* is one of several species that look superficially like the more common, larger, and more widespread smoky jungle frog, *L. pentadactylus*. The back is reddish brown, the sides are pinkish tan, and the belly is grayish. The back and sides are largely devoid of contrasting markings. The limbs bear dark bands; the rears of the thighs are black and usually lack flecks of contrasting color. Except for where there are black triangles, the upper lip is lighter in color than the rest of the face. The dorsal and lateral skin is quite smooth. The dorsolateral folds are well defined and continuous with the supratympanal fold (the fold of skin over the eardrum). The head is proportionally large.

Voice: Males produce a loud whooping note while sitting in or at the mouths of their burrows.

Reproduction: Unknown.

Similar species: The two most similar species, *L. pentadactylus* and *L. knudseni,* usually have dark dorsal markings and have spots or bars rather than triangles on the upper lip.

Habitat/Range: These jungle frogs construct burrows in primary rainforest habitats, usually on the side of a damp slope or near a stream or seep. The chosen burrow site is often largely devoid of leaf litter or other surface debris. Fair numbers of this pretty frog may be present in ideal habitats. The northwestern Amazon Basin is home to this frog.

114. Dwarf Jungle Frog

Leptodactylus wagneri complex

(Including *L. diedrus, L. leptodactyloides, L. petersii,* and *L. wagneri*)

Size: Males are up to 2 inches (5 cm) long; females to 2.75 inches (7 cm).

Identifying features: It was long known that there were several small species of *Leptodactylus* of the *L. podicipinus–L. wagneri* complex that, because of their confusing similarities, were referred to merely as *L. wagneri*. In 1994 W. Ronald Heyer diagnosed this identification problem and assigned names to the various look-alike species. While this work has satisfied taxonomists, laymen are still bewildered by these little brown frogs, whose natural variability and tendency to share characteristics make them extremely difficult to differentiate.

We discuss four species here. All are olive brown to olive green in body color. Darker markings—most prominently a triangle or V between the eyes, vertical labial bars (especially likely to be present on *L. wagneri*), and barring on the rear limbs—are present. The light belly and chin may or may not be patterned with darker mottling. The toe tips may or may not be expanded but do not serve as actual climbing pads.

Leptodactylus diedrus, of the northwestern Amazon Basin, is the only member of the complex that lacks dorsolateral folds. The belly is unmarked white, and the throat is reticulated dark and light. Light lip spots are present along the edge of the lower jaw. The lip barring is usually indistinct.

Leptodactylus leptodactyloides has short dorsolateral ridges with irregular edges. There is often at least some darkening on the belly, and the chin is dark with light spots. The lip bars are usually indistinct. This frog is widely distributed in Amazonia from Bolivia to the mouth of the Amazon River and occurs northward into the Guianas as well.

Leptodactylus petersii also has incomplete dorsolateral folds with irregular edges. The belly is prominently marked with dark mottling against a light ground color. The dark chin usually has light spots. The lip bars—especially posterior ones—are usually indistinct. This species is associated with the eastern and northern Amazon Basin.

Leptodactylus wagneri has long, crisp dorsolateral ridges that may continue uninterrupted to the groin or may be broken just posterior to the sacrum. The belly is (usually) boldly mottled, and the chin may be mottled. The lip bars are usually quite well defined. Expect this species in Amazonian Colombia, Ecuador, and Peru.

Voice: The calls vary by species but are variations on low whooping notes, low whistles, or rapidly repeated *pops*.

Reproduction: The females lay large clutches of eggs in floating foam nests.

Similar species: See the account for *Leptodactylus rhodonotus*.

Habitat/Range: The species of this complex are often terrestrial, and we have found frogs along trails in secondary forests and in forest clearings. We have also encountered them well away from the shore in rafted water hyacinths and water lettuce, and sitting in shallow water at oxbow, river, and stream edges. Vocalizations can be heard both day and night. See the individual species comments in this account for ranges.

Genus *Lithodytes*; Painted Antnest Frog

This is a monotypic genus. During the day these frogs usually remain in the nests of leaf-cutter ants; at night they may wander away in search of food (their diet includes ants and other insects). They are alert and active. If disturbed while at the ant nest the frog quickly dives into the large nest opening.

This species is considered a mimic of the poison frog, *Epipedobates femoralis*.

115. Painted Antnest Frog

Lithodytes lineatus

Size: 1.5–2 inches (3.5–5 cm); females are larger and more robust than males.

Identifying features: This is a brightly marked, terrestrial frog. The black dorsum is separated from the black upper sides by a broad cream or yellow dorsolateral line. The lower sides are cream. Spots of bright red-orange are present in the groin and on the rear of the thighs. The skin is slightly rough dorsally and smooth ventrally.

Voice: A low whistle emitted while the frog sits near or at the mouth of its burrow, often in a leaf-cutter ant nest.

Reproduction: Eggs are deposited in foam nests that are usually constructed at the edges of ephemeral ponds. After hatching, the tadpoles are washed or flip-flop into the pond to complete their development.

Similar species: Superficially, this leptodactylid looks much like *Epipe-dobates femoralis*, a small, not too brightly colored arrow-poison frog. However, the latter has both a dorsolateral stripe *and* a ventrolateral stripe and has only a single well-defined red (or yellow) spot on the upper thigh.

Habitat/Range: Although the painted antnest frog may be found nearly anywhere on the floor of primary forests, as its name implies it is often closely associated with the nests of leaf-cutter ants. This pretty little frog ranges through much of northern South America.

Genus *Physalaemus;* Forest Toadlets

Of the nearly 40 species in this genus, which ranges from Mexico south to Argentina, only a single form is found in the northwestern Amazon Basin. The forest toadlets superficially resemble small toads. Most have a brown dorsum that blends remarkably well with the preferred habitat, leaf litter.

These frogs breed while floating in shallow water, and like most lepto-dactylines they construct a foam nest for their several hundred eggs.

Frogs of this genus appear to be active both by day and by night, but seem to call most persistently after dark. They seem to be prey specialists, with termites being the prey.

116. Painted Forest Toadlet

Physalaemus petersi

Size: Males may be 1.25 inches (3 cm) long; females are adult at 1.5 inches (4 cm).

Identifying features: When viewed from above, nothing about this toad-like frog looks "painted." Its dorsum is some shade of brown, and there are numerous red or orange tubercles present. Underneath, however, the belly is gaudily dabbed with bold black markings on a white background, and the groin is orange with bold black spots. The ventral skin is smooth. Small parotid glands are present.

Voice: The bisyllabic call is usually voiced after nightfall while the males float on quiet waters.

Reproduction: The foam nest, which may hold up to several hundred eggs, floats on the surface of the breeding pond.

Similar species: The more uncommon but similarly colored *Edalorhina* *perezi* has *strongly* tuberculate upper eyelids. Most Amazonian toad species have *prominent* parotid (shoulder) glands and rough ventral skin, and lack the orange and black groin. The two squat eleutherodactyline species, *Ischnocnema quixensis* and *Eleutherodactylus sulcatus,* also lack a black and orange groin.

Habitat/Range: We have found this species in primary forest, but it is also found at least occasionally in secondary forest locations. It may be surface active both day and night. We saw this species in Amazonian Peru, and it may occur in neighboring countries.

Genus *Vanzolinius;* Whistling Frog

The frogs of this monotypic genus are abundant in swampy rainforest areas. At the advent of the rainy season their shrill, repetitive, whistled call may be heard emanating from newly flooded areas. A foam nest is constructed at water's edge for the several hundred eggs.

117. Dark-Blotched Whistling Frog

Vanzolinius discodactylus

Size: Females are 1.25 inches (3 cm) in SVL; males are 1 inch (2.5 cm).

Identifying features: The whistling frog has scattered conical tubercles on an otherwise smooth dorsal skin. The snout is long, tapered, and rounded at the tip. The dorsum is brown to dark gray, usually with large, even darker, blotches. These are often most prevalent between the eyes and on the sides. The dark lips are prominently barred with cream. The belly is cream and is spotted ventrolaterally. The toes are webbed basally, bear lateral fringes, and have small, rounded toe pads.

Voice: A frequently repeated whistled note.

Reproduction: This is a foam-nest breeder. The female lays up to 400 eggs per clutch.

Similar species: The species in the *Leptodactylus wagneri* complex lack toe pads, and the two very similar *Adenomera* species lack any vestiges of lateral toe fringes.

Habitat/Range: This tiny frog voices its repeated whistles from secluded sites at the edges of ponds, swamps, and similar bodies of water. The species is widely distributed in the northwestern Amazon Basin.

Narrow-Mouthed Toads/Sheep Frogs: Family Microhylidae

The narrow-mouths are rather rotund little frogs with short but strong hind legs and a pointed head. Most feed on ants or termites, finding and then sitting and eating at a colony until sated. Microhylids are nocturnal breeders, and huge short-lived or explosive breeding congresses sometimes occur soon after heavy rains have fallen. The calls of most sound like the nasal bleating of a distant sheep.

Collectively, the narrow-mouths are secretive burrowers. The species that dwell in seasonally dry areas are able to withstand extensive periods of drought without becoming seriously desiccated. Most are difficult to see even when surface active. In keeping with their secretive lifestyle, many call from shallow water beneath fallen leaves or other debris. In such positions, even with the vocal sac distended, they remain invisible to a searcher.

When frightened or calling, the frogs inflate themselves with air. Frightened microhylids may also assume a "rump-up" stance by extending the hind limbs. When not inflated they have loose-appearing folds of skin along the sides.

Genus *Chiasmocleis;* Sheep Frogs

This is a small (about a dozen species) genus of Neotropical narrow-mouthed toads. We cannot help but wonder why the members of this family are referred to as frogs when the prefix "sheep" is used, but called toads when the term "narrow-mouth" is affixed. Many of the species are distributed either to the north or the south of the actual Amazon Basin; two may be encountered in the northwestern section of the basin. Of very typical sheep frog appearance, with small eyes and no tympanum in evidence, these anurans are secretive dwellers of damp to swampy, leaf-littered forest habitats. The call is the usual sheep frog bleat.

118. Bassler's Sheep Frog

Chiasmocleis bassleri

Size: Females are slightly larger than males, and both sexes average just under 1 inch (2.5 cm).
Identifying features: Like most microhylids, this species has a narrow

head, pointed snout, and relatively small eyes. The dorsum (including the upper surfaces of the rear limbs) is brown or maroon-brown. A lighter area with somewhat irregular edges extends from the tip of the snout to the rear of each upper eyelid, where it becomes less well defined but continues to the axis of each forelimb. The sides are black and the belly is bluish gray with prominent black spots. The throat is gray with lighter spots. The outer surface of each arm is orange-tan, and the arm is narrowly separated from the darker dorsum by a narrow band of black. The fingers and toes are black, spotted with blue-gray; there is no webbing between the fingers and no extensive webbing between the toes. The anterior surfaces of the thighs are tannish, but not usually quite as contrasting as the arms. A large black spot is present in each groin.

Voice: A penetrating nasal buzz.

Reproduction: Although egg clutches are reported to contain between 100 and 200 eggs, little else is known about the breeding biology.

Similar species: The vestigial toe webbing coupled with belly, throat, and arm color will differentiate this frog from other microhylids of the region.

Habitat/Range: We found a small number of these terrestrial frogs vocalizing on a June night in a recently flooded, leaf-strewn depression in Amazonian Peru. The frogs were beneath the leaves in water only about half an inch deep. Except for this single instance, all known specimens have been found on the ground or on low, horizontal leaves. *Chiasmocleis bassleri* seems equally common in both secondary and primary forests and has been found in Peru and Ecuador.

Genus *Elachistocleis*; Sheep Frogs

The four species in this genus are of Neotropical distribution. At least one, *E. ovalis*, is very brilliantly colored for a narrow-mouth. When threatened, it indulges in the stereotypical microhylid defense posture—posterior elevated on extended hind legs and head down flat against the substrate. The tympanum is not visible.

119. South American Sheep Frog

Elachistocleis ovalis

Size: Both sexes attain an adult SVL of about 1.25 inches (3 cm).

Identifying features: The narrow head and ovoid body immediately identify this frog as a microhylid, although an inordinately colorful one. The dorsum is olive gray finely peppered with tiny black dots. The gray to yellow belly is variously patterned with black, orange, or yellow. There is yellow along the lower sides and at the insertion of the forearms. Brilliant orange patches occur in the groin, on the dorsal and hidden surfaces of the femur, and on the tibia. The tympanum is hidden, and a fold of skin transverses the area immediately behind the tiny head. The frog can actually turn its head—at least partially—beneath this fold to dislodge biting or stinging ants.

Voice: A nasal buzz of short duration.

Reproduction: We saw no amplexus at the breeding site, but a pair collected for photography amplexed in the bag. The female laid about 75 eggs.

Similar species: This is the only narrow-mouth in the area with orange and yellow flash marks.

Habitat/Range: This microhylid seems to occur in a wide variety of habitats ranging from Venezuela south to Brazil and Bolivia.

Genus *Hamptophryne;* Sheep Frog

The single species in this genus is common and widely distributed in the western Amazon Basin. Foraging *Hamptophryne* are often encountered at night on forest trails. The breeding requirements seem broader than those of other species. We have heard this species chorusing in January, March, May, June, September, and December. A terminal toe pad is present on each digit. The tympanum is concealed.

120. Amazon Sheep Frog

Hamptophryne boliviana

Size: This is a moderate-sized sheep frog. Males attain an SVL of about 1.25 inches (3 cm); females may be nearly 1.75 inches (to 4.5 cm).

Identifying features: The dorsum is gray to tan, often with a large, somewhat darker, irregular dorsal figure and a light vertebral line. The sides are brown from snout to groin. The dark lateral coloration passes over the apex of the light-colored forelimb, separating the light-colored arm from the light-colored back. The belly is white. The rear legs are dark-barred.

Voice: A repeated bleating like that of a sheep, often given while the frog is sitting in the water or at the water's edge beneath a fallen leaf.

Reproduction: The clutch consists of about 250 eggs.

Similar species: *Ctenophryne geayi* is very similar but usually grayer, and the dark lateral color does not separate the arm color from that of the back. *Chiasmocleis bassleri,* also superficially similar, has a blue-gray belly.

Habitat/Range: Even when they are at their breeding ponds, these burrowing frogs are more often heard than seen. They may be active after nightfall but are so adept at remaining hidden that finding one is truly an accident. This species seems to be the most common of the sheep frogs in the Iquitos region. It ranges from Bolivia northward and eastward to Peru and Ecuador.

Genus *Syncope;* Pygmy Sheep Frogs

Everything about these frogs is elfin. They are adult at only a half inch in length. Muted by the leaves beneath which they sit when chorusing, their *peeeent*s are so soft that they can barely be heard over the normal forest noises, especially the pitter-pattering of raindrops. The two species of this genus have only three fingers and four toes. Additionally, unlike the other genera of microhylids in the Amazon Basin, at least part of the tympanum is visible.

121. Dusky Pygmy Sheep Frog

Syncope antenori

Size: Tiny! Lilliputian! Minuscule! This frog is fully adult at an SVL of 0.5 inch (1.5 cm).

Identifying features: Three short fingers, four short toes, a brown dorsum (often with sparsely distributed, *very* tiny flecks of bluish white) a light canthal stripe, and a pale blue–flecked gray belly (the color of old enamelware) will identify this easily overlooked microhylid.

Voice: The call is high pitched and of very short duration, yet still has the buzzing quality associated with tiny microhylids.

Reproduction: Gravid females lay from three to seven eggs. It is thought that they utilize water-holding terrestrial plants as a deposition site.

Similar species: The equally small and sympatric *Syncope carvalhoi* has white-spotted brown belly, sides, and back.

Habitat/Range: Those we heard were calling from beneath fallen leaves on the wet bank of a newly freshened old secondary forest stream in Loreto Province, Peru. The species occurs in many areas of the northwestern Amazon Basin.

Tongueless Aquatic Toads: Family Pipidae

The many species in this family are of Neotropical and African distribution. All are aquatic, lack tongues, and eagerly stuff food—be it fish, worm, or insect—into their mouths with their hands.

Several of the African members of the family—the clawed frogs and dwarf underwater frogs—are bred in vast numbers in captivity and are well known to aquarium enthusiasts. The tropical American species are far less familiar to casual enthusiasts. They have unusual breeding habits and, in contrast to their African relatives, are difficult to breed in captivity. The Suriname toads are restricted to tropical South America.

Genus *Pipa;* Suriname Toads

The two species that occur in the Amazonian region are among the world's most unusual frogs in appearance; both look like they lost a battle with a car tire. One, the Suriname toad, seems far more common than the other. They are tongueless and use patting motions of their forefeet to stuff prey into their capacious mouths.

Searching for a mud brown frog in turbid water against a substrate of mud might seem an exercise in futility; indeed, it usually is. But at the advent of the rainy season, when ponds are being cooled and freshened and rivers are beginning to rise, the grassy verges of waterways begin to accumulate clear water, and the Suriname toads come to these areas to forage—and if conditions are right, to breed. Such conditions constitute your best chance of seeing these remarkable anurans.

122. Common Suriname Toad

Pipa pipa

Size: 4.5–6.5 inches (11.5–16.5 cm); females are larger and more robust than males.

Identifying features: Just as the matamata is unmistakable among turtles, the Suriname toads are unmistakable among frogs. The flattened body; tiny, lidless eyes; pointed nose; and flaps of skin from the anterior upper lip and on each side of the broad head are diagnostic. Overall, these toads look more like blobs of mud than living animals. The entire body is muddy tan to brown with or without lighter or darker blotches. The rear feet are broad and fully webbed, the hind legs are flattened but muscular, and the webless fingers are tipped with small but easily visible bifurcate lobes. The venter is lighter than the back and marked by a dark T whose top runs between the apices of the forelimbs.

Voice: Males produce a clicking breeding call while submerged.

Reproduction: The breeding biology is well known and quite interesting. Breeding seems to be initiated by rising water levels. While the pair are amplexing, they make stylized vertical loops or seesawing movements in the water during which the eggs are expelled and fertilized. The male uses his hind feet to brush the eggs forward onto the female's back. The jelly coating that surrounds each egg is sticky, and the eggs adhere to the female's back. The female's dorsal skin swells to cover the 50–80 eggs. The young frogs complete their development within these imbedded egg capsules and then push their way to freedom through a rupture in the female's skin above each egg.

Similar species: In the Amazon Basin, only the smaller *Pipa snethlageae* could be confused with the Suriname toad, but the former lacks the dermal flaps on the head, has simple toe tips, and lacks the dark ventral T.

Habitat/Range: Suriname toads are fully aquatic and may be encountered in quiet waters throughout much of the Amazon Basin. They can be seen after dark in the shallows at grassy river and oxbow edges or at newly flooded depressions. This species ranges from Peru and Colombia east to Venezuela and Brazil.

123. Utinga Suriname Toad

Pipa snethlageae

Size: The SVL is about 3.5 inches (9 cm).

Identifying features: Like the larger common Suriname toad, this amazing creature is clad in rough skin the color of mud. There is no dark T on the venter. The fingertips lack multipointed lobes. The body is horizontally flattened, but not as severely as that of the common Suriname toad. The lidless eyes of *P. snethlageae* are less dorsally directed than are those of its larger relative. There is no flap of skin beneath the lower jaw. The fingers are unwebbed; the toes are fully webbed.

Voice: Males produce a series of weak clicks while submerged.

Reproduction: Unknown.

Similar species: See the account for the common Suriname toad, above.

Habitat/Range: The Utinga Suriname toad is fully aquatic and is found in slow-moving and standing Amazonian waters.

P1. Mammals such as the giant otter prey on small riverine amphibians and reptiles.

P2. Monkeys such as the saki pictured here consume frogs and lizards.

P3. Many birds, including the rufescent tiger heron pictured here, prey on reptiles and amphibians.

P4. The common mussurana (hatchling pictured) eats other species of reptiles and amphibians, including venomous types.

P5. Caiman like this spectacled caiman prey on all manner of smaller amphibians and reptiles.

H1. (left) Many reptiles and amphibians favor trail edge habitats.

H2. (right) Water-holding tree cavities are breeding sites for some frogs (Amazon milk treefrog pictured).

H3. (left) The water-holding cups and leaf axils of bromeliads are the breeding and/or resting sites of many amphibians and some reptiles.

H4. (below) River edge thickets are home to gladiator treefrogs, vine snakes, and other herps.

H5. Cecropias and other fast-growing trees quickly reclaim abandoned clearings or river edge situations, beginning the woody succession.

H6. Temporary rainforest ponds are breeding sites for many amphibians and feeding sites for the reptiles that prey on them.

H7. The closed canopy provided by ceibas and other huge trees offers the muted light and high humidity preferred by many reptiles and amphibians.

H8. Seasonally flooded forests are called *varzeas* in the Amazon Basin.

H9. Human-made clearings and ponds provide habitats for many forest edge reptiles and amphibians.

H10. (left) Treefalls provide suitable habitats for "edge-dwelling" amphibians and reptiles.

H11. (right) Fallen fronds and detritus in the root systems of stilt palms offer habitats for some secretive and fossorial reptiles and amphibians.

H12. Regenerating secondary forests are important habitats.

H13. Floating and emergent vegetation provides breeding sites for many herp species and refuge for others.

F1. The cylindrical, leglike paired fins of the South American lungfish, *Lepidosiren paradoxa,* impart an "unfishlike" appearance.

F2. Baby electric eels, *Electrophorus electricus* (and other knifefishes), may be mistaken for caecilians.

F3. The virtual lack of fins and ability to move overland belie the fact that the marbled swamp eel, *Synbranchus marmoratus,* is a fish—and one capable of biting *hard,* at that. Photo by Dr. Leo G. Nico.

1. Bassler's slender caecilian, *Oscaecilia bassleri* (Loreto, Peru)

2. Amazonian ringed caecilian, *Siphonops annulatus* (Loreto, Peru)

3. Common aquatic caecilian, *Typhlonectes compressicauda* (Loreto, Peru)

4. Amazon climbing salamander, *Bolitoglossa altamazonica* (Loreto, Peru)

5. Dwarf climbing salamander, *Bolitoglossa peruviana* (Amazonas, Colombia)

6. Black-bellied climbing salamander, *Bolitoglossa* species (Loreto, Peru)

7. Cayenne harlequin toad, *Atelopus flavescens* (French Guiana)

8A. Amazon harlequin toad, *Atelopus pulcher* (Rio Apayacu, Loreto, Peru)

8B. Amazon harlequin toad, *Atelopus pulcher*, venter

8C. Amazon harlequin toad, *Atelopus pulcher* (Rio Orosa, Loreto, Peru)

9. Common harlequin toad, *Atelopus spumarius* (Suriname)

10. Eyelashed forest toad, *Bufo ceratophrys* (Loreto, Peru)

11A. Sharp-nosed toad, *Bufo dapsilis,* pink-sided morph (Loreto, Peru)

11B. Sharp-nosed toad, *Bufo dapsilis,* dark morph (Loreto, Peru)

12. Peruvian smooth-sided toad, *Bufo glaberrimus* complex (Loreto Peru); photo by David M. Schleser, Nature's Images, Inc.

13. Eastern smooth-sided toad, *Bufo guttatus* (Suriname)

14A. Crested forest toad, *Bufo margaritifer* complex, broad-crested morph (Loreto, Peru)

14B. Crested forest toad, *Bufo margaritifer* complex, vertebral stripe (Loreto, Peru)

14C. Crested forest toad, *Bufo margaritifer* complex, spiny morph (Loreto, Peru)

15A. Cane (giant) toad, *Bufo marinus,* typically patterned adult female (Loreto, Peru)

15B. Cane (giant) toad, *Bufo marinus,* nonpatterned old female (Loreto, Peru)

16A. Orange-bellied leaf toad, *Dendrophryniscus minutus,* dorsum (Loreto, Peru)

16B. Orange-bellied leaf toad, *Dendrophryniscus minutus,* venter (Loreto, Peru)

17. Amazonian glass frog, *Cochranella ritae*

18. Ucayali rocket frog, *Colostethus marchesianus*

19. Blue poison frog, *Dendrobates azureus* (Suriname)

20A. Biolat poison frog, *Dendrobates biolat* (Madre de Dios, Peru)

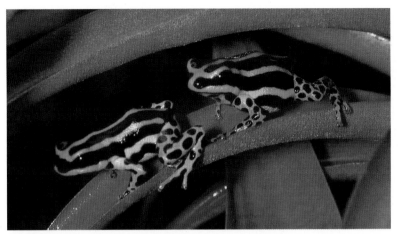

20B. Biolat poison frog, *Dendrobates biolat,* pair in bromeliad (origin unknown); photo by Larry Marshall

21. Brazil-nut poison frog, *Dendrobates castaneoticus* (Brazil)

22A. Fantastic poison frog, *Dendrobates fantasticus,* red morph (Peru)

22B. Fantastic poison frog, *Dendrobates fantasticus*, yellow morph (origin unknown)

23A. Splash-backed poison frog, *Dendrobates galactonotus*, yellow morph (origin unknown)

23B. Splash-backed poison frog, *Dendrobates galactonotus*, red morph (origin unknown)

24A. Mimic poison frog, *Dendrobates imitator* (Peru)

24B. Mimic poison frog, *Dendrobates imitator*, "*intermedius*" morph (origin unknown); photo by Larry Marshall

25. Pasco poison frog, *Dendrobates lamasi* (origin unknown); photo by Larry Marshall

26. Rio Madeira poison frog, *Dendrobates quinquevittatus* (Brazil)

27. Red-backed poison frog, *Dendrobates reticulatus* (Loreto, Peru)

28A. Dyeing poison frog, *Dendrobates tinctorius,* yellow bull's-eye morph (Suriname)

28B. Dyeing poison frog, *Dendrobates tinctorius*, yellow-headed morph (Suriname)

28C. Dyeing poison frog, *Dendrobates tinctorius*, blue morph (Suriname)

28D. Dyeing poison frog, *Dendrobates tinctorius*, green-striped morph (Suriname)

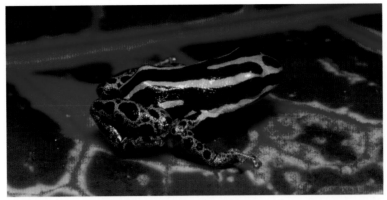

29A. Amazonian poison frog, *Dendrobates ventrimaculatus* complex, with short middorsal stripe forming a Y anteriorly (Loreto, Peru)

29B. Amazonian poison frog, *Dendrobates ventrimaculatus* complex, with nonbranching full-length middorsal stripe (increasingly referred to as *D. duellmani*) (Loreto, Peru)

30. Sky blue poison frog, *Epipedobates azureiventris* (origin unknown)

31. Spotted-thighed poison frog, *Epipedobates femoralis* (Loreto, Peru)

32. Pale-striped Amazon poison frog, *Epipedobates hahneli* (Loreto, Peru)

33. Ruby poison frog, *Epipedobates parvulus* (Loreto, Peru)

34A. Spotted-legged poison frog, *Epipedobates pictus,* dorsum (Loreto, Peru)

34B. Spotted-legged poison frog, *Epipedobates pictus,* venter (Loreto, Peru)

35. Silverstone's poison frog, *Epipedobates silverstonei* (origin unknown)

36A. Three-striped poison frog, *Epipedobates trivittatus,* green two-striped phase (Loreto, Peru)

36B. Three-striped poison frog, *Epipedobates trivittatus,* orange two-striped phase (Suriname)

37. Sanguine poison frog, *Epipedobates zaparo* (Peru); photo by Chris Miller

38. Peruvian casque-headed treefrog, *Hemiphractus helioi* (Loreto, Peru); photo by David M. Schleser, Nature's Images, Inc.

39. Long-nosed casque-headed treefrog, *Hemiphractus proboscideus* (Loreto, Peru)

40. Gladiator treefrog, *Hyla boans* (Loreto Peru)

41. Short-nosed treefrog, *Hyla brevifrons* (Loreto, Peru)

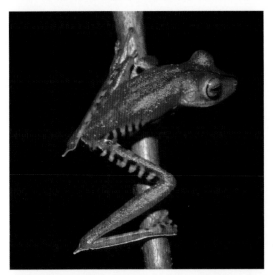

42. Convict treefrog, *Hyla calcarata* (Loreto, Peru)

43. Spotted-thighed treefrog, *Hyla fasciata* (Loreto, Peru)

44. Map treefrog, *Hyla geographica* (Loreto, Peru)

45. Rough-skinned green treefrog, *Hyla granosa* (Loreto, Peru)

46. Many-striped treefrog, *Hyla haraldschultzi* (Loreto, Peru)

47. Cinnamon treefrog, *Hyla koechlini* (Loreto, Peru)

48. Rocket treefrog, *Hyla lanciformis* (Loreto, Peru)

49. Plain-colored treefrog, *Hyla leali* (Loreto, Peru)

50A. Clown treefrog, *Hyla leucophyllata,* clown phase (Loreto, Peru)

50B. Clown treefrog, *Hyla leucophyllata,* giraffe phase (Loreto, Peru)

51A. Neotropical marbled treefrog, *Hyla marmorata,* dorsum (Loreto, Peru)

51B. Neotropical marbled treefrog, *Hyla marmorata,* venter (Loreto, Peru)

52. Yellow-toed treefrog, *Hyla microderma* (Loreto, Peru)

53. Least treefrog, *Hyla minuta* (Loreto, Peru)

54A. Jeweled treefrog, *Hyla miyatai*, night color (Loreto, Peru)

54B. Jeweled treefrog, *Hyla miyatai*, day color (Loreto, Peru)

55. Orange-shanked treefrog, *Hyla parviceps* (Loreto, Peru)

56A. Common polkadot treefrog, *Hyla punctata punctata,* red-spotted morph, day color (Loreto, Peru)

56B. Common polkadot treefrog, *Hyla punctata punctata,* yellow-spotted morph, day color (Loreto, Peru)

56C. Common polkadot treefrog, *Hyla punctata punctata,* red-spotted morph, night color (Loreto, Peru)

57. Chaco treefrog, *Hyla raniceps* (Brazil) ✓ TRC

58. Red-striped treefrog, *Hyla rhodopepla* (Loreto, Peru)

59. Golden-nosed treefrog, *Hyla rossalleni* (Loreto, Peru)

60. Mottled clown treefrog, *Hyla sarayacuensis* (Loreto, Peru)

61A. Variable clown treefrog, *Hyla triangulum,* plain phase (Loreto, Peru)

61B. Variable clown treefrog, *Hyla triangulum,* blotched phase (Loreto, Peru)

61C. Variable clown treefrog, *Hyla triangulum,* spotted phase (Loreto, Peru)

62. Forest bromeliad treefrog, *Osteocephalus cabrerai* (Loreto, Peru)

63. Common bromeliad treefrog, *Osteocephalus leprieurii* (Loreto, Peru)

64. Flat-headed bromeliad treefrog, *Osteocephalus planiceps* (Loreto, Peru)

65. Giant broad-headed treefrog, *Osteocephalus taurinus* (Loreto, Peru)

66A. Amazonian milk treefrog, *Phrynohyas resinifictrix,* adult (Loreto, Peru)

66B. Amazonian milk treefrog, *Phrynohyas resinifictrix,* metamorph (Loreto, Peru)

67. Common milk treefrog, *Phrynohyas venulosa* (Loreto, Peru)

68. Slender treefrog, *Scarthyla ostinodactyla* (Loreto, Peru)

69. Plain narrow-headed treefrog, *Scinax cruentomma* (Loreto, Peru)

70. Brown-thighed treefrog, *Scinax funerea* (Loreto, Peru)

71A. Fringe-lipped treefrog, *Scinax garbei,* dorsum (Loreto, Peru)

71B. Fringe-lipped treefrog, *Scinax garbei*, flash marks on thigh (Loreto, Peru)

72. Two-striped treefrog, *Scinax rubra* (Loreto, Peru)

73A. Pygmy hatchet-faced treefrog, *Sphaenorhynchus carneus*, night color (Loreto, Peru)

73B. Pygmy hatchet-faced treefrog, *Sphaenorhynchus carneus*, day color (Loreto, Peru)

74. Spotted hatchet-faced treefrog, *Sphaenorhynchus dorisae* (Loreto, Peru)

75. Greater hatchet-faced treefrog, *Sphaenorhynchus lacteus* (Loreto, Peru)

76. Jordan's casque-headed treefrog, *Trachycephalus jordani* (Ecuador)

77A. Amazon leaf frog, *Agalychnis craspedopus,* dorsum (Loreto, Peru); photo by Dennis Sheridan

77B. Amazon leaf frog, *Agalychnis craspedopus,* venter (Loreto, Peru); photo by Dennis Sheridan

78. Giant monkey frog, *Phyllomedusa bicolor* (Loreto, Peru)

79. Orange-sided monkey frog, *Phyllomedusa hypocondrialis hypocondrialis* (Brazil)

80A. Warty monkey frog, *Phyllomedusa tarsius*, adult (Guyana); photo by Brice Noonan

80B. Warty monkey frog, *Phyllomedusa tarsius,* metamorph (Guyana)

81. Barred monkey frog, *Phyllomedusa tomopterna* (Loreto, Peru)

82. White-lined monkey frog, *Phyllomedusa vaillanti* (Loreto, Peru)

83. Colombian horned frog, *Ceratophrys calcarata* (Colombia)

84. Amazon horned frog, *Ceratophrys cornuta* (Suriname)

85. Green rain frog, *Eleutherodactylus acuminatus* (Loreto, Peru)

86. Amazonian rain frog, *Eleutherodactylus altamazonicus* (Loreto, Peru)

87. Long-nosed rain frog, *Eleutherodactylus carvalhoi* (Loreto, Peru)

88. Diadem rain frog, *Eleutherodactylus diadematus* (Loreto, Peru)

89. Peeping rain frog, *Eleutherodactylus lacrimosus* (Loreto, Peru)

90. Striped-throated rain frog, *Eleutherodactylus lanthanites* (Loreto, Peru)

91. Luscombe's rain frog, *Eleutherodactylus luscombei* (Loreto, Peru)

92. Red-bellied rain frog, *Eleutherodactylus lythrodes* (Loreto, Peru)

93A. Marti's rain frog, *Eleutherodactylus martiae*, striped dorsum (Loreto, Peru)

93B. Marti's rain frog, *Eleutherodactylus martiae*, nonstriped dorsum (Loreto, Peru)

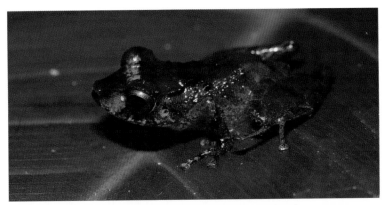

94A. Carabaya rain frog, *Eleutherodactylus ockendeni* (Loreto, Peru)

94B. Carabaya rain frog, *Eleutherodactylus ockendeni* (Loreto, Peru)

95. Peruvian rain frog, *Eleutherodactylus peruvianus* (Loreto, Peru)

96. Broad-headed rain frog, *Eleutherodactylus sulcatus* (Loreto, Peru)

97A. Variable rain frog, *Eleutherodactylus variabilis,* with vertebral stripe (Loreto, Peru)

97B. Variable rain frog, *Eleutherodactylus variabilis,* without vertebral stripe (Loreto, Peru)

98A. Spotted-bellied rain frog, *Eleutherodactylus ventrimarmoratus*, dorsum (Loreto, Peru)

98B. Spotted-bellied rain frog, *Eleutherodactylus ventrimarmoratus*, venter (Loreto, Peru)

99. Tan-legged rain frog, *Eleutherodactylus* species

100. Common big-headed rain frog, *Ischnocnema quixensis* (Loreto, Peru)

101. Cocha chirping frog, *Adenomera andreae* (Loreto, Peru)

102. Forest chirping frog, *Adenomera hylaedactyla* (Loreto, Peru)

103. Eyelashed forest frog, *Edalorhina perezi* (Loreto, Peru)

104. Moaning river frog, *Hydrolaetare schmidtii* (Loreto, Peru)

105. Sharp-nosed jungle frog, *Leptodactylus bolivianus* (Loreto, Peru)

106. Smooth jungle frog, *Leptodactylus diedrus* (Loreto, Peru)

107. Rose-sided jungle frog, *Leptodactylus knudseni,* juvenile (Loreto, Peru)

108. Common jungle frog, *Leptodactylus leptodactyloides* (Loreto, Peru)

109. Smoky jungle frog, *Leptodactylus pentadactylus* (Loreto, Peru)

110. Peter's jungle frog, *Leptodactylus petersii* (Loreto, Peru)

111A. Moustached jungle frog, *Leptodactylus rhodomystax,* adult (Loreto, Peru); photo by Bill Love, Blue Chameleon Ventures

111B. Moustached jungle frog, *Leptodactylus rhodomystax*, juvenile (Loreto, Peru)

112. Warty jungle frog, *Leptodactylus rhodonotus* (Loreto, Peru)

113. Black-thighed jungle frog, *Leptodactylus stenodema* (Loreto, Peru)

114. Dwarf jungle frog, *Leptodactylus wagneri* (Loreto, Peru)

115. Painted antnest frog, *Lithodytes lineatus* (Loreto, Peru)

116A. Painted forest toadlet, *Physalaemus petersi* (Loreto, Peru)

116B. Painted forest toadlet, *Physalaemus petersi* (Loreto, Peru)

117. Dark-blotched whistling frog, *Vanzolinius discodactylus* (Loreto, Peru)

118. Bassler's sheep frog, *Chiasmocleis bassleri* (Loreto, Peru)

119. South American sheep frog, *Elachistocleis ovalis* (Paraguay)

120. Amazon sheep frog, *Hamptophryne boliviana* (Loreto, Peru)

121. Dusky pygmy sheep frog, *Syncope antenori* (Loreto, Peru)

122. Common Suriname toad, *Pipa pipa* (Loreto, Peru)

123. Utinga Suriname toad, *Pipa snethlageae* (Loreto, Peru)

124. Paradox frog, *Pseudis paradoxa* (Suriname)

125. Neotropical green frog, *Rana palmipes* (Loreto, Peru)

126A. Spectacled caiman, *Caiman crocodilus* ssp., juvenile (Loreto, Peru)

126B. Spectacled caiman, *Caiman crocodilus* ssp., juvenile with spectacle bridge crossing the snout (Loreto, Peru)

127A. Black caiman, *Caiman niger* (origin unknown)

127B. Black caiman, *Caiman niger,* skull (Loreto, Peru)

128A. Dwarf caiman, *Paleosuchus palpebrosus* (origin unknown)

128B. Comparison of the hip regions of the difficult to differentiate dwarf caiman (left), with four rows of strongly keeled scutes, and smooth-fronted caiman (right), with two rows of strongly keeled scutes

129A. Smooth-fronted caiman, *Paleosuchus trigonatus*, juvenile (Loreto, Peru)

129B. Smooth-fronted caiman, *Paleosuchus trigonatus,* adult (Loreto, Peru)

130A. Matamata, *Chelus fimbriatus*, juvenile (Loreto, Peru)

130B. Matamata, *Chelus fimbriatus*, adult (Loreto, Peru)

131A. Spotted toad-headed turtle, *Phrynops geoffroanus tuberosus*, carapace (Brazil)

131B. Spotted toad-headed turtle, *Phrynops geoffroanus tuberosus,* plastron (Brazil)

132. Gibba toad-headed turtle, *Phrynops gibbus* (Loreto, Peru)

133. Common toad-headed turtle, *Phrynops nasutus* (Suriname)

134. Amazon toad-headed turtle, *Phrynops raniceps* (Loreto, Peru)

135. Red-faced toad-headed turtle, *Phrynops rufipes* (Brazil)

136. Western twist-necked turtle, *Platemys platycephala melanonota* (Loreto, Peru)

137. Big-headed river turtle, *Peltocephalus dumerilianus* (Venezuela)

138A. Giant river turtle, *Podocnemis expansa,* adult female (Loreto, Peru)

138B. Giant river turtle, *Podocnemis expansa,* juvenile (Loreto, Peru)

139. Red-spotted river turtle, *Podocnemis erythrocephala* (Loreto, Peru)

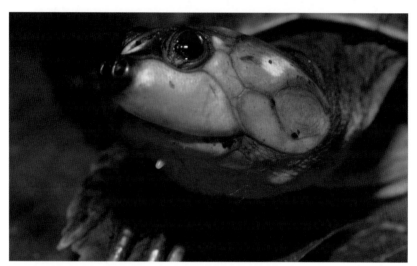

140. Amazon river turtle, *Podocnemis sextuberculata* (Loreto, Peru)

141A. Yellow-spotted river turtle, *Podocnemis unifilis,* adult female (Loreto, Peru)

141B. Yellow-spotted river turtle, *Podocnemis unifilis,* juvenile (Loreto, Peru)

142. White-lipped mud turtle, *Kinosternon leucostomum,* subadult (Loreto, Peru)

143. Amazon mud turtle, *Kinosternon scorpioides scorpioides* (Loreto, Peru)

144. Amazon wood turtle, *Rhinoclemmys punctularia punctularia* (Suriname)

145. Red-footed tortoise, *Chelonoidis (Geochelone) carbonaria,* adult (Suriname)

146. Yellow-footed tortoise, *Chelonoidis (Geochelone) denticulata,* adult pair (Loreto, Peru)

147. Giant amphisbaenian, *Amphisbaena alba* (Brazil); photo by Bill Love

148. Banded amphisbaenian, *Amphisbaena fuliginosa* (Peru); photo by Chris Scott

149A. Collared forest gecko, *Gonatodes concinnatus,* male (Loreto, Peru)

149B. Collared forest gecko, *Gonatodes concinnatus,* female (Loreto, Peru)

150A. Bridled forest gecko, *Gonatodes humeralis,* male in breeding colors (Loreto, Peru)

150B. Bridled forest gecko, *Gonatodes humeralis,* female (Loreto, Peru)

151.Amazon pygmy gecko, *Pseudogonatodes guianensis* (Loreto, Peru)

152.Tropical house gecko, *Hemidactylus mabouia* (Loreto, Peru)

153.Turnip-tailed gecko, *Thecadactylus rapicaudus* (Loreto, Peru)

154. Large-scaled forest lizard, *Alopoglossus angulata* (Loreto, Peru)

155. Black-bellied forest lizard, *Alopoglossus atriventris,* male (Loreto, Peru)

156. Reticulated creek lizard, *Arthrosaura reticulata reticulata* (Loreto, Peru)

157. Brown worm lizard, *Bachia vermiformis* (Loreto, Peru)

158A. Black-striped forest lizard, *Cercosaura ocellata bassleri,* male (Loreto, Peru)

158B. Black-striped forest lizard, *Cercosaura ocellata bassleri,* female (Loreto, Peru)

159. Spectacled forest lizard, *Gymnophthalmus underwoodi* complex (Brazil)

160A. Glossy shade lizard, *Iphisa elegans,* dorsum (Loreto, Peru)

160B. Glossy shade lizard, *Iphisa elegans,* venter of breeding male (Loreto, Peru)

161. Common forest lizard, *Leposoma parietale* (Loreto, Peru)

162. Blue-tailed glossy lizard, *Micrablepharis maximiliana* (Brazil)

163. Common streamside lizard, *Neusticurus ecpleopus* (Loreto, Peru)

164. Elegant eyed lizard, *Prionodactylus argulus* (Loreto, Peru)

165. White-striped eyed lizard, *Prionodactylus oshaughnessyi* (Loreto, Peru)

166A. Amazon forest dragon, *Enyalioides laticeps,* male (Loreto, Peru)

166B. Amazon forest dragon, *Enyalioides laticeps*, female (Loreto, Peru)

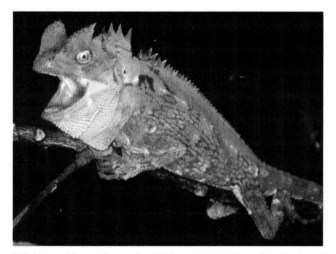

167. Horned forest dragon, *Enyalioides palpebralis* (Acre, Brazil); photo by Laurie Vitt

168. Great green iguana, *Iguana iguana* (Loreto, Peru)

169. Blue-lipped forest anole, *Anolis bombiceps* (Loreto, Peru)

170. Slender anole, *Anolis fuscoauratus fuscoauratus* (Loreto, Peru)

171. Yellow-tongued forest anole, *Anolis nitens scypheus* (Loreto, Peru)

172. Blue-throated anole, *Anolis nitens tandae* (Loreto, Peru)

173. Amazon bark anole, *Anolis ortonii* (Loreto, Peru)

174. Amazon green anole, *Anolis punctatus* (Loreto, Peru)

175. Common forest anole, *Anolis trachyderma* (Loreto, Peru)

176A. Banded tree anole, *Anolis transversalis,* male (Loreto, Peru)

176B. Banded tree anole, *Anolis transversalis,* female (Loreto, Peru)

177. Sharp-nosed monkey lizard, *Polychrus acutirostris* (Paraguay)

178. Common monkey lizard, *Polychrus marmoratus* (Loreto, Peru)

179. Western leaf lizard, *Stenocercus fimbriatus* (Loreto, Peru)

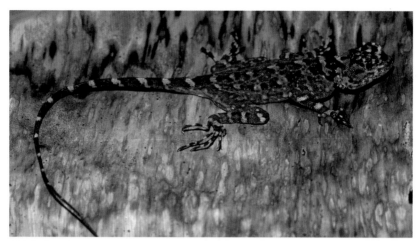

180. Collared tree runner, *Tropidurus (Plica) plica* (Loreto, Peru)

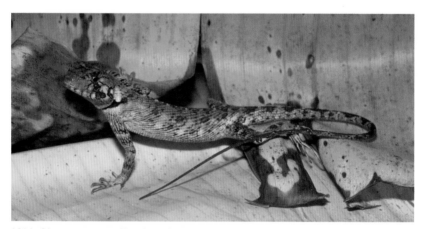

181A. Olive tree runner, *Tropidurus (Plica) umbra ochrocollaris,* male (Loreto, Peru)

181B. Olive tree runner, *Tropidurus (Plica) umbra ochrocollaris,* female (Loreto, Peru)

182. Eastern green thornytail, *Tropidurus (Uracentron) azureum azureum* (Suriname)

183. Amazon thornytail, *Tropidurus (Uracentron) flaviceps,* male (Loreto, Peru); photo by James L. Castner

184. Diving lizard, *Uranoscodon superciliosus* (Brazil); photo by Laurie Vitt

185. Black-spotted skink, *Mabuya nigropunctata* (Loreto, Peru)

186. Amazon whiptail, *Ameiva ameiva* (Loreto, Peru)

187A. Rainbow whiptail, *Cnemidophorus lemniscatus,* male (Suriname)

187B. Rainbow whiptail, *Cnemidophorus lemniscatus*, female (Suriname)

188A. Crocodile tegu, *Crocodilurus amazonicus (lacertinus)*, adult (Loreto, Peru)

188B. Crocodile tegu, *Crocodilurus amazonicus (lacertinus)*, juvenile (Loreto, Peru)

189. Northern caiman lizard, *Dracaena guianensis* (Loreto, Peru)

190. Cocha whiptail, *Kentropyx altamazonica* (Loreto, Peru)

191. Forest whiptail, *Kentropyx pelviceps* (Loreto, Peru)

192A. Black and white tegu, *Tupinambis merianae*, subadult (Argentina)

192B. Black and white tegu, *Tupinambis merianae*, hatchling (Argentina)

193A. Golden tegu, *Tupinambis teguixin*, subadult (Loreto, Peru)

193B. Golden tegu, *Tupinambis teguixin,* subadult (Colombia)

194. Coral pipesnake, *Anilius scytale scytale* (Loreto, Peru)

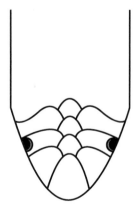

195. Blind snakes, families Leptotyphlopidae and Typhlopidae (diagrammatic sketch)

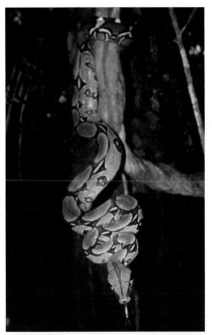

196A. Red-tailed boa, *Boa constrictor constrictor,* adult (Loreto, Peru)

196B. Red-tailed boa, *Boa constrictor constrictor,* juvenile (Loreto, Peru)

197. Common boa, *Boa constrictor imperator,* adult (Amazonas, Colombia)

198A. Emerald tree boa, *Corallus caninus*, adult (Suriname)

198B. Emerald tree boa, *Corallus caninus*, unpatterned adult (Suriname)

198C. Emerald tree boa, *Corallus caninus*, juvenile (Loreto, Peru)

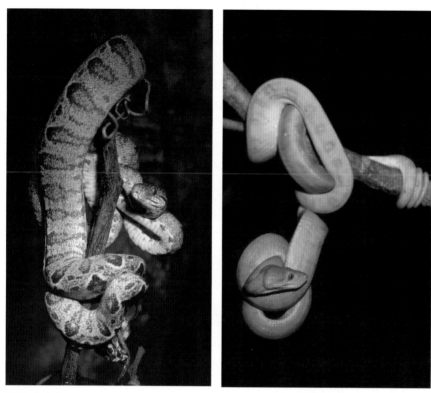

199A. (*left*) Amazon tree boa, *Corallus hortulanus,* typical coloration (Loreto, Peru)

199B. (*right*) Amazon tree boa, *Corallus hortulanus,* yellow adult (Loreto, Peru)

199C. Amazon tree boa, *Corallus hortulanus,* red subadult (Loreto, Peru)

200A. Brazilian rainbow boa, *Epicrates cenchria cenchria,* adult (southern Suriname)

200B. Brazilian rainbow boa, *Epicrates cenchria cenchria,* juvenile (southern Suriname)

201A. Peruvian rainbow boa, *Epicrates cenchria gaigei,* subadult (Loreto, Peru)

201B. Peruvian rainbow boa, *Epicrates cenchria gaigei,* subadult (Loreto, Peru)

202A. Green anaconda, *Eunectes murinus murinus,* 14-foot adult in stream (Loreto, Peru)

202B. Green anaconda, *Eunectes murinus murinus,* juvenile (Loreto, Peru)

203. Wedge-tailed earth snake, *Atractus latifrons,* brilliantly colored subadult (Loreto, Peru)

204. Ring-necked earth snake, *Atractus* species cf. *collaris* (Loreto, Peru)

205A. White-naped earth snake, *Atractus* species, juvenile (Loreto, Peru)

205B. White-naped earth snake, *Atractus* species, melanistic adult (Loreto, Peru)

206. Rusty earth snake, *Atractus torquatus* (Loreto, Peru)

207A. Common whipsnake, *Chironius exoletus* (Loreto, Peru)

207B. Common whipsnake, *Chironius exoletus* (Loreto, Peru)

208. Olive whipsnake, *Chironius fuscus*

209. Rusty whipsnake, *Chironius scurrulus,* juvenile (Loreto, Peru)

210A. Common mussurana, *Clelia clelia clelia,* large juvenile (Brazil)

210B. Common mussurana, *Clelia clelia clelia,* hatchling (Loreto, Peru)

211. Tawny forest racer, *Dendrophidion dendrophis* (Loreto, Peru)

212. Ornate snail-eating snake, *Dipsas catesbyi* (Loreto, Peru)

213. Big-headed snail-eating snake, *Dipsas indica indica* (Loreto, Peru)

214. Variegated snail-eating snake, *Dipsas variegata variegata* (Suriname)

215A. Amazon egg-eating snake, *Drepanoides anomalus,* adult (Loreto, Peru)

215B. Amazon egg-eating snake, *Drepanoides anomalus,* hatchling with extensive white on its head (Loreto, Peru)

216. Yellow-tailed cribo, *Drymarchon corais corais,* adult (French Guiana)

217. Common glossy racer, *Drymoluber dichrous,* adult (Loreto, Peru)

218A. Common false coral snake, *Erythrolamprus aesculapii aesculapii* (origin unknown)

218B. Common false coral snake, *Erythrolamprus aesculapii aesculapii,* note reduced ringing (Rodonia, Brazil); photo by Laurie Vitt

219A. Banded South American water snake, *Helicops angulatus,* dark-banded morph (Loreto, Peru)

219B. Banded South American water snake, *Helicops angulatus,* bright-banded morph (Loreto, Peru)

220A. Spotted water snake, *Helicops leopardinus,* dorsum (Loreto, Peru)

220B. Spotted water snake, *Helicops leopardinus,* venter (Loreto, Peru)

221. Giant false water cobra, *Hydrodynastes gigas*

222. Coral mud snake, *Hydrops martii* (Loreto, Peru)

223. Common blunt-headed tree snake, *Imantodes cenchoa* (Loreto, Peru)

224. Amazon blunt-headed tree snake, *Imantodes lentiferus* (Loreto, Peru)

225. Common cat-eyed snake, *Leptodeira annulata annulata* (Loreto, Peru)

226A. Black-skinned parrot snake, *Leptophis ahaetulla nigromarginatus,* adult in tree (Loreto, Peru)

226B. Black-skinned parrot snake, *Leptophis ahaetulla nigromarginatus,* defensive gaping (Loreto, Peru)

227. Tricolored swamp snake, *Liophis breviceps breviceps* (Loreto, Peru)

228. Common swamp snake, *Liophis reginae semilineatus* (Loreto, Peru)

229A. Velvety swamp snake, *Liophis typhlus typhlus*, green morph (Loreto, Peru)

229B. Velvety swamp snake, *Liophis typhlus typhlus*, olive brown morph (Loreto, Peru)

229C. Velvety swamp snake, *Liophis typhlus typhlus,* defensive posture with hood spread (Suriname); photo by Bruce Morgan

230. Tan racer, *Mastigodryas boddaertii,* adult (origin unknown); photo by R. Wayne Van Devender

231. Brown vine snake, *Oxybelis aeneus* (Suriname)

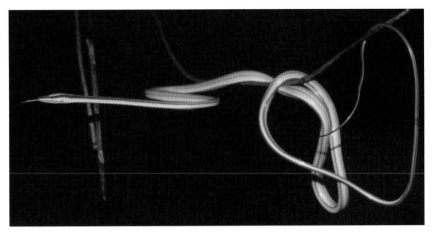

232A. Green-striped vine snake, *Oxybelis (Xenoxybelis) argenteus* (Loreto, Peru)

232B. Green-striped vine snake, *Oxybelis (Xenoxybelis) argenteus,* head (Loreto, Peru)

233. Green vine snake, *Oxybelis fulgidus* (Loreto, Peru)

234. Yellow-headed calico snake, *Oxyrhopus formosus,* adult (Loreto, Peru)

235A. Black-headed calico snake, *Oxyrhopus melanogenys melanogenys,* typically banded adult (Loreto, Peru)

235B. Black-headed calico snake, *Oxyrhopus melanogenys melanogenys,* nonbanded adult (Loreto, Peru)

235C. Black-headed calico snake, *Oxyrhopus melanogenys melanogenys,* melanistic adult (Loreto, Peru)

236A. Banded calico snake, *Oxyrhopus petola digitalis,* adult (origin unknown); photo by David M. Dennis

236B. Banded calico snake, *Oxyrhopus petola digitalis,* juvenile (Loreto, Peru)

237. Brazilian calico snake, *Oxyrhopus trigeminus* (Brazil)

238. Emerald palmsnake, *Philodryas viridissimus viridissimus* (Suriname); photo by Bruce Morgan

239. Amazon scarlet snake, *Pseudoboa coronata* (Loreto, Peru)

240. Eastern scarlet snake, *Pseudoboa neuweidii* (Suriname)

241A. Dusky mud snake, *Pseudoeryx plicatilis,* adult (Loreto, Peru)

241B. Dusky mud snake, *Pseudoeryx plicatilis,* juvenile (Loreto, Peru)

242A. Common bird snake, *Pseustes poecilonotus polylepis,* adult in defensive display (Loreto, Peru)

242B. Common bird snake, *Pseustes poecilonotus polylepis,* juvenile (Loreto, Peru)

243. Giant bird snake, *Pseustes sulphureus sulphureus,* adult (Loreto, Peru)

244. Amazon ringed snake, *Rhinobothryum lentiginosum* (Suriname); photo by Bill Love, Blue Chameleon Ventures

245. Common liana snake, *Siphlophus cervinus* (origin unknown); photo by R. Wayne Van Devender

246A. Tiger rat snake, *Spilotes pullatus pullatus,* normally patterned adult (Loreto, Peru)

246B. Tiger rat snake, *Spilotes pullatus pullatus,* nonbanded juvenile (Loreto, Peru)

247. Short-nosed leaf-litter snake, *Taeniophallus brevirostris* (Loreto, Peru)

248. Common mock viper, *Thamnodynastes pallidus* (Loreto, Peru)

249. Red vine snake, *Tripanurgos (Siphlophis) compressus* (Loreto, Peru)

250A. Common false viper, *Xenodon rhabdocephalus rhabdocephalus,* juvenile (Loreto, Peru)

250B. Common false viper, *Xenodon rhabdocephalus rhabdocephalus,* feigning death (Loreto, Peru)

251A. Giant false viper, *Xenodon severus*, black adult banded anteriorly (Loreto, Peru)

251B. Giant false viper, *Xenodon severus*, brown-speckled adult (Loreto, Peru)

251C. Giant false viper, *Xenodon severus*, brown-speckled adult head (Loreto, Peru)

252. Flat-headed snake, *Xenopholis scalaris* (Loreto, Peru); photo by David M. Schleser, Nature's Images, Inc.

253. Northwest black-backed coral snake, *Leptomicrurus narduccii melanotus;* computer image by Dale Johnson

254. Pygmy black coral snake, *Leptomicrurus scutiventris;* computer image by Dale Johnson

255. White-banded coral snake, *Micrurus albicinctus* (Brazil); photo by Laurie Vitt

256. Black-headed coral snake, *Micrurus averyi* (Brazil); photo by Laurie Vitt

257. Slender coral snake, *Micrurus filiformis* (Loreto, Peru); photo by David M. Schleser, Nature's Images, Inc.

258. Orange-ringed coral snake, *Micrurus hemprichii ortonii* (Amazonas, Brazil); photo by Laurie Vitt

259. Langsdorff's coral snake, *Micrurus langsdorffi* (Amazonas, Brazil); photo by Laurie Vitt

260. Western ribbon coral snake, *Micrurus lemniscatus helleri*; photo by Brad Smith

261A. Eastern ribbon coral snake, *Micrurus lemniscatus lemniscatus* (Rodonia, Brazil); photo by Laurie Vitt

261B. Eastern ribbon coral snake, *Micrurus lemniscatus lemniscatus,* albino (Para, Brazil); photo by Laurie Vitt

262. Sooty coral snake, *Micrurus putumayensis* (Loreto, Peru); photo by David T. Roberts, Nature's Images, Inc.

263. Remote coral snake, *Micrurus remotus (=psyches)* (Brazil); photo by Laurie Vitt

264. Western Amazon coral snake, *Micrurus spixii obscurus* (Loreto, Peru)

265A. Central Amazon coral snake, *Micrurus spixii spixii* (Amazonas, Brazil); photo by Laurie Vitt

265B. Central Amazon coral snake, *Micrurus spixii spixii*, head and eggs (Colombia);
photo by Harry W. Greene

266A. Aquatic coral snake, *Micrurus surinamensis surinamensis* (Brazil); photo by
R. Wayne Van Devender

266B. Aquatic coral snake, *Micrurus surinamensis surinamensis* (Loreto, Peru)

267. Eastern striped forest pit viper, *Bothriopsis bilineata bilineata* (Suriname)

268A. Western striped forest pit viper, *Bothriopsis bilineata smaragdina,* adult (Rondonia, Brazil); photo by Laurie Vitt

268B. Western striped forest pit viper, *Bothriopsis bilineata smaragdina,* neonates (Loreto, Peru)

269A. Speckled forest pit viper, *Bothriopsis taeniata* (origin unknown)

269B. Speckled forest pit viper, *Bothriopsis taeniata* (Brazil); photo by Laurie Vitt

270A. South American lancehead, *Bothrops atrox,* adult (Loreto, Peru)

270B. South American lancehead, *Bothrops atrox,* neonate (Loreto, Peru)

271. Velvety lancehead, *Bothrops brazili* (origin unknown)

272. Amazonian hog-nosed lancehead, *Bothrops hyoprora,* male (Loreto, Peru)

273. Amazonian rattlesnake, *Crotalus durissus dryinas* (Suriname)

274. Tropical rattlesnake, *Crotalus durissus terrificus* (origin unknown)

275. Amazon bushmaster, *Lachesis muta muta* (Loreto, Peru)

Paradox Frogs: Family Pseudidae

In general form, the pseudid frogs are very like the typical ranids in appearance. Their digits, however, are more like those of the treefrogs. A separate family (whose validity is still questioned by some systematists) has been erected for the two Neotropical species. Both are very aquatic and seldom stray far from the water. Although it requires a permanent water source, the common paradox frog is not at all restricted to river basins; it occurs far to the north and south of the Amazon Basin, and is more accurately a species of seasonally inundated regions.

Genus *Pseudis;* Paradox Frogs

Both species in this genus are restricted to northeastern South America and can be abundant in suitable aquatic habitats. Breeding usually occurs either during the passage of a frontal system that lowers barometric pressure or at the advent of the rainy season as ponds are freshened. The egg clusters are placed in frothy floating nests, usually among surface vegetation, very similar to those constructed by the leptodactylid frogs. Prior to metamorphosis the tadpoles grow to an immense size, at times up to four times the snout-to-vent length of the adult frog. For example, a 9–inch-long (23–cm) tadpole may metamorphose into a 3–inch-long (7.5–cm) adult frog. Thus arises the paradox that gives this frog its common name: it shrinks in size, rather than growing, when it assumes adulthood.

124. Common Paradox Frog

Pseudis paradoxa

Size: Males attain 3 inches (7.5 cm) in SVL; females may slightly exceed 4 inches (10 cm).
Identifying features: This is a short-nosed, broad-headed frog. The upper body is green to brown (often with combinations of both colors dorsally). If dorsal markings are present, they are oriented lengthwise. The hind legs are barred with dark pigment. The lower sides are lighter in color than the dorsum, and the venter is white to yellow. This frog has dorsolaterally directed eyes, slimy skin, very muscular hind legs, and fully webbed hind feet.
Voice: Often-repeated hoarse grunts.

Reproduction: Large females lay several hundred eggs within a protective frothy nest. Amplexus occurs while the frogs are floating on the water surface. The tadpoles are much larger than the adults.

Similar species: No other typical-appearing frog in the area has such dorsally directed eyes, fully webbed feet, or the habit of floating quietly amid or atop floating and emergent vegetation.

Habitat/Range: These very aquatic frogs may abound in suitable quiet waters. Weedy ponds, oxbows, and other such habitats are preferred. They occur in many watersheds from Trinidad and Venezuela southward to Argentina.

True Frogs: Family Ranidae

This is the family to which our most familiar "typical" frogs belong. The bullfrog and the leopard frog of North America, the edible frog of Europe, and the red-eared frog of Asia are all ranids.

Although the family is highly variable and speciose in the cooler temperate climates, remarkably few species occur in the Neotropics. We will discuss only a single, very typical-appearing species.

Genus *Rana;* True Frogs

One of the larger genera of anurans, the genus *Rana* contains upward of 225 species. They are most diverse in temperate areas, and comparatively few enter the Neotropics; only one *Rana* species is present in the Amazon Basin.

Most ranid frogs could as well be called semiterrestrial as semiaquatic. They are creatures of water edges and often sit for long periods on pond or river banks. Only a very few species climb, but those that live in fast-moving streams or river rapids may have toe pads to assist them in finding secure footing on waterswept rocks or logs. Most ranids actively forage throughout the hours of daylight but breed under the comparative safety offered by darkness.

For the most part, breeding is typical, with males amplexing the females as both float in shallow water. The egg clusters are deposited in shallow-water situations. Egg clusters of some of the largest species may contain more than 10,000 eggs. Tadpoles hatch, develop, and metamorphose in the water.

125. Neotropical Green Frog

Rana palmipes

Size: Males reach about 3 inches (7.5 cm) in SVL; females may barely exceed 4.5 inches (11.5 cm).

Identifying features: This ordinary-looking frog is usually green to greenish tan on the dorsum and has well-defined dorsolateral ridges. The flanks are light with dark spots, and the belly is off-white. The hidden surfaces of the thighs are dark with light reticulations. The forefeet are not webbed; the hind feet are fully webbed.

Voice: A series of chuckles.

Reproduction: An average-sized clutch contains more than 5000 eggs, laid in small clumps.

Similar species: The various jungle frogs of the genus *Leptodactylus* have basically unwebbed toes. The infrequently seen leptodactylid *Hydrolaetare schmidtii* has more dorsally oriented eyes and usually a broad, dark dorsal stripe running from between the eyes to the vent.

Habitat/Range: This is an abundant species that is active both day and night. It may wander into the forest but is most common along the edges of ponds, streams, and rivers. It is an alert and agile jumper as well as an excellent swimmer. The species ranges from Central America southward to Peru and Brazil.

CLASS REPTILIA

7

Crocodilians

Of the four groups of crocodilians—the gharials, the crocodiles, the alligators, and the caimans—only two, the crocodiles and the caimans, occur in South America. Only the caimans are found in the Amazon Basin.

Family Alligatoridae

Four species of caiman occur in the basin. All are semiaquatic, with the emphasis being on aquatic. All construct nests that provide varying degrees of parental care to both eggs and young. The four vary dramatically in size. The dwarf caiman and the smooth-fronted caiman are adult at about 5 feet (1.5 m) in total length. The adult spectacled caiman attains a length of about 8 feet (2.5 m). But the adult black caiman may exceed a truly impressive 12 feet (3.7 m) in total length. The black caiman and the spectacled caiman seem to prefer quiet or slow-flowing water, whereas the two strongly armored species of dwarf caiman are often associated with rapidly flowing, sometimes turbulent, shaded forest streams.

Since the dwarf caiman and the smooth-fronted caiman seldom stray far from their forest home streams, and often remain hidden in bank undercuts and burrows of their own making, both may be more common than casual observations indicate.

Genus *Caiman;* Typical Caiman

The two members of this genus are the most alligator-like in appearance of the crocodilians of the Amazon Basin. The black caiman even approaches the American alligator in size, and is very like it in coloration.

The snout of both species is relatively broad and flat, but less so than that of the American alligator.

The spectacled caiman, named for the "spectacle bridge" that crosses the snout immediately anterior to the eyes, is the more widespread of the two, ranging from Mexico to the Amazon Basin. The black caiman ranges from southern Venezuela southward throughout the northern and eastern Amazon Basin. Both species prefer rivers and oxbows. The diet includes all sorts of smaller creatures, from insects and fish to water birds and mammals. Adult black caiman are large enough to overpower domestic livestock of considerable size, and because of this are often slaughtered on sight.

126. Spectacled Caiman

Caiman crocodilus ssp.

Size: Adults range from 5 to 7 feet (1.5–2.1 m) in total length; rarely to more than 8 feet (2.4 m).

Identifying features: Young animals are yellowish to olive; adults are olive drab with black cross bands. This species can change color to a degree, and is darker by day, when cold, or when frightened than it is at night or when content. The common name derives from the curved bony ridge (resembling the bridge of a pair of eyeglasses) that crosses the snout immediately anterior to the eyes. The upper eyelids are corrugated and bear a slightly raised "knob" posteriorly. There may be several dark spots along each side of the lower jaw.

Voice: Babies produce high-pitched croaks, often in series. Males produce spluttering "roars."

Reproduction: More than 30 eggs may be laid in a nest constructed of vegetation debris. Females protect the nest, but their exact role in assisting in the hatching of the eggs and the escape of the young from the nest is poorly understood. Hatchlings are 6.5–8 inches (17.6–20.3 cm) in total length.

Similar species: All other crocodilians in the area lack the spectacle bridge.

Habitat/Range: Habitats include open areas and exposed banks of rivers, oxbows, lakes, and other permanent water sources. This species ranges from central Brazil to the northern tip of the continent.

Comments: Many Amazon tours take participants into flooded oxbows at night in search of this species. Baby spectacled caiman are sold in U.S. pet shops. The species is now established in small breeding colonies in the canal systems of southern Florida. It is a rather small but aggressively defensive crocodilian.

127. Black Caiman

Caiman (Melanosuchus) niger

Size: Adults range from 8 to 10 feet (2.4–3.1 m)—rarely to more than 13 feet (4 m)—in total length.

Identifying features: This immense crocodilian is quite alligator-like in appearance. Juveniles are dark with yellow bands that fade with growth and age but often remain visible into adulthood. The jaws of hatchlings are gaudily blotched with black on yellow(ish). Adults appear black, especially when wet (which they usually are). However, the sides of the head are often brownish. The skull is massive, and the snout is broad but pointed at the tip.

Voice: Juveniles and females produce rather high-pitched croaks. Adult males produce deep-toned bellows.

Reproduction: The female deposits 30–40 eggs into a nest made of vegetation debris. Hatchlings are 8–9 inches (20.3–22.9 cm) in length. Females defend the nest, but their role, if any, in assisting in the hatching of the young and their subsequent departure from the nest is unknown.

Similar species: No other Amazonian crocodilian equals an adult black caiman in size. Juveniles lack both a bony spectacle bridge on the snout (spectacled caiman) and greatly enlarged nape scales (dwarf and smooth-fronted caiman).

Habitat/Range: Black caiman are often encountered along heavily forested river shallows; they also inhabit isolated ponds, lakes, seasonally flooded areas (from which they retreat with receding waters), oxbows, and other water sources. The species ranges from the northern and eastern Amazon Basin northward to southern Venezuela.

Comments: If this crocodilian is present, it is most easily found at night by its eyeshine. In the beam of a flashlight held at eye level, the black caiman's eyes shine red. Adults of this endangered species are aggressively defensive and should be considered potentially dangerous.

Genus *Paleosuchus;* Armored or Forest Caiman

The two species of armored caiman are very similar in appearance—or, said another way, are very difficult to differentiate, particularly hatchlings and juveniles. Armored caiman are often associated with muddy-banked small streams with a fair current, and occasionally with relatively turbulent water; however, they also inhabit quiet backwaters and small forest ponds. They dig quite extensive burrows in stream or pond banks. They eat any smaller creatures they can catch and overpower, but seem particularly fond of fish. The back, neck, and tail are clad in prominent, bony scales.

This genus ranges over much of northwestern, north-central, and northeastern South America. It is absent along the Pacific coast.

128. Dwarf Caiman

Paleosuchus palpebrosus

Size: To 4.5 feet (1.4 m), but usually smaller. This is the smallest of the Neotropical crocodilians.

Identifying features: The dwarf caiman is mud brown with several broad, darker cross bands dorsally. It is somewhat lighter in color ventrolaterally and ventrally. Overall the snout is rather broad and comparatively bluntly rounded (vaguely alligator-like). The sides of the lower jaw have dark and light bands. The irises are brown. The armored nape scales are less well developed than those on the smooth-fronted caiman. Besides the nape, the dorsum, the tail, and even the eyelids are protected by bony raised scales. The keeling on all rows of dorsal scales is rather uniform, and four rows of scales lie above the pelvis. This species and the slender-snouted smooth-fronted caiman are among the world's most heavily armored crocodilians.

Voice: Babies produce high-pitched croaks. Adult males produce longer, deeper grunts.

Reproduction: Females pull together mounds of ground vegetation to form nests, and lay only five to nine eggs. Hatchlings are similar to adults in appearance, but their markings contrast more sharply.

Similar species: The appearance and color of this small but defensively feisty crocodilian are closely paralleled by the congeneric *P. trigonatus*. However, the smooth-fronted caiman has a more tapered (crocodile-like) snout, the outermost rows of dorsal scales are the most strongly keeled, and there are usually (but not invariably) two rows of scales above the pelvis. The spectacled caiman has a bony ridge across the base of the snout. The gigantic *Caiman niger* has a broader snout, and smaller individuals still bear traces of yellow bands. Neither the spectacled nor the black caiman typically inhabits the deeply shaded streams preferred by both *Paleosuchus* species.

Habitat/Range: This is a caiman of shaded forest streams. It may prefer somewhat quieter water than the related smooth-fronted caiman. Both species may be found in deeply shaded streamside pools. This species is thought to be very rare in the Peruvian Amazon region, but is regularly encountered farther east. It ranges from the northern and eastern Amazon Basin northward to Venezuela.

129. Smooth-Fronted Caiman

Paleosuchus trigonatus

Size: To 6 feet (1.8 m); rarely larger. Males are the larger sex.

Identifying features: The body is dark brown overall with obscure darker bands. Except for its more slender, tapering snout and more heavily armored nape, this caiman is very similar to *P. palpebrosus*. Like its congener, the smooth-fronted caiman is heavily armored dorsally and has brown irises. The outermost rows of dorsal scales are much more heavily keeled than the center rows. There are often (but not invariably) only two rows of scales above the pelvis.

Voice: Babies produce high-pitched croaks. Adult males produce longer, deeper grunts.

Reproduction: The eggs of crocodilians require an incubation temperature of about 87°F (31°C) to ensure proper development. The temperatures along the shady streams preferred by these caiman, however, are often below 80°F. *Paleosuchus trigonatus* females may solve this problem by building their vegetation-mound nests against the terrestrial nests of termites, which help to raise the caiman nest temperature by the several necessary degrees.

Similar species: See the *Paleosuchus palpebrosus* account, above.

Habitat/Range: This small crocodilian is found in deeply shaded forest streams and generally seems to prefer more turbulent water than its congener, but individuals have been found in quiet stretches of large rivers and quiet forest pools. The species ranges from Venezuela to Peru and eastern Brazil.

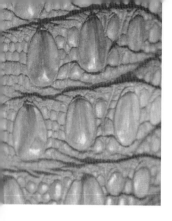

8

Turtles

The order Chelonia—the turtles and tortoises—contains 13 families. Only 4 families are represented in the Amazon Basin, and the 2 families of sideneck turtles (the pleurodines) predominate. The sideneck turtles are so named because they do not withdraw the neck and head straight back into the shell in a vertical S as most turtles do. Rather, the neck and head are tucked sideways under the comparative protection of the overhanging front of the carapace.

We discuss three Amazonian turtles that are essentially terrestrial: the Amazon wood turtle and the two tortoise species, the yellow-footed and the red-footed. The others are essentially aquatic.

Advanced Sideneck Turtles: Family Chelidae

The chelids show a number of structural differences from the sideneck turtles of the family Pelomedusidae. From the viewpoint of the casual observer, however, there is little difference between the two.

Chelid turtles occur in South America, Australia, and Indonesia. The South American types include the matamata, the toad-headed turtles, the Neotropical snake-necked turtle, and the twist-necked turtles, a total of about 20 described and several not yet described species.

All are persistently aquatic. Many are powerful swimmers and may be seen in rivers both large and small. Others are weak swimmers; although they may be found in large bodies of water, they are almost always in the shallows.

In size these turtles range from the 6- or 7-inch (16–18-cm) shell length of the twist-necked turtle to the 15-plus-inch (38-cm or more) matamata.

Genus *Chelus;* Matamata

The matamata of the monotypic genus *Chelus* is probably the world's most unforgettable turtle. The head is broad, flattened, and strongly triangular when viewed from above. The nose is long and snorkel-like. The eyes are small, but even were they large they would probably be of little help in the turbid waters of the Amazon Basin. Fringes of skin bedeck the neck and chin. The carapace is strongly keeled and so rough that algae easily attach to and grow on it, providing added camouflage to an already almost invisible turtle. The feet are webbed, but this turtle is a weak swimmer that prefers to sit in water shallow enough for it to breathe merely by stretching its long neck upward until its nose breaks the surface.

The matamata ranges from central Brazil and Bolivia north to Venezuela and eastern Colombia.

Its bizarre appearance has made the matamata a popular display turtle in zoological gardens and one coveted by private hobbyists. Over the years, a great many of these turtles—babies especially—have been exported for the pet trade.

130. Matamata

Chelus fimbriatus

Size: The carapace length is generally 9–12 inches (23–30 cm), but lengths slightly more than 16 inches (41 cm) have been recorded. Females are larger than males.

Identifying features: The flattened, triangular head; fringed throat and neck; elongated cylindrical snout; and heavily keeled, mud-colored carapace combine to make the matamata the world's most unmistakable turtle. A darker or lighter vertebral stripe may be present. Hatchling matamatas can have extensive pink or rose coloring on the throat, beneath the neck, and on the plastron, but this coloration invariably fades with growth. The top of the head and neck may be a somewhat richer brown than the carapace. Although it is exclusively aquatic, this turtle is not a powerful swimmer and is usually associated with shallow water.

Reproduction: Females dig nests close to the water on sand or clay beaches or dig horizontally into exposed riverbanks. Large females may produce more than 20 eggs that resemble Ping-Pong balls in size and shape.

Similar species: None.

Habitat/Range: Because it is so easy to overlook, this fully aquatic turtle may actually be more common than is thought. It occurs in river edge situations as well as in oxbows and other slow water or protected Amazonian habitats.

Comments: Small specimens of this unique turtle are often seen in aquarium shops in Iquitos and may be offered to tourists by Iquitos street vendors. Its cryptic coloration, dermal camouflage, and sedentary habits serve this wait-and-ambush predator well. The diet consists primarily of fish, which are literally vacuumed into the capacious mouth by a sudden expansion of the throat. Excess water is expelled and the fish is swallowed. It is likely that the innervated dermal fringes help the turtle find fish in the silty waters of its homeland rivers.

Genus *Phrynops;* Toad-Headed Turtles

There are currently about a dozen described species in this genus, and several Amazonian forms are distinct enough to warrant critical evaluation. This genus ranges over most of the South American continent. The *Phrynops* are very aquatic turtles; they seldom leave the water to bask and are accomplished swimmers. Appearance is variable. Some are quite small (*P. gibba* tops out at about 8 inches [20 cm] in shell length) with only slightly enlarged heads, while others (the extralimital *P. hilarii* among them) attain a shell length of about 16 inches (40 cm) and have a very enlarged head. Their large size and agility in the water make species such as *P. geoffroanus* popular with hobbyists and zoological gardens. A few species are easy to keep and are captive-bred in small numbers. Others, such as the beautiful *P. rufipes*, are frustratingly difficult to maintain. The turtles in this genus are carnivorous.

131. Spotted Toad-Headed Turtle
Phrynops geoffroanus tuberosus

Size: Adults of both sexes may near 1 foot (30 cm) in carapace length.
Identifying features: The rather flat carapace of this pretty turtle is olive green to olive black. The scutes on the carapace may be rough centrally. The plastron has a pattern of dark markings over a ground color of red or orange-red. The red coloration dulls with advancing age and may, on some individuals, be yellow or yellow-brown. The head is dark above and patterned with light markings. The cheeks are lighter but are broadly streaked with dark pigment. The chin and throat are yellow with black spots or mottling. There is a pair of prominent light barbels on the chin. The snout is rounded, giving a "pug-nosed" look. The limbs are dark but outlined with yellow.

Reproduction: The reproductive biology of this turtle in the wild is not well known. Well-nourished captive specimens have laid up to 20 eggs. Incubation lasts for about 120 days. Hatchlings are about 1.5 inches (3.8 m) in carapace length.

Similar species: No other sideneck turtle has a primarily red plastron.

Habitat/Range: This aquatic species is found in, and to the north and south of, the eastern Amazon Basin.

132. Lesser Toad-Headed Turtle

Phrynops gibbus

Size: Carapace length 5–6.5 inches (13–16 cm; rarely *slightly* larger); this is one of the smaller members of the genus.

Identifying features: Unlike many other *Phrynops*, this species does not have an enlarged, toadlike head. The carapace and limbs are mud brown to nearly charcoal. The head and neck are dark brown dorsally and yellowish ventrally. The top of the head is usually patterned with lighter olive brown vermiculations. There are very small chin barbels. The plastron is dark with a yellowish margin, and the submarginals (the scutes that rim the upper shell) are also yellow. The posterior marginal scutes of this species tend to flare outward and turn upward.

Reproduction: The female lays one to five eggs, but little is known about the nesting habits in the wild.

Similar species: The other commonly seen dark-shelled turtles in the region (also of the genus *Phrynops*) have very enlarged heads that are olive with dark or yellow(ish) vermiculations.

Habitat/Range: The lesser toad-headed turtle is persistently aquatic and may be found in both still and flowing waters. Some individuals may bask in the early morning hours. The species ranges from northern Brazil and central Peru northward to Colombia and Venezuela.

Comments: This species is often referred to as the "Gibba turtle," which is derived from the term for bent or hunched, probably referring to the neck.

133. Common Toad-Headed Turtle

Phrynops nasutus

Size: This large turtle attains a carapace length of about 1 foot (30 cm).

Identifying features: Almost every part of this turtle is some shade of gray. The carapace is grayish brown to olive gray. The pale yellowish plastron is suffused with grayish brown. The limbs are gray (lightest on the undersides). The gray head is often lightest ventrally, and there may be a dark cheek stripe.

Reproduction: A clutch contains up to eight eggs; the incubation time is about 65 days. The hatchlings have a carapace length of just over 2 inches (5 cm).

Similar species: The identification of these aquatic turtles is made difficult by a certain natural variability in color as well as by the presence of what appear to be several unidentified species. It is often better to attempt to identify the more subtly colored members of this genus by first ruling out the species that they cannot be.

Habitat/Range: Oxbows or *cochas*, swamps, and slow-moving creeks and river edges are the habitats preferred by this turtle. The species ranges from eastern Amazonian Brazil west to Colombia, Ecuador, and, perhaps, northern Peru.

134. Amazon Toad-Headed Turtle

Phrynops raniceps

Size: Females are the larger sex, growing to nearly 9 inches (23 cm) in carapace length. Males reach shell lengths of 5.5–6.5 inches (14–16.5 cm).

Identifying features: This quietly colored turtle has a carapace of olive to dark olive black and may have highlights of brown. Juveniles are often rimmed with yellow. The bridge and plastron are lighter, often yellow olive. The forelimbs are dark with olive markings; the rear limbs are dark. The head is olive with black vermiculations and a yellow chin.

Reproduction: Virtually nothing is known about the breeding habits. Closely allied species lay three to seven eggs per clutch.

Similar species: See the discussion of the somewhat similar *Phrynops nasutus*, above.

Habitat/Range: This moderate-sized turtle is often caught and eaten by river fishermen. Individuals are frequently seen along the edges of rivers; they are powerful swimmers well able to negotiate considerable currents. The actual range is poorly delineated, but this species is common in the northwestern Amazon Basin.

Comments: This genus of confusingly similar turtles is widespread in tropical South America. It is probable that as now described, several of the species are actually species complexes. The characteristics delineating *P. raniceps* will become progressively more specific as other forms are defined and separated.

135. Red-Faced Toad-Headed Turtle

Phrynops rufipes

Size: Carapace length about 10 inches (25 cm).

Identifying features: This is the most brightly colored member of the genus. The face and forelimbs are rosy red. A black bridle extends from the neck and passes through each eye and over the snout. A black V is usually present on the crown of the head. The carapace is gray, sometimes with a very pale rose suffusion. A vertebral keel is present. The plastron is creamy yellow.

Reproduction: Clutches seem to average about nine eggs, which hatch after a 90–120-day incubation period. Hatchlings measure about 1.5 inches (4 cm) in length.

Similar species: This is the only toad-headed turtle with a red face. The red on the face of the red-spotted river turtle is in the form of spots rather than a general suffusion.

Habitat/Range: *Phrynops rufipes* is a species of rainforest creeks in the Amazonian provinces of Colombia and western Brazil.

Genus *Platemys*; Twist-Necked and Swamp Turtles

Of the five species in this genus, only one is an Amazonian form; the others occur south of the Amazon Basin. The resident of the Amazon is the twist-necked turtle, one of the smaller of the region's chelonians. This is the only sideneck turtle you are likely to find roaming far from water. The common name refers to the sideways turning of the neck as the head is withdrawn beneath the overhanging anterior of the carapace. The carapace bears two prominent but smooth keels bordering a longitudinal central depression.

Although they do eat some vegetation, twist-necked turtles are preferentially carnivorous.

136. Western Twist-Necked Turtle

Platemys platycephala melanonota

Size: The carapace length is about 6 inches (15 cm); males may be marginally larger than females.

Identifying features: This is a pretty and rather unique-looking turtle. The somewhat depressed carapace is primarily dark brown with muddy brown highlights; the legs are dark. The top of the head and neck are a rather bright orange. The head is proportionally small. The plastron is also dark but edged with yellow-orange. The scutes of the bridge and the submarginals are mostly yellow-orange. There is a pronounced, smooth keel on each side at the upper edge of each row of costal scutes.

Reproduction: The clutch size is two to six eggs. The nest may be little more than a depression in the leaf litter. Females may travel quite a substantial distance from standing water to deposit their eggs.

Similar species: This is the only turtle in the region with the top of its head a nearly solid orange.

Habitat/Range: Although essentially aquatic, twist-necked turtles wander far overland during the rains and when water levels are high. They may be left high and dry as the waters recede.

Primitive Sideneck Turtles: Family Pelomedusidae

Although the pelomedusids are structurally different from the more advanced chelids, to a casual observer everything about the turtles in these two families is identical. All are strongly aquatic. Unlike most of the chelids, however, which shun above-water thermoregulation, many of the pelomedusids bask. The largest Amazonian turtles are members of this family.

The babies of many species of river turtles (genus *Podocnemis*) have head markings of pale to brilliant yellow, orange, or red. These colors fade quickly with growth and age but are better retained by the males than by the females.

Genus *Peltocephalus;* Big-Headed River Turtle

This monotypic genus is restricted in distribution to the Amazon and its tributaries from Peru to eastern Brazil. At a casual glance this rather high-domed turtle looks like a mud turtle on steroids, but it is far more closely allied to the river turtles of the genus *Podocnemis. Peltocephalus* is big (close to huge, in fact), has a big head and powerful—*very* powerful—jaws, and is persistently aquatic. It retracts its head sideways and lacks plastral hinges.

Most often associated with black water, *Peltocephalus* may also be found in whitewater habitats and forest pools. Population densities are unknown, but over large portions of its range this seems to be an uncommon turtle.

The turtles of this genus are omnivorous, but adults seem particularly fond of fallen ripe palm fruits, which they pick from the water's surface.

137. Big-Headed River Turtle

Peltocephalus dumerilianus

Size: This big river turtle can attain a length of more than 2 feet (63 cm).
Identifying features: The big-headed river turtle is aptly named. Even in young animals, the head is proportionally large. The nose is sharply pointed. The highly domed carapace is keeled, most prominently on young animals. The carapace varies in color from gray to black. The plastron varies from brown to yellow. The top of the head is dark (gray to olive brown), but the sides of the head may be lighter.
Reproduction: A clutch may contain up to 25 eggs. Incubation duration is a few days more than three months. Hatchlings measure about 2 inches (5 cm).
Similar species: None. When small, this turtle is reminiscent of a mud turtle, but it lacks the plastral hinges of the latter.
Habitat/Range: This very aquatic turtle favors black-water rivers (that is, rivers whose water is darkened by tannins) but could ostensibly be found in almost any waterhole or river from Colombia and Venezuela to Peru.

Genus *Podocnemis;* River Turtles

Of the six species in this genus, four occur in the Amazon drainage and two are found north of the region. *Podocnemis expansa* is the largest turtle found in the Amazon; females routinely exceed a shell length of 30 inches (78 cm).

Two of the Amazonian forms, *P. expansa* and *P. unifilis,* are now considered endangered species. Prior to that designation, the babies of both were collected in immense numbers for the pet trade. The eggs and the adults are still important foods for Amazonian villagers.

The carapace is smooth and gently domed. The characteristics that distinguish some species of this genus are subtle and must be carefully evaluated, particularly in older individuals, whose facial markings tend to be obscured.

Omnivorous when young, these turtles become increasingly herbivorous with age. Some use a skimming method termed neustophagia, in which water is taken into the mouth and then expelled, to extract small particulate matter from the surface water film.

Although these river turtles are not as commonly seen in captivity as they once were, a few zoological institutions and some herpetoculturists are breeding some species.

138. Giant River Turtle

Podocnemis expansa

Size: This Amazonian specialty is the largest member of the genus. Females may be sexually mature at somewhat less than 2 feet (61 cm) in length but routinely exceed 30 inches (76 cm); some near a carapace length of 36 inches (91 cm). Males can breed at 8 inches (20 cm) and seldom exceed a carapace length of 12–14 inches (30–36 cm).

Identifying features: The carapace is gray to grayish brown. The head markings of juveniles are off-white, pale butter yellow, or even almost lemon yellow. The facial markings quickly fade with growth. There is no spot on the top of the pointed snout, which has a prominent interorbital groove extending forward to its tip. The outer edges of the groove are demarcated by a light line that runs from the tip of the snout to the eyes and continues around the posterior of the orbit in a J. The colors pale with age, and large individuals are nearly uniform gray to brown. There are two chin barbels. When viewed from above, the carapace is widest posterior of mid-length.

Reproduction: Once, this species congregated in immense breeding aggregations known as *arribadas* as river waters receded during the dry season, and nested on the exposed sandbars. Although fair-sized breeding aggregations continue to occur, the very large numbers are long past. A large female *P. expansa* may lay more than 100 eggs per clutch. Some females produce a second clutch. Despite this fecundity, hunting of the hatchlings for the pet trade and of the adults as food has decimated most populations.

Similar species: Size alone should identify the adult females of this species. The smaller *P. unifilis* has an orange spot on the top of the snout. *Podocnemis sextuberculata* is smaller still (4–11 inches, 10–28 cm) and, except for very small individuals, which have white spots on the head, is nearly a uniform mud gray.

Habitat/Range: *Podocnemis expansa* inhabits the larger river systems, where it may occasionally be seen floating or paddling slowly at the water's surface. Widespread in the Amazon Basin.

Comments: These turtles cannot be exported from their countries of origin, but river edge villagers utilize them as food.

139. Red-Spotted River Turtle

Podocnemis erythrocephala

Size: Adult females attain a shell length of only about 11.5 inches (29 cm); males are often smaller.

Identifying features: As is the case with all members of the genus, the juveniles are the most brightly colored. Babies have bright red head spots. Males often retain these spots until very late in life, but they become brown or are lost by the females as they mature. The carapace is some shade of brown. The plastron is brown with a grayish overcast. The limbs are gray to brownish gray, as is the head except for the patches of brighter color. A prominent interorbital groove is present on top of the snout.

Reproduction: Clutches contain 4–15 eggs. Artificial incubation takes about 90 days. Hatchlings are about 1.5 inches (4 cm) long.

Similar species: The bright red head spots will identify most specimens. *Very rarely* the spots may shade toward yellow, making the identity more questionable.

Habitat/Range: Although not usually thought of as an Amazonian species, this turtle is occasionally found in village marketplaces downriver from Iquitos, Peru. It occurs in various drainages from Colombia to Venezuela and in Brazil.

140. Amazon River Turtle

Podocnemis sextuberculata

Size: Females occasionally near 1 foot (30 cm) in carapace length, but they, and the males, are usually smaller.

Identifying features: Juveniles of this small, grayish sideneck have poorly delineated white head markings; adults are even more nondescript. The carapace is mud gray to brownish. The plastron is lighter, occasionally almost yellow, and bears six prominent tubercles—three on each side along the outer perimeter. The limbs are gray. The gray to brown head is pudgy and rounded but not overly large. The mandibles are lighter in color than the head. There may be either one or two chin barbels. Three large scales occur on each heel.

Reproduction: The clutch size is 6–20, and healthy females usually produce more than a single annual clutch.

Similar species: The presence of an interorbital groove will separate this species from all but its larger congeners. In their smaller sizes, both other species of *Podocnemis* found in the Iquitos region have contrastingly colored orange to yellow head markings.

Habitat/Range: This species seems largely restricted to riverine habitats in the Amazon drainage of Brazil, Peru, and Colombia. River edge villagers often keep small specimens as pets.

141. Yellow-Spotted River Turtle

Podocnemis unifilis

Size: Adult females may be 26 inches long (66 cm); males are usually not more than 13 inches (33 cm).

Identifying features: The gray head of juveniles is distinctively marked with nine rather precisely outlined yellow (or orange) spots. One, on top of the snout, is diagnostic for the species. The spots fade to near obscurity with growth and age. This is the only *Podocnemis* that may *lack* an interorbital groove. The gray, smoothly convex carapace has flaring posterior marginal scutes and, when viewed from above, is widest at the halfway mark. The gray plastron may have a rosy or horn-colored blush. There may be either one or two chin barbels. Adult males have a heavy, elongated tail. All four feet are fully webbed.

Reproduction: This strongly aquatic turtle nests communally (but not in large *arribadas*) on exposed sandy riverbanks and river sandbars where haul-out conditions are suitable, as well as on the banks of the ponds and oxbows they inhabit. Nest densities can be high in suitable areas. Females lay 12–30 eggs and typically produce multiple clutches each year. The largest females produce the largest clutches.

Similar species: Juveniles of the much larger *P. expansa* have pale yellow head spots and lack a spot on top of the snout. The upper mandible of the latter species is yellow, and a yellow J encircles each eye with the shaft extending forward to the tip of the nose. The smaller *P. sextuberculata* has no brilliant markings at any stage of its life, and six rather prominent tubercular projections rim its plastron.

Habitat/Range: This turtle tends to be more common in oxbows, lakes, and smaller tributaries than in the Amazon River itself.

Comments: In the late 1950s and 1960s hatchlings of this and other sideneck turtles were prominent in the American pet trade. Despite their diminished numbers and the fact that the species is now protected by international treaties, eggs and hatchlings are still seen in Peruvian marketplaces.

Mud Turtles: Family Kinosternidae

These are small carnivorous turtles with strong jaws. Two well-developed plastral hinges allow the plastron to be closed tightly against the carapace. Both Amazonian species display a willingness to bite when restrained.

Genus *Kinosternon;* Mud Turtles

There are about 15 species of these primarily aquatic turtles, but only 2 inhabit the Amazon Basin. As a genus mud turtles are found from the northeastern and north-central United States southward to Paraguay.

Some mud turtles roam far from water and are capable of feeding both on land and in the water. There are records of mud turtles consuming vegetation, but the Amazonian turtles seem to prefer animal matter.

Their elongate but domed carapace and two well-developed plastral hinges allow easy identification of the mud turtles to genus. The white-lipped mud turtle has a single vertebral keel that is prominent in young individuals but less so in older ones. Babies and young of the scorpion mud turtle have three carapacial keels, but these too become less well defined with age.

142. White-Lipped Mud Turtle

Kinosternon leucostomum

Size: The carapace length of males can reach 6.5 inches (16.5 cm); females are slightly smaller.

Identifying features: Except for the white on the face and the yellow-orange plastron, this is a dark turtle. The top of the head and the carapace are very dark brown to black. The face and lips are yellow-white, cream, or occasionally almost snow white. The limbs are dark, but often with a grayish cast. The plastral sutures (the areas where the scutes adjoin) may be dark. The supramarginals (the outermost scutes of the carapace) may have a yellowish cast. Hatchlings, juveniles, and subadults have a vertebral keel. This becomes more indistinct with age and growth and is virtually lacking in adults. Adults have well-developed plastral hinges; these are indistinct on hatchlings.

Reproduction: The female lays one to three eggs in a moist, but not wet, nest that she digs into an exposed bank or similar location. Hatchlings, which emerge after about three and a half months of incubation, are about 1.25 inches (3 cm) in carapace length.

Similar species: No other turtle that withdraws its neck in a *vertical* S has extensive amounts of white on its head.

Habitat/Range: This turtle is found in aquatic habitats as far south as Ecuador and northern Peru.

143. Amazon Mud Turtle

Kinosternon scorpioides scorpioides

Size: The carapace length is about 6 inches (15 cm).

Identifying features: This aquatic turtle has a heavy, rather highly domed but elongate shell and a double-hinged plastron. The carapace is dusky to mud brown and has three weak keels. The keels of young specimens are more accentuated than those of older adults. The plastron is yellowish. The top of the head often has a yellowish spot or figure, and may be speckled with black pigment. The neck, limbs, and tail are gray.

Reproduction: Other than the fact that females seem to lay from one to three eggs per clutch, and may lay two or three clutches annually, nothing is known about the reproductive biology of this species in Peru.

Similar species: This is one of the larger mud turtles, and the only one in the Iquitos region, where it seems to be rare. The white-cheeked mud turtle is similar but has white on its head. The big-headed river turtle is a sideneck species and lacks white on the head. Except for the terrestrial yellow-footed tortoise, the mud turtle is the only one of the Iquitos region turtles to withdraw its head into the carapace in a vertical S.

Habitat/Range: Amazon mud turtles are occasionally seen in shallow waters in ponds, swamps, oxbows, and slow rivers. They may wander well away from water in rainy weather and disperse farther during times of high water. Those unable to follow the receding water back to the rivers in the dry season probably burrow into the ground litter to conserve body moisture and await the return of the water.

Basking Turtles: Family Emydidae

Although this family is well represented in temperate areas, only a single species is found in the Amazon Basin, and it occurs only in eastern Brazil. Several other forms are found to the north of the Amazon Basin, and one species occurs to the south. The common name is an apt one, for most semiaquatic members of this family ascend logs or clamber onto banks or floating vegetation periodically to bask (thermoregulate) in the sunshine. All members of this family withdraw their neck in a vertical S.

Genus *Rhinoclemmys;* Tropical Wood Turtles

This genus, represented by eight species, ranges southward from Mexico to northeastern Brazil. Only *R. punctularia* occurs within the area covered by this guide. The genus *Rhinoclemmys* is unique in being the only New World member of the otherwise Old World subfamily Batagurinae. This means nothing to the casual observer (who will see a basking turtle no different in overt appearance from any other), but it is of interest to systematists.

For the most part, the Neotropical wood turtles are habitat generalists. Some species, such as the Amazon wood turtle, which swims well, are more closely tied to water than others are. The wood turtles are generally dark with dull to bright red stripes on the crown and yellow edges on the plastron scutes. The members of this genus are omnivorous.

144. Amazon Wood Turtle

Rhinoclemmys punctularia punctularia

Size: The shell length may be up to 10 inches (25 cm), but most specimens seen are in the 6–8-inch (15–20-cm) size range.

Identifying features: The smooth to insculpted carapace of the adult wood turtle varies from dark brown to black. A vertebral keel with a darker spot at the posterior center of each scute is often present. The plastron is also brown-black, but yellow pigment follows each scute suture. The dark head is adorned with red bars that run along the snout and terminate on each upper eyelid. A second stripe begins just centrally from each orbit and extends posteriorly onto the nape. A pair of red spots may be present on the back of the head. The forelimbs are primarily yellow (sometimes red) with the anterior scales narrowly edged with black. The hind limbs are primarily gray but may have scattered yellow spots. Juvenile specimens may be considerably brighter than adults in color, having light radiations from the center of each costal scute.

Reproduction: Only one or two eggs are produced in each clutch, but healthy adult females may lay several clutches a year at 30-day intervals. The females are not avid nesters, often laying their small clutches in moist leaf litter rather than in a carefully prepared nest. Incubation of eggs laid in captivity has varied from 78 to 120 days. Hatchlings are about 1.5 inches (4 cm) long.

Similar species: None within our scope.

Habitat/Range: This semiaquatic wood turtle frequents shallow swamps, marshes, oxbows, and river edges. It ranges widely in eastern South America, from eastern Venezuela to Brazil's Amazon drainage. It is also found on Trinidad.

Tortoises: Family Testudinidae

The wholly terrestrial turtles of this large tropical and subtropical family are usually referred to in America as tortoises. Most shun water except for a very occasional soak in the shallows or for drinking. They have clublike hind feet and flattened, vaguely spadelike forefeet. Most species have highly domed shells.

Only two species, both in the same genus, occur in the Amazon Basin.

Genus *Chelonoidis;* Neotropical Tortoises

This small genus contains only the three South American mainland species (one of which is a chacoan species from south of the Amazon Basin) and the gigantic insular forms from the Galápagos Archipelago. It is rather newly elevated from the large genus *Geochelone.*

There are two tortoise species in the Amazon Basin, each with several definitive populations. Although most are medium sized, some populations of the red-footed tortoise can attain a shell length of 18 inches (45 cm), and certain Amazonian populations of the yellow-footed tortoise may attain or actually exceed a 30-inch (75-cm) carapace length.

The red-foot is a savanna and clearing species, while the yellow-foot prefers the comparative humidity of rainforest habitats. Both species are kept as pets by villagers—until they reach a size suitable for the stewpot.

Tortoises are predominantly vegetarians but also eat animal matter when it becomes available.

145. Red-Footed Tortoise

Chelonoidis (Geochelone) carbonaria

Size: Adults of some populations near 18 inches (45 cm) in length, but most are much smaller.

Identifying features: This highly domed tortoise may appear elongate (sometimes even dumbbell shaped) when viewed from above. The carapace is black with the centermost area of each scute (the areola) orange. The insculpted growth rings are usually plainly evident on all but the oldest and most worn specimens. The plastron is yellow to orange, with each scute outlined by dark pigment along the growth lines. The head and the large scales on the anterior of the forelimbs are orange to red. The head coloration is often paler than that of the limbs.

Voice: Males cluck when breeding.

Reproduction: A clutch may contain a dozen eggs—rarely a few more, usually a few less. The eggs hatch after about four months of incubation.

Similar species: The only other tortoise of the region is the forest-dwelling yellow-foot, which is paler and often rounder (when viewed from above), and which when young has denticulate (toothed) margins on the posterior and anterior marginal scutes.

Habitat/Range: Although red-footed tortoises may enter forest edges, this is essentially a savanna species. It is found over much of the South American continent.

146. Yellow-Footed Tortoise

Chelonoidis (Geochelone) denticulata

Size: Both males and females in this population near 15 inches (38 cm) in straight carapace length (with tortoises, carapace length is measured alongside the tortoise, not over the curved carapace).

Identifying features: This is the only truly terrestrial chelonian of the Amazon rainforests. The carapace is highly domed, somewhat elongate, and brownish. The head and limbs are brownish with yellowish tan highlights that occur on numerous individual scales on the head and limbs, and as central areas on each of the costal and vertebral scutes and the outer edges of all marginals. The plastron is yellowish with some brown along the scute edges. Although the fore and aft marginals become smoother with growth and age, these areas are prominently dentate on small specimens.

Reproduction: Females lay 6–15 eggs several times annually.

Similar species: The red-footed tortoise is a savanna species that has smooth-edged posterior marginals, spots of red-orange on the head, and red-orange scales (rather than yellow) on the anterior surface of the forelegs.

Habitat/Range: This large tortoise is an inhabitant of the Amazonian primary forests.

Comments: Some Amazonian populations show a tendency toward gigantism, with females reaching or slightly exceeding 30 inches (75 cm) in carapace length!

9

Worm Lizards

Order Squamata

Amphisbaenians: Suborder Amphisbaenia

Amphisbaenids ("Worm Lizards"): Family Amphisbaenidae

Only one of the world's four families is represented in Amazonas. Because of the arrangements of the scales in annuli (circular rings around the body), the species of this family look superficially like gigantic—truly gigantic—earthworms.

Like earthworms, the amphisbaenians burrow persistently in yielding soils. They occasionally emerge in the evening, when flooded from their tunnels by heavy rains, and at other times in response to cues known only to themselves.

Amphisbaenians lack limbs and functional eyes and have a short, blunt tail and a countersunk lower jaw. The lack of external eyes and the ringed arrangement of the scales differentiate them from all other reptiles.

Genus *Amphisbaena;* Amphisbaenians or Worm Lizards

This genus comprises about 45 species, all of fossorial habit. Most are small or intermediate sized; a few are quite large. The giant of the genus, the heavy-bodied, 2.5-foot-long (75-cm) *A. alba,* is of Amazonian distribution. Amphisbaenians feed on annelids (earthworms) and arthropods (centipedes and ants). They are oviparous, but virtually nothing else is known about their breeding biology.

147. Giant Amphisbaenian

Amphisbaena alba

Size: This is one of the largest of the amphisbaenians. Adults can attain a length of 2.5 feet (75 cm).

Identifying features: The coloration is buff, tan, or reddish tan above and white below. The head and tail are usually lighter in color than the body. The eyes appear as dark indentations. There are no vestiges of limbs. The scales are arranged in prominent rings.

Reproduction: This species is oviparous; nothing else is known about the reproductive biology.

Similar species: The smaller, black and white–blotched (often with a pinkish head) *A. fuliginosa* is also found in the region. Color alone differentiates the two.

Habitat/Range: These amphisbaenians burrow through moist—but not wet—yielding soils. They are often found near or amid the root systems of trees.

148. Banded Amphisbaenian

Amphisbaena fuliginosa

Size: The maximum size is 12–16 inches (30–40 cm).

Identifying features: The body is white with irregular black bars and blotches. The belly may have a vague pink overcast and is also marked with blotches of dark pigment. The head and tail are usually pinkish. The eyes appear as dark indentations. There are no vestiges of limbs. The scales are arranged in prominent rings.

Reproduction: This species is oviparous, but little else is known about the reproductive biology. Females may lay their eggs in ant nests.

Similar species: The larger and proportionally heavier *A. alba* lacks black blotches or bands.

Habitat/Range: These creatures burrow through moist—but not wet—yielding soils. They are occasionally unearthed near or amid the root systems of trees. This amphisbaenid may become surface active by day during heavy rains or on warm, wet nights. It is found throughout most of the Amazon Basin from Bolivia to Ecuador and the Guianas.

10

Lizards

Order Squamata

Lizards: Suborder Sauria

Worldwide, there are 16 families of lizards and some 3,800 species, with more being described each year. In the Amazon Basin there are 8-plus families and a mere 75-plus species. Although relatively few in number, they are very diverse in appearance and habits. In the Iquitos region there are both nocturnal and diurnal species. There are insectivores, omnivores, and herbivores. There are arboreal species, terrestrial species, fossorial species, and semiaquatic species. They vary in size from 2.5-inch-long (6-cm) geckos to the iguana, adult males of which often exceed 6 feet (1.8 m) in total length.

Most lizards are easily recognized as lizards, and most can even be relatively easily assigned to the correct family. Species identification is a bit more difficult. In the anoles, the color of the dewlap of the male is often the most diagnostic characteristic. Since females of most anole species lack dewlaps, they can be difficult to identify. Other species, such as the gymnophthalmids ("microteiids"), whether male or female, require careful evalutation of *all* characteristics, and even then some uncertainty may remain. Immature lizards and the anoles *Anolis bombiceps* and *A. nitens tandae* are especially difficult to identify. We urge you to do the best you can, then sit back and relax. Perhaps the next specimen will be a little easier.

Geckos: Family Gekkonidae

The geckos of Amazonas are small, delicate lizards. Most are leaf litter dwellers. Two subfamilies are represented: the Sphaerodactylinae and the Gekkoninae. The sphaerodactylines are voiceless and lack expanded toe pads. The gekkonids are capable of voicing clicks and squeaks (these are often given during territorial squabbles) and have expanded toe pads.

Geckos autotomize (discard) their tails with remarkable ease, and the regenerated tail often looks nothing at all like the original. In fact, it is probable that the species and common names of the largest gecko of the area, *Thecadactylus rapicaudus,* the turnip-tailed gecko, reflect the aberrant appearance of a specimen's bulbous regenerated tail. All species in both subfamilies lack eyelids. Their eyes are protected instead by a transparent scale called a brille. Although most geckos are nocturnal, a few, including some from the Iquitos region, are diurnal.

Subfamily Sphaerodactylinae

Genus *Gonatodes;* Forest Geckos

This genus contains about 17 species of small, often sexually dichromatic, arboreal geckos that lack toe pads. The males of many species are brightly colored, especially during the breeding season. The females of most are tan to brown, often with a collar or other nuchal marking. Both sexes often have ringed tails.

These alert and fast-moving geckos are diurnal. They are frequently seen a few feet up the trunk of a forest tree (some species colonize human dwellings), usually in a head-down position, and often draw attention to themselves by slowly writhing the tail. If approached they quickly dart around the trunk or run into a hole in the ground.

Only a single egg is laid in each clutch, but several clutches are laid annually.

149. Collared Forest Gecko

Gonatodes concinnatus

Size: Adults range from 2.5 to 3 inches (6–7.5 cm) in total length, of which the tail constitutes slightly less than half.
Identifying features: Females are clad in various shades of mottled browns

and have an incomplete white collar (broken vertebrally) that is bordered anteriorly by a wide dark blotch. Breeding males are spectacularly colored. Light spots adorn the orangish head and neck. The white collar (incomplete middorsally) is wide (almost blotchlike laterally), prominent, and bordered anteriorly by a narrow black band. A reddish reticulum overlies the olive green body. The tail is very dark and may be patterned with white rings. There are neither toe pads nor eyelids.

Voice: None.

Reproduction: Females lay a single hard-shelled egg at intervals, probably throughout the year. The eggs are deposited in tree holes or behind bark shards. Communal nesting is probable.

Similar species: The males are unmistakable. Females have a ground color similar to many leaf litter geckos, but the broken white collar and the lack of even a vestige of a light bridle are diagnostic.

Habitat/Range: This beautiful gecko seems largely restricted to the buttresses and trunks of medium to large primary forest trees. It is replaced on smaller trees and in more open areas by the almost equally colorful *G. humeralis*. *Gonatodes concinnatus* ranges from Venezuela to Amazonian Brazil, Colombia, Ecuador, and Peru.

Comments: Although this gecko may leave its daytime habitat to sleep on low horizontal leaves and stems, we have found several females behind bark shards at night.

150. Bridled Forest Gecko

Gonatodes humeralis

Size: 2.5–3.25 inches (6–8 cm) in total length.

Identifying features: This small, sexually dichromatic gecko shows its brightest colors and most contrasting patterns when in breeding condition and when sleeping quietly at night. Females are gray with darker spots and reticulations dorsally and with one or two rows of distinct black spots (about five to a row) laterally. A light-edged black spot is also usually apparent on each side of the neck. Males show complex coloration and variable markings. The light olive dorsal ground color (this may be dark olive drab by day) is peppered or vermiculated with black. Paired raspberry red spots are present dorsolaterally. A prominent row of black spots is present laterally. A light-edged black spot is present on each shoulder. The head bears raspberry and gray-blue to off-white vermiculations and several discrete light spots. A gracefully curved, rearward-directed light bridle extends from eye to eye. The iris of the male is yellowish; the female's is orange. The dark olive tail has six darker bands. The dark limbs bear light vermiculations. The dorsal and lateral scales are tiny and granular; the ventral scales are larger. The skin tears readily if the animal is carelessly grasped. The members of this genus do not have toe pads.

Voice: None.

Reproduction: Females lay a single hard-shelled egg at variable intervals throughout most of the year. The single hatchling we have seen (sex unknown) was colored very like the adult female.

Similar species: The larger and even more brightly colored *Gonatodes concinnatus* occurs in fewer numbers throughout the region and seems more restricted to the boles and buttresses of medium to large trees in primary forests.

Habitat/Range: Although it is found in primary forests, this pretty little gecko seems most common low on the trunks of small to moderate-sized trees in secondary forests. It is also found on trees at the edges of forest clearings, and even in human habitations. The species ranges from Brazil and Bolivia north to Venezuela and Colombia.

Comments: This fast, agile, and alert gecko is not easily approached by day but may be easily caught at night while sleeping on the leaves of broad-leaved plants or on horizontal stems.

Genus *Pseudogonatodes;* Pygmy Geckos

This is a small genus of tiny, primarily terrestrial (leaf litter) geckos. The three to five species (according to which systematist's views you accept), clad in earthen colors, are of Neotropical distribution. *Pseudogonatodes* is differentiated from other gecko genera by toe scale differences, criteria difficult to assess in the field. Pygmy geckos are diurnal and lack the dilated toe pads so typical of many other geckos. Only a single egg is produced in each clutch, but egg deposition occurs at intervals throughout much of the year.

151. Amazon Pygmy Gecko

Pseudogonatodes guianensis

Size: The total length of this elfin lizard is somewhat more than 2 inches (5 cm), of which an unregenerated tail constitutes about half.

Identifying features: The velvety, earthen-toned skin is iridescent when seen in the proper light. A light-bordered dark line runs rearward from above each hind limb to a point about one-third of the way down the tail. A light bridle, usually rather well defined on males but often quite obscure on females, loops across the back of the head. Tiny, paired light spots, more pronounced on females than on males, begin on the nape, where they are well defined, and become more diffuse as they progress rearward. This gecko does not have expanded digital discs.

Voice: None has been attributed to this species.

Reproduction: A single hard-shelled egg is produced in each clutch.

Similar species: There are several geckos with nonexpanded toes in Peruvian Amazonia, but this one is the darkest and least ornamented.

Habitat/Range: *Pseudogonatodes guianensis* is restricted to primary forests, where it seems most common in areas of dense leaf litter, especially around the bases of trees or near clumps of bromeliads or herbaceous growth. The species is found over much of Amazonian South America.

Comments: Although size alone ensures that this elfin, diurnal lizard will be easily overlooked by most ecotourists, it is not uncommon in certain areas of the Peruvian Amazon. The skin tears very easily but repairs itself quickly.

Subfamily Gekkoninae

Genus *Hemidactylus;* House Geckos

The single species of this tropicopolitan genus found in our area has been introduced to the Amazon, and to a great many other regions as well. It is now common in South Florida and is expanding its range yearly. It is of African origin. The hemidactylines (there are 80 or more species) have strongly dilated toe tips with paired laminae (the scales across the bottom of the toes).

House geckos are persistently arboreal but, as indicated by their common name, are often associated with dwellings. The eggs are adhesive when first laid, and are often attached to walls near the roofline. Several two-egg clutches are laid at several-week intervals each season.

152. Tropical House Gecko

Hemidactylus mabouia

Identification: This house gecko commonly attains a robust 4 inches (10 cm) in total length and occasionally reaches 5 inches (13 cm).

Identifying features: The dorsal color is darker by day than by night. Day colors vary from tan to gray or olive brown. There are usually several darker, backward-pointing chevrons on the dorsum. Tuberculate scales are liberally scattered over the dorsum and are especially abundant laterally. The venter is light. At night on white walls, tropical house geckos often have an unpatterned ghostly white appearance. The claws in their sheaths are very visible.

Voice: This is a garrulous species. Males squeak quite audibly if restrained or when involved in territorial disputes.

Reproduction: Eggs and hatchlings have been found year-round in the Iquitos region. The tropical house gecko is a communal nester. The incubation period is 45–55 days. Females produce several sets of two eggs each. Hatchlings are about 2 inches (5 cm) in total length.

Similar species: The equally nocturnal gecko *Thecadactylus rapicaudus* is larger and usually darker, and its claws barely extend beyond the toe pads.

Habitat/Range: Tropical house geckos may be seen at night clinging tightly to the trunks of trees or high on the walls of dwellings and other buildings. They often assume a head-down position. They are wary and quick to seek refuge if approached. This is now a common species in many Amazonian cities as well as in some outlying areas.

Comments: This prolific African "hemi" is aggressively and rapidly expanding its range throughout the tropical and subtropical regions of the world. It is predaceous and has been known to affect populations of smaller geckos. Its impact, if any, on the native Amazonian herpetofauna is not yet known.

Genus *Thecadactylus;* Turnip-Tailed Gecko

The single species in this monotypic genus occupies a wide variety of habitats from Mexico to the Amazon Basin and Trinidad.

This large gecko is persistently arboreal and may be seen in villages as well as in secondary and primary forests; it is often found in some numbers at the edges of forest clearings. The granular scales give this lizard a velvety look. The claws barely extend beyond the tips of the expanded toe pads. As is the case with all geckos, the tail is easily broken off (autotomized) but quickly regenerates. The regenerated tail is often bulbous in appearance and probably gave rise to the common and scientific names.

Despite being persistently arboreal, this gecko usually descends to the ground to lay and bury its eggs. Some females use the debris in the bottom of a tree cavity as an egg deposition site.

153. Turnip-Tailed Gecko

Thecadactylus rapicaudus

Size: This is the largest gecko of the region. Adults of both sexes range in length from 6 to 8 inches (15–20 cm), of which almost half is tail.

Identifying features: Although very changeable, the dorsum and sides are some shade of brown. This may be a light grayish tan or a brown so deep that it appears nearly black. When the ground color is at its lightest, prominent dark bands and blotches are visible on the dorsum and a dark stripe runs from the snout to the anterior nape. When the ground color is darkest, the markings, if present, are lighter. A dark ventrolateral stripe may be visible. The tail is usually prominently banded. The belly is off-white to cream. The greatly expanded toes and toe pads permit this essentially arboreal lizard to climb and cling to smooth vertical surfaces and to easily traverse rough horizontal surfaces, inverted. The claws barely extend beyond the tips of the toe pads. The eyes have no functional lids, being protected instead by the transparent brille (spectacle). This gecko will open its mouth widely and display its blue tongue in a defensive display.

Voice: Males are capable of squeaking loudly if stressed or involved in territory disputes with other males.

Reproduction: Females lay one or two eggs at intervals through the summer months.

Similar species: The only other nocturnal gecko species through much of the region is *Hemidactylus mabouia*, which is smaller and has prominent claws.

Habitat/Range: The turnip-tailed gecko inhabits forest huts, houses, and lodges as well as palms and other trees in both secondary and primary forests. It is an abundant species in a wide variety of habitats from Mexico to the Amazon Basin.

Comments: We have encountered this species on trees (including palms) edging forest trails and in clearings. This gecko is alert even at night, and will quickly ascend if approached.

Gymnophthalmines (Microteiids): Family Gymnophthalmidae

Until quite recently these small lizards were considered members of the family Teiidae and were frequently referred to as "microteiids." The latter name is still used despite the familial redesignation.

Many gymnophthalmids have a semitransparent scale (a window, if you will) in the lower eyelid. Generic differences can be subtle (such as the comparative shape of certain head scales). Specific differences within a genus are even less obvious. Add to this the seasonal color enhancements, most conspicuous during the breeding season, and the normal sexual dichromatism, and you may wind up with an identification that is "iffy" at best. Most of these lizards are skulkers par excellence and dwell in and beneath the leaf litter on the forest floor. Many prefer areas *covered thickly* by moist leaf litter; others are restricted to streamside areas. Most species inhabit primary and secondary forests. Many are nocturnal.

Genus *Alopoglossus;* Forest Lizards

The seven or eight species in this genus are retiring forest dwellers that do not seem to be uncommon but are not often seen. This genus is defined by the lack of keeling on the head scales, the straight posterior edge of the parietal scales (the rearmost pair of enlarged head shields), and the lack of an unpigmented "window" in the lower eyelid. Various *Alopoglossus* species occur in Brazil, Ecuador, the Guianas, and Peru.

These are oviparous lizards that probably lay only one or two eggs per clutch, but little else is known or conjectured about their reproductive biology.

154. Large-Scaled Forest Lizard

Alopoglossus angulata

Size: Adults are about 4–5 inches (10–13 cm) in total length. The tail length is a bit more than 1.5 times the SVL.

Identifying features: This is a very rough-scaled lizard. The dorsal scales cross the back in diagonal rows. The dorsal, lateral, and ventral scales are keeled. Each head scale is slightly rough rather than keeled. The limbs are well developed. The dorsal and cranial colors are some shade of brown, but not usually dark brown. The head is often paler than the body. The dark lateral color is often poorly defined and compromised by an infiltration of brown. The cheeks may be brown. A thin, off-white (seldom pure white) stripe runs ventral to the dark side stripe. The belly is cream to gray, either with or without a few darker spots. The ventral scales may be smooth or weakly keeled. The lower eyelid has semitransparent scales. The irises are yellow to yellow-orange.

Reproduction: This species is oviparous, but little else is known about its breeding biology. Only one or two eggs may be laid in each clutch.

Similar species: See the account for *Alopoglossus atriventris*, below.
Habitat/Range: This rather nondescript forest lizard occurs throughout most of the Amazon Basin. It is very firmly associated with moist habitats near a permanent water source. The species may be found in Amazonian Peru, Ecuador, and Colombia, and probably in adjacent areas of contiguous countries.

155. Black-Bellied Forest Lizard

Alopoglossus atriventris

Size: The adults are 4–5 inches (10–12.5 cm) in total length. The tail is a little less than 1.5 times the SVL.
Identifying features: This is another small, rough-scaled microteiid. The dorsal scales cross the back in diagonal rows. The dorsal, lateral, and ventral scales are keeled. Each head scale is slightly rough rather than keeled. The limbs are well developed. The dorsum and cranium are dark brown. A broad, deeper brown (sometimes with a pinkish blush) to black lateral stripe is present, bordered beneath by a thin white stripe. The venter is light (in females and juveniles) to black (in breeding males). The lower eyelid has a series of semitransparent scales. The irises are an intense orange.
Reproduction: Virtually nothing is known about the reproductive biology of this oviparous lizard. It is thought the clutch size is small (one or two eggs) and that more than a single clutch is produced annually.
Similar species: Three other *Alopoglossus* species occur in the Iquitos region. The differences between them are subtle (especially when you are trying to identify a female or nonbreeding male). Breeding males of *A. atriventris* seem to be the most intensely colored and to have the brightest orange eyes. *A. atriventris* also has the most prominently keeled ventral scales.
Habitat/Range: This is a leaf litter species of forested areas, where it is active both day and night. It occurs in Amazonian Peru, Ecuador, and Colombia.
Comments: Because all the lizards of this genus look so similar, it may be possible to field-identify specimens only to genus.

Genus *Arthrosaura;* Creek Lizards

There are about four species in this genus, which is found over much of the northern half of South America. They are very similar in appearance to the various species of *Alopoglossus,* but the arthrosaurs have a transparent window in the lower eyelid and lack postparietal and occipital head scales (the scales that surround the parietal eye and the scales on the rear of the head).

Other than the fact that these are oviparous lizards that probably lay only one or two eggs per clutch, little is known about their reproductive biology.

156. Reticulated Creek Lizard

Arthrosaura reticulata reticulata

Size: Adults are about 5.25 inches (13 cm) in total length. The tail length is more than 1.5 times the SVL.

Identifying features: This is a rather robust, fast-moving, dark lizard. The dorsum is olive tan to dark brown. The venter may vary from reddish cream to brilliant orange. The sides are darker than the back and variably patterned with tiny light spots that are usually most densely clustered and in greatest contrast on the sides of the neck and the anterior sides. Old males may be very dark overall and the light spots difficult to see. The irises are orange.

Reproduction: This species is oviparous, but little else is known about its breeding biology. It is speculated that only one or two eggs are laid in each clutch.

Similar species: Similar lizard species lack the clustered light spots on the sides of the neck and shoulders.

Habitat/Range: This lizard occurs throughout most of the Amazon Basin. It is very firmly associated with moist habitats near permanent water. We have found it active at virtually all hours of the day and night.

Genus *Bachia;* Worm Lizards

The 18–20 species in this genus are slender burrowers or leaf litter inhabitants with tiny forelimbs and even more degenerate hind limbs, no ear openings, and reduced eyes.

The genus occurs throughout most of northern South America east of the Andes, as well as on Trinidad, the Grenadines, and Grenada. The body scales are *not* in whorls.

At the risk of sounding repetitive, we can only state that little is known about the reproductive biology. These are oviparous lizards that probably lay only one or two eggs per clutch.

157. Brown Worm Lizard

Bachia vermiformis

Size: Adults are 7–10 inches (18–25 cm) in total length.

Identifying features: This is a greatly attenuate, cylindrical lizard with very reduced yet functional legs. The tail has a blunt tip. There is no dorsal pattern or external eardrum. The lower eyelid contains a transparent disk.

Reproduction: It is probable that only two eggs are produced per clutch.

Similar species: Other *Bachia* species have well-defined paravertebral stripes.

Habitat/Range: *Bachia vermiformis* has been found beneath forest logs and in rotting stumps at forest edges. This species also makes use of fallen and terrestrial termite nests. It is most often found during land-clearing and logging operations. Found in Amazonian Peru; exact range imperfectly delineated.

Comments: Most researchers consider this an uncommon—or at least uncommonly seen—species.

Genus *Cercosaura;* Forest Lizards

The single species in this genus is broken into three subspecies that are widely distributed in Peru, Brazil, and the Guianas.

Cercosaura has windowed lower eyelids, lacks small granular scales mixed in with the larger scales dorsally, and has both postparietal and occipital scales. The dorsal scales are in longitudinal rows.

One or two eggs are laid in each clutch, and several clutches are laid each breeding season.

158. Black-Striped Forest Lizard

Cercosaura ocellata bassleri

Size: This small lizard attains a total length of 6.5 inches (16.5 cm). The tail length is nearly twice the SVL.

Identifying features: Females and juveniles are grayish dorsally with four thin dorsal stripes and scattered black spots. The sides are usually lighter than the dorsum and may be patterned with variably intense ocelli. Non-breeding males are somewhat darker than females and have an orange flush on the sides. The belly is white centrally and brilliant red-orange along each side. Breeding males are brown dorsally and have a well-defined dorsolateral stripe on each side. The sides are bright red-orange below the stripe and contain several white ocelli edged by broad rings of black. The irises are gold.

Reproduction: Females apparently lay two eggs at a time. It is probable that more than one clutch is produced annually.

Similar species: Many of the microteiids look at least vaguely similar, particularly juveniles, females, and nonbreeding males. *Cercosaura ocellata bassleri* is the most prominently striped of all.

Habitat/Range: Like several other microteiid species, this one is closely associated with leaf litter in primary forests. We have found them in the litter near the buttresses of large trees.

Genus *Gymnophthalmus;* Spectacled Forest Lizards

This genus currently contains eight species, but critical evaluation of the characteristics defining them is needed. Superficially, these little lizards look very much like diminutive skinks. They are shiny, smooth scaled, and usually have a blue or pinkish tail. The lower eyelids are spectacled and immovable. The forefeet have four digits.

These oviparous lizards lay only one or two eggs in a clutch. The hatchlings look very much like the adults but are brighter in color.

The genus ranges from southern Mexico to Argentina and includes some of the Caribbean islands.

159. Spectacled Forest Lizard

Gymnophthalmus underwoodi complex

Size: Most of this lizard's total length (up to 4 inches, or 10 cm) consists of slender tail. The SVL is only about 1.5 inches (4 cm).

Identifying features: This slender, pretty lizard is wary and agile. When moving quickly it folds its legs back against its body and squirms vigorously away. The legs are short and the scales are smooth and shiny. The dorsum is warm brown to gray, and the sides are brown to black. A variably defined light (often tan) stripe may separate the dorsal and lateral colors. The tail may be orangish, brown, or blue. The belly is light, but variably so. Each eye is covered by an immovable, transparent spectacle.

Reproduction: It is thought that each clutch consists of only one or two eggs. Nothing is known about the duration of incubation or hatchling size.

Similar species: Except for *Micrablepharis maximiliana*, other striped, blue-tailed microteiids have movable eyelids. In addition, the spectacled forest lizard has prefrontal scales (paired scales on the top of the head between the eyes and the nostrils; use a lens to ascertain this fact), and these are lacking in *Micrablepharis*.

Habitat/Range: This savanna (and village and garden) lizard is seldom seen far from grasses or similar cover. Although it is easy to spot, it is difficult to catch, and it can be difficult to identify even when in hand. Much about this species complex, including its actual range in Amazonas, is badly in need of study.

Comments: At least two full species (and probably one hybrid form) may be currently contained in this species designation. Parthenogenesis is known to occur in some members of this group.

Genus *Iphisa*; Shade Lizard

Its scale pattern makes this monotypic genus one of the best defined in the family Gymnophthalmidae. The shade lizard is a small, short-legged, active leaf litter dweller with only two rows of scales on its back and on its belly. The lower eyelid is movable and has a transparent window.

160. Glossy Shade Lizard

Iphisa elegans

Size: The maximum total length is about 5.25 inches (13 cm), of which about 3 inches (7.5 cm) is tail.

Identifying features: This is another of the slender-bodied, short-legged, shiny, smooth-scaled gymnophthalmines; yet it is also one of the easiest Amazonian lizards to identify. There are only two rows of dorsal scales and two rows of ventral scales. The glossy shade lizard is brown dorsally, black laterally, and white (with a peachy suffusion) ventrally. The dorsal and lateral colors are separated dorsolaterally by an often poorly defined tan stripe. The tail is brown above, lighter below. The eyelids are functional.

Reproduction: Clutches seem to consist of one or two eggs. Nothing is known about the duration of incubation. Hatchlings are about 2.75 inches (7 cm) in total length.

Similar species: None.

Habitat/Range: The preferred habitats are swamp edge and pond edge forests. When alerted, the glossy shade lizard is quite likely to fold its legs back against its body and squirm vigorously as it effects its escape. This very secretive and seldom seen lizard is widely distributed in Amazonia.

Genus *Leposoma;* Forest Lizards

The 11 species in this genus range from Costa Rica southward to Brazil. With their cylindrical body, long tail, and strong legs, these lizards of the forest litter are of very typical appearance. The windowed lower eyelids are movable. The dorsal and lateral scales are keeled and cross the back and sides in oblique rows. The head scales are strongly keeled.

One or two eggs constitute a clutch, and multiple clutches are laid each season. Some species are parthenogenetic.

The lizards of this genus are easily confused with those of the genus *Cercosaura.*

161. Common Forest Lizard

Leposoma parietale

Size: Adults near 4 inches (10 cm) in total length. The maximum SVL is 1.75 inches (4.5 cm).

Identifying features: This is a small, keeled-scaled gymnophthalmid. Except for males in breeding colors, *L. parietale* is basically a brown on brown lizard. The dorsum is medium brown and the top of the head and the sides are dark brown. Nonbreeding males have a pale orange belly. This becomes an intense orange at breeding time. Several light "portholes" (not dark-rimmed ocelli) are present along the lower sides. Females have a pale belly.

Reproduction: Several two-egg clutches may be laid during each breeding season.

Similar species: Many of the rough-scaled microteiids look quite similar. *Cercosaura ocellata bassleri* tends to be more prominently striped dorsally. In addition, both it and *Neusticurus ecpleopus* have well-defined, dark-outlined, light lateral ocelli. *Alopoglossus atriventris* has a white ventrolateral stripe.

Habitat/Range: This microteiid seems less persistently tied to primary forest habitats than many other gymnophthalmids. It also occurs in secondary forests and at the edges of agricultural clearings. It seems to be primarily a diurnal species but has also been found moving actively about after nightfall. It is found in Amazonian Colombia, Ecuador, and Peru.

Genus *Microblepharis;* Glossy Lizards

Of the two species in this genus, one, *M. dunni,* is known from only a single specimen and its range is unknown. The second, *M. maximiliana,* occurs in the southern and eastern regions of the Amazon Basin. This is a very small and slender lizard with shiny scales. It has a long tail and short but well-developed legs, and is adept at evading capture. The windowed lower eyelids are immovable.

The glossy lizard is often associated with the nests of leaf-cutter ants. As is the case with other gymnophthalmids, one or two eggs are produced in each clutch, and several clutches are produced each breeding season.

162. Blue-Tailed Glossy Lizard

Micrablepharis maximiliana

Size: Up to about 4 inches (10 cm) in total length. The tail length is more than 1.5 times the SVL. Thus, from nose to vent the lizard is only about 1.5 inches (4 cm) long.

Identifying features: Slender of body, short of leg, and shiny and smooth of scale describe this wary little lizard. When frightened, it is likely to fold its legs back against its body and wriggle away. The dorsum is warm brown and the sides are black. The dorsal and lateral colors are separated dorso-laterally by a pale yellow to tan stripe. The tail is blue, brightest distally. The belly is off-white and may bear some darker spots. Rather than functional lids, each eye is covered by an immovable, transparent spectacle.

Reproduction: It is thought that each clutch consists of only one or two eggs. Nothing is known about the duration of incubation or hatchling size.

Similar species: Except for the *Gymnophthalmus underwoodi* complex, other striped, blue-tailed microteiids have movable eyelids. *G. underwoodi* has prefrontal scales (use a lens to ascertain this fact), which are lacking in *Micrablepharis*.

Habitat/Range: It is usually possible to see a blur of movement in the poor light as this lizard skitters quickly from beneath one fallen leaf to the next. *Micrablepharis* is often found in and around the terrestrial nests of leaf-cutter ants. Currently it is thought to be a species of the Brazilian eastern Amazon region, but its actual range is poorly understood.

Genus *Neusticurus;* Streamside Lizards

Nine species are currently assigned to this genus, but future research may disclose another two or more. The streamside lizards are larger than most gymnophthalmids. Many attain a length of 9 inches (22.5 cm), and a few may near a foot (30 cm) in overall length. They are active diurnal foragers of streamside habitats. These lizards swim well and do not hesitate to enter the water, either to secure an insect or to escape danger. The movable lower eyelids are windowed, and the legs are strongly developed. The dorsum of many species is studded with tubercles that are scattered among small scales. Two eggs are laid per clutch, and breeding apparently occurs throughout the year.

The range of the genus is discontinuous. One species is found in a limited area of Costa Rica; others occur throughout northern South America.

163. Common Streamside Lizard

Neusticurus ecpleopus

Size: This robust gymnophthalmid may exceed 10 inches (25 cm) in total length.

Identifying features: Unlike many other gymnophthalmids that move with the head held close to the ground, the streamside lizard often sits and moves with its head held high. The dorsal scalation is heterogeneous, with longitudinal rows of large scales interspersed among the small scales. Adults are olive tan to olive brown dorsally and lighter laterally, and the belly is creamy, sometimes with an orange blush antero-laterally. The throat may be yellow(ish). One large ocellus with a light center is present above the female's arm; males have four ocelli on each side.

Reproduction: Clutches probably contain no more than two eggs each, but given suitable conditions a female may produce multiple clutches.

Similar species: No other small forest-dwelling lizard has the distinctively heterogeneous scalation of *N. ecpleopus*.

Habitat/Range: All specimens of *Neusticurus ecpleopus* that we have found have been in the proximity of forest streams. These lizards do not hesitate to enter water and are strong swimmers. They are active diurnally and often sleep on streamside vegetation at night. The species ranges from central Bolivia north to southern Colombia. It also occurs in Amazonian Brazil.

Genus *Prionodactylus;* Eyed Lizards

The genus *Prionodactylus* comprises six primarily terrestrial species of lizards that often bask atop fallen trunks in patches of morning light. All dwell in leaf litter in rainforest habitats, and some are confusingly similar. Uncertainty continues about the differentiating features of *P. argulus* and

P. oshaughnessyi, which appear to show a wide degree of geographic variability, especially the females (note the femoral pore count in the chart below).

These are very slender and attenuate lizards with short, well-developed legs. The lower eyelids are movable and windowed. Young specimens often have bright orange tails, but the color fades with age. Females lay only one or two eggs per clutch, but lay several clutches in a season.

The genus ranges from Panama south through most of the northern half of South America.

164. Elegant Eyed Lizard

Prionodactylus argulus

Size: The total length is about 5.5 inches (14 cm). The tail is twice as long as the body.

Identifying features: The two species of *Prionodactylus* in western Amazonia are so similar in external appearance that it is impossible to differentiate them if they are not in hand. Even then it is very likely to be difficult.

Prionodactylus argulus is an elongate, rather flat lizard. The dorsum is clad in large scales of warm brown; a wide longitudinal field of small granular scales separates the large dorsal scales from the ventral scales. The granular scales are brighter, often an attractive reddish brown (and are brightest during the breeding season). Males have small black ocelli on the sides; these are best defined anteriorly. A prominent white stripe runs from snout to groin. The belly is off-white to yellowish. The underside of the tail is intense red-orange.

Reproduction: One or two eggs are laid in each clutch. It is probable that females produce multiple clutches when conditions are suitable.

Similar species: *Prionodactylus oshaughnessyi;* see the comparison chart below.

	P. argulus	*P. oshaughnessyi*
femoral pores (male)	6–10	8–14
femoral pores (female)	1–3	8–15 or 0
preanal pores	0	2
ventrals separating femoral pores	4	2
scale rows at midbody	27–35	31–45
size of lateral scales	slightly smaller than dorsals	noticeably smaller than dorsals

Habitat/Range: This diurnal lizard is found in leaf litter in primary and secondary forests. We have found it sunning on logs in the morning. It is known to occur in Amazonian Bolivia, Brazil, Colombia, Ecuador, French Guiana, and Peru.

165. White-Striped Eyed Lizard

Prionodactylus oshaughnessyi

Size: The total length is a slender 5.5 inches (14 cm); the tail length is twice the SVL.

Identifying features: This is an attractive keeled-scaled lizard. The dorsum is clad in large scales of warm brown; a wide longitudinal field of small granular scales separates the large dorsal scales from the ventral scales. The granular scales are darker, often a pretty reddish brown. There are small black ocelli, best defined anteriorly, in the dark side area. A well-defined white stripe runs below the dark side area from snout to groin. The belly is off-white to yellowish. The underside of the tail is an intense red-orange. The irises are reddish tan.

Reproduction: One or two eggs are laid in each clutch. It is probable that females lay multiple clutches when conditions are suitable.

Similar species: See also *Prionodactylus argulus* (above). The bright orange-red subcaudal area will differentiate this lizard from other micro-teiids.

Habitat/Range: This diurnal species inhabits the leaf litter in primary forests. We have also found individuals in vegetation debris at clearing edges and sleeping on tall emergent grasses in shallow ephemeral pools in cleared areas. This species is known to occur in Amazonian Brazil, Colombia, Ecuador, French Guiana, and Peru.

Iguanian Lizards

Once all members of the huge, diverse, and confusing family Iguanidae, the iguanian lizards of the Amazon Basin have now been broken into four more workable families. Still usually referred to as iguanian lizards, the four families we will discuss are the Hoplocercidae (forest dragons), Iguanidae (iguanas), Polychrotidae (anoles and relatives), and Tropiduridae (tree runners). All are diurnal, but many are so well camouflaged that they are difficult to see. Among these lizards are canopy dwellers, tree trunk inhabitants, and leaf litter species.

Family Hoplocercidae; Forest Dragons and Spiny-Tailed Lizard

This small family comprises three genera of lizards of diverse appearance. The two Amazonian genera are *Hoplocercus* (not pictured), a small, terrestrial, spiny-tailed creature from eastern Brazil; and *Enyalioides*, with its several species of forest dragons. The forest dragons are at least semiarboreal, although they seldom go much higher than a few feet up a tree. Insofar as is known, all members of this family are egg layers. *Hoplocercus* is said to be at least partially crepuscular; *Enyalioides* is diurnal.

Genus *Enyalioides;* Forest Dragons

The seven species are pretty, big-headed lizards with a pronounced vertebral crest. Some are of almost bizarre appearance. They are diurnal. The inside of the mouth is pink or yellow, and some forest dragons indulge in interesting threat displays, facing an intruder and opening the mouth widely to show the bright coloration. These lizards are most often seen by day clinging to the trunks of small trees, including palms and bamboo. They may sleep at night still clinging to the trunk but are more apt to choose a leafy horizontal branch or frond.

The genus ranges from Panama south to Brazil and Peru.

166. Amazon Forest Dragon

Enyalioides laticeps

Size: Adults attain a total length of 1 foot (30 cm) or slightly more. The tail length is about twice the SVL. There is some sexual dimorphism.
Identifying features: Males are green to brown dorsally and have orange, green, and brown–striped throats with a large, dark gular spot. A dark-edged orange(ish) bar runs from the angle of the mouth to beneath the tympanal opening. The belly is orange. The vertebral crest is better defined in males than in females. Females are paler and have a reddish gular spot, and the belly is tan suffused with pink blush. Juveniles are paler yet (green or tan dorsally and laterally) and have dark lateral barring. The belly is white. A longitudinal lateral skin fold is often present. There are three or more femoral pores on each hind leg.
Reproduction: This is an oviparous species.
Similar species: *Enyalioides microlepis*, the brown forest dragon (not pictured), has proportionally smaller dorsal and lateral scales and only one or two femoral pores on each hind leg.

Habitat/Range: This species is most commonly seen in primary forest but may also be encountered in secondary forest situations. Although often seen quite low on trunks of trees, these lizards climb well and are often found sleeping several feet above the ground on lateral branches at night. The Amazon forest dragon is found in Amazonian Ecuador, Brazil, Peru, and Colombia.

167. Horned Forest Dragon

Enyalioides palpebralis

Size: Both sexes reach a total length of 10–11 inches (25–28 cm), about half of which is tail.

Identification: "Of spectacular appearance" would be an accurate way to preface any description of this Amazonian lizard. The horned forest dragon is not brightly colored. Within their spectrum of light to dark brown dorsal coloration, however, individuals are capable of considerable change. When the color is at its lightest, a reticulum of dark pigment is usually visible both dorsally and laterally. The belly is off-white to brown. An orange-red spot is present on each side of the neck. Both sexes have a gular (throat) pouch that is weakly distensible. This is yellowish on males and some shade of brown on females. The head is large, and is made to look even more so by the enlarged, pointed, and outwardly diverging scales above each eye. A vertebral crest, discontinuous above the shoulders and highest on the nape, is very prominently developed. The scales on the legs are strongly keeled. The interior of the mouth is bright orange shading to bright yellow at the juncture of the jaws. Overall, this lizard blends so remarkably well with its habitat that it is small wonder that few are seen.

Similar species: None.

Habitat: This cryptic lizard ranges through terra firma and river edge rainforests in Peru and Brazil. It seems to prefer to position itself low on tree trunks by day, and to sleep on lateral branches a few feet above the ground at night.

Comments: Very little is known about the life history or reproductive biology of the horned forest dragon. It relies on its cryptic coloration to escape detection, a ploy that seems to serve it in good stead. When disturbed it is more apt to turn toward the disturbance and open its brilliantly colored mouth in defensive display than to flee.

Iguanas: Family Iguanidae

Because of the mass trade in these bright green lizards in the pet markets of the world, there is probably no more instantly recognized group of lizards. While the hatchlings are only about 8 inches (20 cm) in total length, adult males can exceed 6 feet (1.8 m). The young spend much time on the ground or low in shrubs. Adults climb into the canopy to bask and feed. The iguanas are folivorous (foliage or leaf eaters).

Genus *Iguana*; Green Iguanas

This genus includes two species: the great green iguana of much of tropical Latin America and the endangered Antillean green iguana. The great green iguana is one of the many "pet" species that doesn't make a suitable pet. When hormonally stimulated during the breeding season, normally placid males can become veritable buzz saws of teeth, claws, and whipping tail, dangerous even to their human keepers.

Once very common through much of the Amazon Basin, green iguanas are now difficult to find in many areas. Boat crews navigating rivers near the shore are more likely than others to see them.

The distensible gular pouch and high vertebral crest readily identify adult iguanas. The babies can be the brightest green of any lizard species in the Amazon. This is a diurnal, oviparous lizard.

168. Great Green Iguana

Iguana iguana

Size: This is the largest lizard in the Amazon Basin. Hatchlings are about 8 inches (20 cm) long; adult males may exceed 6 feet (1.8 m); females are seldom more than 4.5 feet (1.5 m). The length of the original tail is somewhat more than twice the SVL.

Identifying features: Babies have rather small heads and are bright green, perhaps slightly less intensely green ventrally. There may be vertical dark lateral bars. There is a low dorsal crest. Adults are paler, often becoming olive or gray-green; the lateral markings may or may not remain. Sexually active adult males may become strongly suffused with orange anteriorly. The vertebral crest becomes proportionally higher with age. The crest of the male consists of more attenuate scales than that of the female. There is a single huge, round scale on each jowl.

Reproduction: Usually during the dry season, females construct well-formed nests in yielding soil and bury their 10–36 eggs. The largest females lay the largest clutches and the largest eggs.

Similar species: Size alone will identify the adults of this huge lizard. Only *Enyalioides laticeps* or the two tree runners of the genus *Tropidurus* are likely to be mistaken for hatchling iguanas.

Habitat/Range: These beautiful lizards occur in most riparian habitats but seem noticeably less common than they were 30 or 40 years ago. Finding one may involve a concerted search. Iguanas can run fast on open ground, climb agilely, swim efficiently, and may drop from a high perch to the ground or water.

Anoles: Family Polychrotidae

The anoles and their relatives make up the huge family Polychrotidae. Anoles, known erroneously in the past as American chameleons, are more easily overlooked in the Neotropics than they are in the southeastern United States. We will take a look at seven species of anoles plus two large anole relatives. Some are lizards of clearing edges, some are primarily terrestrial inhabitants of the deeper forests, and some are beautifully colored arboreal acrobats.

Anoles have elongated digital pads that assist them in climbing and clinging tightly to vertical surfaces. Most are capable of climbing a vertical pane of glass.

Many of the canopy anoles are capable of extensive color changes between shades of bright green and brown. Most of the more terrestrial species and some of the tree trunk dwellers also change color, but only through various shades of brown.

Male anoles (and the females of some species) have distensible throat fans called dewlaps. Although dewlap colors may vary somewhat within a species, many anole species can be more easily identified by their dewlap colors than by body color or pattern. *Anolis bombiceps* is especially easy to confuse with the various subspecies of *A. nitens*, and *A. fuscoauratus* with *A. trachyderma*.

Genus *Anolis*; Anoles

The genus *Anolis* is most diverse in Caribbean and Middle America. It includes some 225 species plus a great many subspecies. Attempts to break this genus into five genera—*Anolis, Dactyloa, Norops, Phenoco-saurus,* and *Xiphocercus*—have thus far met with considerable resistance. Comparatively few species occur in North and South America. Four Amazonian species are persistently arboreal. The remainder can climb well but spend most of their time either on the leaf litter of the forest floor or low on rotting or fallen tree trunks. As mentioned earlier, two of the species, *A. nitens* and *A. bombiceps,* are very similar in external appearance (even down to dewlap colors) and can be difficult to differentiate.

All Amazonian anoles are diurnal, although some are active at very low light levels in primary rainforest. All are oviparous, although their reproductive biology is very poorly known. If they follow the pattern of better-known species, the eggs probably number from one to several per clutch. Female anoles prepare a minimal nest at best, more often than not merely scattering their egg(s) in the damp leaf litter.

All species are primarily insectivorous, but some eat fruit and blossoms as well.

169. Blue-Lipped Forest Anole

Anolis bombiceps

Size: This large and heavy-bodied anole reaches a total length of about 10 inches (25 cm). The tail length is about 1.75 times the SVL.

Identifying features: The dorsum is often deep brown with darker brown blotches and spots; the belly is lighter. The vertebral scales are not enlarged. Both females and males have dewlaps, but the female's is smaller. The dewlap color is blue to nearly black with scattered white scales.

Reproduction: One to two eggs make up a clutch; laying occurs throughout the rainy months (perhaps throughout most of the year) at about three-week intervals.

Similar species: Two confusingly similar subspecies of *Anolis nitens* are sympatric with *A. bombiceps. Anolis nitens scypheus* has a blue dewlap edged in red. The dewlap of *A. nitens tandae* is often similar to that of *A. bombiceps,* but the former has enlarged vertebral scales.

Habitat/Range: *Anolis bombiceps* is a species of terrestrial situations in primary and secondary forests. Individuals are often seen sitting quietly on top of the leaf litter or clinging to a low buttress in a patch of sunlight. At night, these lizards have been found sleeping low on forest shrubs in Colombia and Peru.

170. Slender Anole

Anolis fuscoauratus fuscoauratus

Size: This small anole is adult at 5.5 inches (14 cm) total length.

Identifying features: The dorsal ground color is pale gray, tan, or brown. Females often have a paler tan or yellowish vertebral stripe. The belly is grayish. The proportionally large dewlap is orange-red with white scales, some of which may have a vaguely dark edging.

Reproduction: A single egg is laid at intervals throughout the rainy season.

Similar species: *Anolis ortonii* and *A. trachyderma* can be easily confused with this species. *Anolis ortonii* has a much larger and redder dewlap with elongate areas of orange outlining rows of white scales. *Anolis trachyderma* usually has a much darker dorsum and two light transverse bars (which may be hard to discern) on the chin, and the *small* dewlap is red with brown scales.

Habitat/Range: Slender anoles are often seen in leaf litter but quickly dart up a tree if frightened. They are found in secondary forest more often than primary, and are also abundant in agricultural clearings, fields, and at the periphery of logged areas. They may be found at night sleeping low on shrubs and on tall grasses and canes. Widespread in the Amazon Basin.

171. Yellow-Tongued Forest Anole

Anolis nitens scypheus

Size: This is one of the larger terrestrial anoles, attaining a length of about 11 inches (28 cm). The tail length is about twice the SVL.

Identifying features: This deep to pale brown anole may have a lighter dead leaf pattern or a series of obscure darker marks dorsally. A light vertebral stripe, often most prominent posteriorly, may be present. Both sexes have a tricolored dewlap—blue in the center, orange-red along the edge, with white scale rows across the fields of both colors. The male's dewlap is proportionally much larger than the female's.

Reproduction: Females lay one or two eggs per clutch and may nest at (approximately) three-week intervals through much of the year.

Similar species: *Anolis bombiceps* is of very similar appearance but has a blue dewlap that lacks the red edge.

Habitat/Range: These robust anoles are found in primary and secondary forests. They are primarily terrestrial but regularly ascend buttresses, stumps, fallen trunks, and other such elevated objects throughout the northwestern and central Amazon Basin.

172. Blue-Throated Anole

Anolis nitens tandae

Size: The total length is about 11 inches (28 cm), with the tail constituting about two-thirds of that. Females are the smaller sex.

Identifying features: This is a big, brown anole with darker chevrons. The belly is somewhat lighter than the dorsum. The vertebral scales are noticeably larger than the scales below them. Females have a cream dewlap with a central blue spot and lighter scales running in stripes across both color fields. Males' dewlap color varies geographically. It may be blue in the center and reddish or pinkish elsewhere, or entirely blue. In all cases lines of light scales run across the field of the dewlap.

Reproduction: Females lay one or two eggs per clutch and apparently nest at (approximately) three-week intervals through much of the year.

Similar species: Neither *Anolis bombiceps* nor *A. n. scypheus* has enlarged vertebral scales.

Habitat/Range: This is a primarily terrestrial anole of the central Amazon Basin.

173. Amazon Bark Anole

Anolis ortonii

Size: This small anole is about 4.5 inches (11.5 cm) in total length. The tail length is about 1.4 times the SVL.

Identifying features: *Anolis ortonii* usually displays irregular longitudinal light and dark streaks (vermiculations) on the gray to brown back, sides, limbs, and tail. The venter is olive gray with brownish spots. The dewlap of the male is large, richly colored, and of complex pattern. The distal edge is orange, orange streaks enclose the rows of white scales on the distended dewlap, and the remaining areas are dark to bright red.

Reproduction: One to two eggs are produced in a clutch, and several clutches are produced each year.

Similar species: The dark and light vermiculations present on both dorsal and lateral surfaces and the distinctive orange and red–streaked dewlap of the males should allow you to identify this anole.

Habitat/Range: The Amazon bark anole may be encountered in secondary and primary forests, in and on forest dwellings, along trails, and at the edges of clearings, usually on or close to the ground. They have been seen on fallen trees, the buttresses of standing trees, thatched roofs, fallen palm fronds, low shrubs, and other such situations. At night they sleep on horizontal and diagonal branches of low bushes. Widespread throughout the Amazon Basin.

174. Amazon Green Anole

Anolis punctatus

Size: At its largest, this anole nears 1 foot (30 cm) in total length. The length of the tail is somewhat more than twice the SVL.

Identifying features: Often a beautiful moss to leaf green, if cold or otherwise stressed this bulbous-nosed anole may turn splotchy green and deep olive or even purplish brown. Sparse pale blue, white, or pale yellow spots are present on the dorsum and lower sides. The large dewlap is red with lines of white to gray scales across it.

Reproduction: The female lays one or two eggs per clutch, and produces several clutches during the year. The smallest specimen we have seen was 3 inches (7.5 cm) in total length and had a well-healed umbilical scar.

Similar species: None.

Habitat/Range: Although occasionally seen low on the trunks of slender trees, this is considered a canopy-dwelling anole. It occurs throughout most of the central, northern, and eastern Amazon Basin.

175. Common Forest Anole

Anolis trachyderma

Size: This small anole may reach 5.5 inches (14 cm) in total length.

Identification: By day, this is the darkest of the three small brown anoles in the region. The dorsum is brown with poorly defined darker markings. The belly is light. There are narrow light bands on the legs. At night, the ground color lightens to tan or pale brown and the markings are further obscured. There are two transverse light markings across the dark chin.

The relatively narrow dewlap is red with a paler edging and is patterned with rows of dark (usually brown) scales.

Reproduction: Only one egg is produced per clutch, but several depositions occur during the year.

Similar species: This is the only one of the basin's anoles with dark (rather than light) scale rows across the distended dewlap.

Habitat/Range: The common forest anole may be found in primary and secondary forests. It seems less common in clearings and agricultural holdings than the other brown anoles. Individuals are usually seen on or close

to the ground and commonly sleep on low shrubs. Widespread throughout the Amazon Basin.

176. Banded Tree Anole

Anolis transversalis

Size: This species attains a total length of about 7 inches (18 cm). The tail
length is about 1.25 times the SVL.

Identifying features: This is perhaps the prettiest of the two moderately large
green anoles of the region. It is a persistently arboreal species that is capable
of considerable color changes. The ground color is usually some shade of
green but may vary at times from pale reddish buff (females) to bright yellow-green (males). Females are prominently barred with broad transverse
markings that are broadest dorsally. Broken lines of dark transverse marks
may border the primary bars. The males are often less prominently barred.
At their darkest the primary markings are thin, unbroken bars; as often as
not, however, they are represented merely by small, dark spots. Both sexes
have a dewlap. The female's is small, whitish, and transversely barred with
dark markings. Males have an immense yellow dewlap.

Reproduction: Females lay one egg (rarely, two) per clutch. Although little
else is known about the reproductive biology, it is suspected that, like most
anoles, females produce eggs at intervals through the suitable months of
the year.

Similar species: None. Although the common monkey lizard (*Polychrus
marmoratus*) has transverse barring, it is bulkier and lacks both a distensible dewlap and the expanded toe pads common to the lizards in the
genus *Anolis*.

Habitat/Range: This species seems primarily a canopy form of primary
forests, but several have been found sleeping at night about 6 feet above
the ground on the horizontal branches of small trees. Widespread throughout the Amazon Basin.

Genus *Polychrus;* Bush Anoles, Monkey Lizards

These anoline lizards lack distended toe pads but are very much at home
in shrubs and trees. They usually move rather slowly along their arboreal
highways in a curious hand-over-hand fashion. The genus ranges from
Nicaragua to Argentina. The very long tail is moderately prehensile and
provides support and stability, especially on breezy days.

Lizards of this genus have a distensible gular pouch, and some have a moderate ability to change color shades. Like the anoles, the six species in this genus are diurnal and oviparous. However, unlike the anoles, which lay only one to a few eggs, the monkey lizards produce reasonably large clutches (5–20 eggs) and dig nests in a suitable substrate.

The diet consists of both insect and plant materials.

177. Sharp-Nosed Monkey Lizard

Polychrus acutirostris

Size: The overall length is about 15 inches (38 cm), 11 inches (28 cm) of which is tail. Females are the larger sex.

Identifying features: This is a relatively slender, often slow-moving anole with a very long, semiprehensile tail. The dorsal ground color is olive gray to gray or gray-brown, and darker markings may be prominent or obscure. The belly and lower sides are lighter than the dorsum. Dark lines radiate rearward from the eye. There are no distended toe pads.

Reproduction: Little is known about the reproductive biology, but a maximum clutch size of 23 eggs has been recorded.

Similar species: None.

Habitat/Range: This species barely reaches southern Amazonia in eastern Brazil. It is far more abundant in seasonally dry habitats southward to Paraguay.

178. Common Monkey Lizard

Polychrus marmoratus

Size: This is a large lizard with a very attenuate tail. Adults may attain 14 inches (35 cm) in total length. The tail length can be up to 2.5 times the SVL. Females are the larger sex.

Identifying features: Although this lizard does occasionally change its ground color to olive or olive brown, it is usually rather bright green dorsally with golden brown to yellow-olive diagonal cross bands. A white ventrolateral line is present. The belly is greenish. One dark line extends rearward from the eye to the top of the tympanum and another extends from the eye to the angle of the jaw. When the lizard is not moving, the tip of the long, slender tail may be wrapped loosely around a branch for support.

Reproduction: Females lay up to 7 eggs per clutch. It is not known whether this lizard produces multiple clutches.

Similar species: *Anolis transversalis* could conceivably be confused with this species, but the former has a distensible dewlap and broadly expanded toe pads, whereas *Polychrus marmoratus* does not.

Habitat/Range: The bush anole probably spends most of its life in forest trees. It is a persistently arboreal species that, when unhurried, moves in a methodical hand-over-hand style along branches and twigs. This unusual lizard remains motionless for long periods and moves *very* slowly when not frightened, but can hop from branch to branch when rushed. They may occur in primary and secondary forests, but most specimens are seen along the edges of clearings or trails in the western Amazon Basin.

Leaf Lizards and Tree Runners: Family Tropiduridae

The members of this family differ morphologically from other iguanians. The dead-leaf lizard is distinctive and easily identified. The two tree runners are similar to the forest dragons (genus *Enyalioides* of the family Hoplocercidae) in general appearance but have proportionally smaller heads and a more spraddle-legged stance. If in hand, the two tree runners are easily differentiated from the pink-mouthed forest dragons by their dark mouth linings. The tree runners might also be mistaken for baby green iguanas, but the latter are bright leaf green.

Because of their remarkable tail morphology, another group of tree-dwelling tropidurines is known as the thornytails. As a group they are unmistakable.

Genus *Stenocercus*; Leaf Lizards

Depending on whose authority you accept, there are between 30 and 46 species in this genus. Among them are very "normal"-appearing, easily seen lizards and others so well camouflaged that they are almost invisible (unless moving) even at close range. Only three species inhabit the Amazon Basin. The others range from Argentina to Ecuador and Colombia.

All members of the genus are diurnal and oviparous. Although they are alert, at least some species will remain in place as you approach, depending on their camouflage to protect them and running only at the last minute.

179. Western Leaf Lizard

Stenocercus fimbriatus

Size: The total length ranges from 9.5 to 11.5 inches (24–29 cm); the SVL is up to 3.5 inches (9 cm). Females are somewhat larger than males. Juveniles have proportionally shorter tails than adults.

Identifying features: This attractive lizard is a remarkable dead-leaf mimic. The head and dorsum are dried-leaf tan with a series of rearward-pointing darker chevrons that simulate leaf ribs. These marks are best defined above the pelvis and at the base of the tail. A (usually) weakly defined dark line crosses the top of the head between the eyes or orbits; it becomes prominent and strongly defined beneath the eye, extends to the labials, and merges into the dark throat color. The irises are orange. A low but prominent vertebral crest is present. Dorsolateral and antehumeral crests (ridges) precisely delimit the light dorsal color from the soil brown throat, sides, and limbs. The belly is brown to pinkish brown. The dorsal and lateral scales are imbricate, keeled, and sandpapery to the touch. The limb scales are heavily keeled.

Reproduction: Leaf lizards are oviparous, but little else is known about their reproductive biology. Like other members of the genus, females probably produce one to six eggs per clutch.

Similar species: The more infrequently seen rose-bellied leaf lizard, *S. roseiventris* (not pictured), also occurs in Amazonian Peru. It is a darker, more heavily patterned lizard that has anterior dorsolateral folds rather than dorsolateral crests.

Habitat/Range: *Stenocercus fimbriatus* is one of the most cryptically colored of all primary forest lizards. If startled, it moves in short bursts of motion and halts very abruptly, becoming virtually invisible within the litter of the forest floor. We saw one large specimen sleeping on vegetation about a foot above the ground, but it dropped to the ground and disappeared when we were trying to photograph it. Despite an extensive search of the surrounding area we were unable to relocate the specimen. This species is restricted to western Brazil and adjacent eastern Peru.

Comments: *Stenocercus fimbriatus* was formerly placed in the genus *Ophryoessoides* and was long considered synonymous with *O. aculeatus*.

Genus *Tropidurus;* Tree Runners, Thornytails, and Relatives

The genus *Tropidurus* comprises about 24 species of diverse appearance.

As currently defined, it includes not only the traditional longtime members of the genus but the lizards once in the genera *Plica* and *Uracentron* as well. About half a dozen species occur in the Amazon Basin. Others are found throughout northern South America. Some are seen very infrequently.

The tree runners are typically lizardlike in appearance. They are extensively arboreal and move with ease up and down even smooth-trunked trees. These lizards have a curious "spraddle-legged" look. One species seems to dwell on very large trees while the other prefers smaller trees.

The thornytails are equally arboreal, tending to be found very high up in very large trees, and seem particularly fond of the tree species *Macrolobium acacaefolium*. These interesting lizards live in colonies with a single dominant male and several females. Subordinate males, if present, are usually colored like the females and are never as bright as the dominant male.

As a group, these lizards are diurnal and oviparous. They seem well adapted to ambient forest temperatures and do not sun themselves for long periods. Most feed primarily or almost exclusively on arboreal ants.

180. Collared Tree Runner

Tropidurus (Plica) plica

Size: The total length is about 15 inches (35 cm), of which about 9 inches (23 cm) is tail. Males are the larger sex.

Identifying features: Coloration is variable; in most cases, an alert tree runner will be quite similar in color to the bark of the tree on which it is resting. The dorsal ground color may vary from olive to gray, with darker bands that may be from barely to very visible and are best defined vertebrally and on the limbs. A darker collar, usually broken laterally with lighter blotches, is present. The belly is usually grayish and not banded. The throat *may* have a brownish wash over the gray. The mouth lining is blue. The nuchal crest is prominent; the vertebral crest, though obvious, is low.

Reproduction: This is an oviparous species.

Similar species: *Tropidurus umbra ochrocollaris* is more olive green than gray, has a better-defined dark collar, and lacks patches of enlarged, spiny scales behind the ears.

Habitat/Range: The common tree runner preferentially selects large-diameter trees. It may remain motionless until quite closely approached, depending on its camouflage for protection. Once frightened, however, the lizard will dart quickly up (or, more rarely, down) the tree, usually circling around to the side most distant from the observer. It is seen primarily on vertical trunks by day and positions itself on horizontal limbs and fronds to sleep at night. This abundant lizard occurs over most of the northern half of South America.

181. Olive Tree Runner

Tropidurus (Plica) umbra ochrocollaris

Size: This species attains a total length of 9.5–11 inches (24–28 cm). The tail length is about twice the SVL.

Identifying features: The dorsum and sides are grayish brown to olive. Cold individuals are often darker than warm ones. The black collar is thin and broken vertebrally. A thin, dark line runs rearward from the eye to, or nearly to, the collar. A dark spot is present beneath the eye, and there is another at the corner of the mouth. The mouth lining is blue. The throat may be orangish or greenish. The belly is often pale orange.

Reproduction: Females of this oviparous species lay only a few large eggs in each clutch.

Similar species: *Tropidurus plica* is similar in appearance but has proportionally larger and more strongly keeled body scales, is usually much grayer, and has a patch of enlarged (spinose) scales posterior to the ear opening. *Enyalioides laticeps* has a pink mouth lining and a proportionally larger head.

Habitat/Range: This tree runner usually prefers trees of smaller diameter than those chosen by *T. plica*. Individuals are most often seen on the trunks by day, but usually choose horizontal perches on limbs and fronds on which to sleep at night. As a species *T. umbra* is found from Bolivia and Brazil north to Ecuador and the Guianas. The subspecies *T. o. ochrocollaris* is the predominant race in the northwestern Amazon Basin.

182. Eastern Green Thornytail

Tropidurus (Uracentron) azureum azureum

Size: Adults are about 5 inches (13 cm) in total length; the very spiny tail is about 2 inches (5 cm) long.

Identifying features: The dominant color on this little ant eater is lime green. There are up to eight wide, black, curved cross bands dorsally, the first on the back of the head and the last above the pelvis. There is a large, black supraocular blotch over each eye. The lime green limbs are mottled with black. The belly may be green with a bluish tinge. The body and tail are broad and somewhat flattened. The caudal scales are heavily keeled and prominently spinose.

Reproduction: This is an egg-laying lizard, but little else is known about its reproductive biology. A female from Suriname produced two eggs, but neither hatched.

Similar species: There are three races of this thornytail; this one is the most strongly patterned and the easternmost in distribution. The two more westerly races tend to be weakly reticulated, not banded, dorsally. Other species of thornytail are not green.

Habitat/Range: Although it has been found low on tree trunks, on fallen trees, and even on rock formations, this thornytail is generally thought to be a canopy dweller associated with tree holes. It occurs in the eastern Amazon Basin.

183. Amazon Thornytail

Tropidurus (Uracentron) flaviceps

Size: This large thornytail may near 7.5 inches (19 cm) in total length; the tail constitutes about one-third of that.

Identifying features: This is a dark but variable lizard. Many specimens have a buff head and a buff-speckled dark gray to black body and tail. A prominent white collar may be present. The belly, although variable, is often creamy buff. Both body and tail are depressed, the tail especially so. The forelimbs are lighter in color than the rear limbs. Juveniles may be more brightly colored than adults. The tail bears strongly keeled, very spinose scales.

Reproduction: Two eggs are produced in each clutch. Several clutches are laid annually. Incubation duration and hatchling size are unknown.

Similar species: None. Other thornytails are predominantly green.

Habitat/Range: This canopy-dwelling lizard is occasionally seen only a few feet above the ground on large trunks. It feeds on large ants and lives in family groups on suitable trees. Look for it in the northwestern Amazon Basin.

Genus *Uranoscodon*; Diving Lizard

The single species ranges widely through the northern and eastern Amazon Basin in well-shaded habitats that are very near water. The common name is appropriate, for if near the water when threatened, diving lizards often dive. They are capable of swimming either submerged or on the surface, and can run across the surface film like a basilisk, gradually sinking and swimming away when they slow. Alternatively, they may remain entirely motionless, relying on their dark coloration to render them invisible in the shaded forest against a dark trunk. Diving lizards are diurnal and strongly arboreal, although their idea of arboreality is to cling low on the trunks of standing trees. Most of those seen are between 1 and 6 feet (30–180 cm) up the trunk. If surprised on the ground, they often dash off bipedally.

This species is oviparous. The diet includes many species of arthropods.

184. Diving Lizard

Uranoscodon superciliosus

Size: This large tropidurine may near 18 inches (45 cm) in overall length, of which the SVL is about 6 inches (15 cm).

Identifying features: Except for the light throat, venter, and flecking, this is usually a dark lizard. The dorsum is olive brown to brown, often with tiny, irregularly arranged buff or golden spangles. Occasional specimens may have some orange on the surfaces of the hind limbs. A dentate vertebral crest begins on the anterior nape and continues well onto the tail. The sides, also spangled, lighten in color ventrally.

Reproduction: Clutches of 4–10 eggs are known. Incubation seems to take about 100 days. Hatchlings are slightly more than 5 inches (13 cm) in total length.

Similar species: None.

Habitat/Range: This tree-dwelling species of the eastern Amazon Basin seems most often associated with creekside or swampy habitats. It is capable of bipedal locomotion and can run across the surface of quiet water; it swims well and dives readily from high perches if disturbed.

Skinks: Family Scincidae

Representatives of this huge family are found almost worldwide. Some dwell in the driest desert habitats (sandfish), some are waterside lizards that do not hesitate to swim or dive (coal skinks), others are common "backyard" species (broad-headed skinks), and many are forest dwellers.

Among the latter are the five very similar-looking skink species of the Amazon Basin.

With few exceptions, skinks are shiny-scaled lizards of small to moderate size. The common skink of the northwestern Amazon Basin, *Mabuya nigropunctata*, typifies this appearance. The black-spotted skink is a pretty, agile, and alert lizard.

Genus *Mabuya*; Rainbow Skinks, Sun Skinks

Skinks of this genus may be encountered from Africa to Asia, and from Latin America to Florida (where one species is introduced). They also occur on Caribbean islands. All told, there are more than 80 species, and all, including the South American forms, are typically "skinklike" in appearance. Mabuyas are from 8 to 10 inches in overall length; are primarily brown with darker stripes; and have smooth scales and windowed, but movable, lower eyelids. The Latin American mabuyas are viviparous.

185. Black-Spotted Skink

Mabuya nigropunctata

Size: Adults are generally between 7 and 9 inches (17–23 cm) in total length, although some reach 10 inches (25 cm). The tail length is about 1.35 times the SVL.

Identifying features: The coppery brown dorsum is bordered beneath by a broad, unevenly edged lateral stripe, which is in turn bordered ventrally by an uneven white stripe. Below this is a series of dark spots. The limbs are black, banded with brown. The venter is greenish white. The tail is dark, but on young specimens may show a vague bluish tint. The scales are smooth and shiny.

Reproduction: This is a viviparous lizard (embryonic nutrition occurs through a primitive placenta) that births three to eight young.

Similar species: *Mabuya nigropunctata* is the only skink currently known from the Iquitos region. From there its range extends eastward throughout the Amazon Basin.

Habitat/Range: Skinks may be encountered in habitats as diverse as tree trunk crevices and hollows, forest floors, and village trash heaps. These short-legged lizards climb well but are also found in leaf litter in open areas. The rustling of dry leaves as the skink forages may draw your attention to it. The black-spotted skink often thermoregulates in isolated patches of sunlight and is shiningly beautiful when seen. This species is common throughout the Amazon Basin.

Teiids: Family Teiidae

The teiids are alert, fast lizards. The many smaller lizards once referred to as microteiids have now been reclassified into the family Gymnophthalmidae (representative species are discussed above).

With the exception of the persistently aquatic caiman lizard (also called alligator tegu) and crocodile tegu, the teiids we will discuss are terrestrial and diurnal. They vary in overall length from the 7-inch (18-cm) forest whiptails to the more than 3-foot-long (90-cm) caiman lizard and tegu. All have long tails that are rather easily autotomized but do not necessarily regenerate well or fully. Many of the species colonize the environs of Amazon villages, and some become excessively abundant in these situations. The various whiptails of the genus *Ameiva* are common components of the herpetofauna in large cities such as Leticia, Iquitos, and Belém.

Genus *Ameiva;* Whiptails

The 20 or so species of *Ameiva* are distributed from Florida (introduced) through Latin America and are found on many Caribbean islands. Grasslands, grassy riverbanks, and village environs are among their favored habitats. These strictly diurnal lizards are (usually) larger counterparts of the racerunners and whiptails (genus *Cnemidophorus*) that are so familiar to North Americans. All are oviparous.

Whiptails are very alert, very fast, quite agile, and *very* difficult to approach closely. If in hand, the *Ameiva* species are easily distinguished from those of the genus *Cnemidophorus* by counting the rows of belly plates—10–12 on *Ameiva*, 8 on *Cnemidophorus*.

186. Amazon Whiptail

Ameiva ameiva

Size: In western Amazonas, these lizards seldom exceed 14 inches (35 cm) in total length. Specimens from eastern Amazonas may be a few inches longer. The tail length is about 2.2 times the SVL.

Identifying features: The populations of green-rumped ameivas (once designated *A. a. petersi*) that occur over much of the Amazon include lizards that usually have a dorsum of warm tan anteriorly shading to brilliant green posteriorly. Some, however, may have the anterior green and the rump brown, and others are entirely green. In all cases the sides are darker and liberally peppered with prominent, dark-edged white spots. The belly has brilliant blue spots on the outermost rows of ventral scales. There are 12 rows of large belly scales.

Reproduction: Females are thought to lay single (rarely two) clutches of up to four eggs in the early summer. The eggs hatch in a bit more than two months. Hatchlings are nearly 5 inches (13 cm) in total length.

Similar species: Compare accounts and pictures (photos 190 and 191) of the tropical whiptails of the genus *Kentropyx*.

Habitat/Range: Amazon ameivas are locally common over much of the region. They prefer open areas such as fields, parklands, weedy canal banks, and the low vegetation at the edges of villages and forest lodges. They are fast, alert lizards that nervously move between patches of cover. If hard-pressed, they quickly dart for their burrows. Once up to speed, they are capable of bipedal movement. They are found throughout most of the northern half of South America, in Panama, and have been introduced into Dade County, Florida.

Comments: A second, very different color phase of this lizard occurs in some parts of the range but is not known from the Iquitos region. On this morph the dorsum is charcoal to bluish gray with rather regular cross rows of pale blue to yellowish or whitish spots. The belly has numerous blue spots on the outer several rows of scales. Blue(ish) spots also appear on the limbs.

Genus *Cnemidophorus;* Racerunners, Whiptails, and Rainbow Lizards

This is a confusing genus to define. There are probably about 40 species, many of which are hybrid "species" (some with three parental forms). Many of the hybrids are parthenogenetic. All species are oviparous.

"Cnemies" are a common component of the herpetofauna over much of the United States, Central America, and northern South America. Those in South America belong to the *C. lemniscatus* (rainbow lizard) complex, which currently exemplifies taxonomic confusion.

Like the larger ameivas, the rainbow lizards are strictly diurnal. They are at least as alert and fast as their larger relatives, and because they are smaller they are even more agile and difficult to approach. The rainbow lizards have eight longitudinal rows of belly plates.

The intricacy of color combinations and patterns on male rainbow lizards is quite amazing.

187. Rainbow Whiptail

Cnemidophorus lemniscatus complex

Size: A total length of 9–10 inches (23–25 cm) is most common, but occasional males may near 1 foot (30 cm) in length. Females are smaller.

Identifying features: This is a busily patterned and beautifully colored, sexually dimorphic lizard. Adult males have a blue face, chin, and forelimbs. The top of the head, the shoulders, the belly, and the tail are greenish. The back is buff. The sides are golden. Yellowish stripes are visible on the back, and the sides and anterior tail are liberally spangled with golden flecks. Females and juveniles are brownish above and have six or seven buff dorsal stripes, a brown tail, a greenish venter, and, sometimes, a yellowish face.

Reproduction: From three to four clutches of two to five eggs are laid annually. Incubation takes about 55 days. Hatchlings are about 3.5 inches (9 cm) in total length.

Similar species: As currently described, this is a complex of at least four species. Additional study is badly needed.

Habitat/Range: Savannas and dry village fields are the general habitats of this complex of colorful lizards, which may be found over much of the eastern Amazon Basin and southern Central America. An introduced population is in Dade County, Florida.

Genus *Crocodilurus;* Crocodile Tegu

The single species in this Neotropical genus is extensively aquatic. Its distribution is tightly tied to the meandering courses of the Amazon and Orinoco Rivers and their tributaries. Watch for crocodile tegus basking on river edge snags while your craft is in smaller waterways. The babies are intricately and beautifully colored; adults are considerably duller.

This is an oviparous, diurnal species with "normal" rather than strongly tuberculated dorsal scales and a low keel along each side of the tail.

Crocodile tegus eat all types of smaller creatures. They are very adept at catching small fish and amphibians. Besides these, they feed on insects, worms, spiders, and virtually anything else they can overpower.

188. Crocodile Tegu

Crocodilurus amazonicus (lacertinus)

Size: This is a large lizard. The SVL is about 8 inches (20 cm), and the length of the double-keeled (alligator-like) tail is more than twice that, giving a total length of just over 2 feet (60 cm).

Identifying features: In Amazonian Peru, this beautiful, attenuate teiid tends toward overtones of green but is darkest dorsally. Aged individuals appear to be the darkest. From top to bottom, the face and anterior sides shade from brown to light-spotted green. The throat and belly are yellow, reticulated or spotted with dark pigment; the lips are barred with black. The back is dark olive green shading to brown on the sides, where dark-bordered light ocelli are apparent. Posteriorly and on the limbs and anterior tail the ocelli become tinged with orange. The feet and toes are banded in orange and black. Distally the tail is suffused with orange dorsally and is darker laterally and ventrally. The teeth are conical anteriorly and tricuspid posteriorly.

Reproduction: Little is known about the reproductive biology of this teiid, other than that it is oviparous. One imported female laid a clutch of three eggs. Although apparently fertile, the eggs did not hatch.

Similar species: The northern caiman lizard, *Dracaena guianensis,* is more robust and has inordinately heavy dorsal scaling, an orangish head, and a nonspotted greenish body and tail. Baby caiman are olive tan to olive gray with black bands, or black with yellow bands.

Habitat/Range: Persistently aquatic and, apparently, very locally distributed, the crocodile tegu basks for extended periods on floating or emergent rafts of vegetation or limbs. It is a powerful swimmer, moving through the water with sinuous grace. Look for it near vegetation and on potential basking sites along the edges of quiet oxbow lakes, lagoons, backwaters, or flooded savannas. This lizard is quite capable of climbing and may bask well above the surface of the water. You may be lucky enough to see it anywhere between the upper reaches of the Peruvian Amazon and the mouth of the river at Belém, Brazil. It also occurs along the Rio Orinoco and its drainage.

Comments: Although the species is considered rare in many areas, populations of crocodile tegus may exist in some lagoons in eastern Peru and adjacent Brazil.

Genus *Dracaena;* Caiman Lizard

This is the larger and by far the bulkier of the two aquatic Amazon lizard species. It has scattered, strongly enlarged scales on its back and a triple-keeled tail anteriorly. The overall body color is some shade of green. The head and shoulders are orange to buff. The head is proportionally large and very deep (from top to bottom). The immensely powerful jaws are well adapted for crushing the shells of the snails and other shelled creatures on which this lizard feeds.

The genus *Dracaena* is bitypic. One species occurs in the Amazon Basin and the other is from Paraguay and adjacent non-Amazonian regions. Both species are oviparous and diurnal.

189. Northern Caiman Lizard

Dracaena guianensis

Size: This is a large and unmistakable lizard. The total length may approach 3 feet (90 cm). The tail length is about 1.8 times the SVL.

Identifying features: The body scales are heterogeneous, with several longitudinal rows of large scales interspersed among the small ones. The tail bears several rows of enlarged scales. The body and tail may vary from olive brown to forest green, and the head from olive brown to orange. Older specimens are often more dully colored than young ones. Adult males have a yellowish belly and a yellowish and gray throat. Females have a gray belly. The head is massive.

Reproduction: Females usually lay only a few (occasionally as many as 8–15) large, parchment-shelled eggs. One reported clutch of two eggs was found in a river edge termite nest.

Similar species: None; the color and scalation are diagnostic.

Habitat/Range: This is a species of the flooded forests, where it may be seen basking in patchy sunshine or in comparatively open sites along backwaters and riverbanks. *Dracaena guianensis* may be found from Peru to eastern Brazil along most of the major river systems.

Comments: The caiman lizard climbs well and may bask sprawled on a branch, a muddy bank, or a protruding log or trunk. It is agile in the water and if closely approached readily dives and swims to safety or hides beneath bottom debris. The diet consists of snails, which the lizard swallows after crushing and spitting out the shells.

Genus *Kentropyx;* Tropical Whiptails

The eight species of this genus range throughout South America southward to northern Argentina.

Like the other whiptails—in fact, like all other teiids—the tropical whiptails are strictly diurnal. They differ from the other whiptails (genera *Ameiva* and *Cnemidophorus*) in having keeled, rather than smooth, belly plates. They are oviparous.

Although they are very alert, these lizards will often allow close approach when they first emerge to thermoregulate in the morning. Once fully warmed they are quite ready to dash to safety the moment they sense a disturbance. They often run bipedally.

190. Cocha Whiptail

Kentropyx altamazonica

Size: Although adults occasionally reach lengths of 14 inches (35 cm), most specimens are adult at 9–11.5 inches (22.5–29 cm). The tail length is about 2.25 times the SVL.

Identifying features: This is the more subtly colored of the two common *Kentropyx* of the western Amazon Basin. The limbs, sides, and posterior dorsum are olive tan to olive brown. Anterodorsally there is a broad vertebral stripe of bright green. A row of large, dark dorsolateral spots is present. Each spot is bordered ventrally for at least its anterior half by a thin, light tan stripe. Small light spots are present on the face and ventrolaterally. The belly is cream.

Reproduction: Clutches of up to six eggs are known. It is probable that females lay more than a single clutch during periods of low water.

Similar species: The Amazon whiptail lacks a vertebral stripe. Although it fades as it progresses posteriorly, the vertebral stripe of *K. pelviceps* usually continues onto the tail and is scalloped on its inner edges. The dark dorsolateral stripes have uneven edges and are not bordered dorsally by a light line.

Habitat/Range: Although a forest lizard, this species is often seen in more open areas than its congener, *Kentropyx pelviceps*, but it is not as fond of wide-open spaces as *Ameiva ameiva*. Look for *K. altamazonica* in sunny patches on the forest floor, especially near tree falls and in newly cleared areas throughout the Amazon Basin.

Comments: This fast, agile lizard can run quickly over mud, is not uncommon in flooded areas, and is said to be able to run across the surface of quiet water (like the iguanian basilisk). It climbs well and may be extensively arboreal during the seasonal high water. Insects and blossoms are the primary foods.

191. Forest Whiptail

Kentropyx pelviceps

Size: Although adults occasionally exceed 14 inches (35 cm) in total length, most are between 9 and 11.5 inches (23–29 cm). The sexes are about equal in size. The tail length is about twice the SVL.

Identifying features: Despite their subtle colors, these forest speedsters are among the prettiest of lizards. They are dull in color when cold, inactive, or frightened, but few species can equal in beauty a thoroughly warmed and active whiptail. The broad middorsal stripe, scalloped along the edges, is bright greenish bronze on the snout and fades first to gold and then to obscurity as it progresses rearward. The head is brown, the limbs are tan, and an irregular brown stripe borders the middorsal stripe. Turquoise spots are present on the sides. The throat is gray, but the belly is salmon to pinkish tan. The rear toes are fringed.

Reproduction: Clutches consist of as many as six eggs, and several clutches may be laid annually.

Similar species: The Amazon whiptail lacks a middorsal line. The cocha whiptail is similar, but the middorsal line is often greener (it may occasionally be yellow) on that species and terminates more anteriorly than does the stripe of *K. pelviceps*. The dark dorsolateral stripes have even edges and are bordered ventrally by a thin light line.

Habitat/Range: This is a lizard of sunny spots on the forest floor, forest edges, and other similar habitats. It is much more closely associated with forest habitats than either the larger giant ameiva or the cocha whiptail. It is found in the western and central Amazon Basin.

Comments: This lizard swims well and can run quickly on the slick, muddy surfaces left by fluctuating water levels. It climbs well, too, and may be found in the trees during times of high water. Although it is primarily insectivorous, this lizard may also accept blossoms and other plant material.

Genus *Tupinambis;* Tegus

Of the five species in this genus, two are found in the Amazon Basin. Tegus are the largest predatory terrestrial lizards of the basin. They are common along many open forest trails and clearings, agricultural plots, near rainforest lodges, and at village edges. They lie-up in burrows in inclement weather or at night. Besides feeding on smaller animals, tegus also eat a considerable amount of vegetation.

The largest examples of the largest species attain an overall length of more than 3.5 feet (1 m). In addition to their notable length, tegus are heavy-bodied, big-headed, strong-jawed lizards. Although they usually move about on all fours, when startled they may run bipedally, forequarters lifted well away from the ground.

Tegus are diurnal and oviparous. Dark colors predominate on all except specimens from the driest chaco habitats.

192. Black and White Tegu

Tupinambis merianae

Size: This hulking lizard may near 4 feet (1.2 m) in total length. The tail comprises about two-thirds of the total.

Identifying features: Adults are variably patterned in black and white, usually with a well-defined longitudinal black shoulder stripe. There is a tendency for adult males from drier savannas to have more white on their heads than tegus from wetter habitats. This is a heavy-bodied lizard. Adult males develop huge, pendulous jowls. The jaws have immense strength. Hatchlings are tinged with lime green dorsally but are otherwise colored and patterned much like the adults.

Reproduction: Females lay from 15 to more than 30 eggs. Incubation seems to be in the vicinity of three and a half months. Hatchlings are about 8 inches (20 cm) in total length.

Similar species: The golden tegu is black and gold rather than black and white and usually lacks a well-defined black shoulder stripe.

Habitat/Range: Trail edges, village environs, open woodlands, well-drained hills, and slopes are all home to this huge lizard. It is also found in forested habitats but is associated therein with areas of patchy sunlight. The species occurs from the southern Amazon Basin southward to Argentina.

193. Golden Tegu

Tupinambis teguixin

Size: This is the largest primarily terrestrial lizard of the northern Amazon Basin. Adults can be more than 3 feet (95 cm) in total length, of which just under two-thirds is tail.

Identifying features: Tegus are dark (deep brown to black) lizards with a variably intense and intricate pattern of light to dark golden yellow. Some populations are black and white, and a few are black and bluish white. The light coloration is usually arranged in uneven-edged rings from nape to tail tip. The dark head is variably reticulated with gold. There is often a dark horizontal ocular stripe. A black shoulder stripe of variable prominence is present. The limbs are often heavily patterned with gold. The dorsal and lateral scales are smooth and shiny and more or less of the same size. The nonkeeled, cream-colored ventral scales are larger and arranged in longitudinal rows.

Reproduction: Females lay 4–12 (occasionally more) eggs. These apparently undergo a diapause after being laid, which results in a lengthy (five–seven-month) incubation.

Similar species: None. This is the only big, gold-reticulated black lizard in the region. The aquatic (greenish or olive brown) caiman lizard and the great green iguana are the only other lizards here that equal or exceed an adult tegu in size.

Habitat/Range: This is a lizard of all kinds of habitats, from openings and pond edges in primary forests to agricultural areas. When not basking or hunting, the tegu often seeks seclusion in a burrow. This powerful predator ranges throughout most of the northern half of South America.

Comments: The golden tegu is both a powerful predator and an opportunistic feeder that accepts both animal and vegetable matter.

11

Snakes

Snakes: Suborder Serpentes

The Amazon Basin is blessed with a remarkable diversity of snake species. These run the gamut from the small to the large (actually, to the *huge*), from the drab to the gaudy, and from the innocuous to the potentially deadly. They may be encountered in villages, in lakes, in clearings, and in rainforest. They live in trees, on the surface of the ground, in the water, and in burrows. In short, snakes are almost everywhere. But, paradoxically, snakes are also among the very hardest of the basin's herpetofauna to find.

Representatives of eight snake families may be encountered in the Amazon Basin. All of the species in two families—the Elapidae (coral snakes) and the Viperidae (pit vipers)—must be considered dangerously venomous. In addition, several colubrine species have venom of undetermined potency.

The members of three burrowing families—the Anomalepidae, the Leptotyphlopidae, and the Typhlopidae—are so tiny, so confusingly similar in external appearance, and so seldom encountered that we make only cursory mention of them. All lack functional external eyes and enlarged belly scales.

The coral pipesnake (family Aniliidae) has functional eyes but only slightly enlarged ventral scales.

The boa constrictor and its relatives (family Boidae) vary in size and habits. Two species found in the Amazon Basin are extensively arboreal, and most of the others can climb well. The boa constrictor is perhaps the most readily recognized snake of Amazonia. The green anaconda is extensively aquatic. Adults reach a size at least equal to—and a weight far greater than—any other snake found in the region.

The majority of the snakes found in this region belong to the very diverse family Colubridae. Although members of this family are often called "harmless snakes," that can be a misnomer. The saliva of some species with nonspecialized teeth contains toxic enzymes, and other species with enlarged teeth in the rear of the upper jaw ("rear fangs") produce toxins of unknown virulence. Humans' reactions to the bites of "harmless" snakes can be quite diverse. For instance in the United States, the bite of the common garter snake can cause reddening of the skin and intense itching in some people, and no reaction other than bleeding in others. Use care when approaching—and especially when handling—all snakes.

When a snake's length is stated, it is total length.

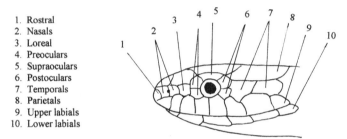

1. Rostral
2. Nasals
3. Loreal
4. Preoculars
5. Supraoculars
6. Postoculars
7. Temporals
8. Parietals
9. Upper labials
10. Lower labials

Pipesnakes: Family Aniliidae

According to the classification in Zug, Vitt, and Caldwell's *Herpetology,* this is a monotypic family. The single member is referred to as the coral pipesnake because of its color and the fact that it is cylindrical in cross section. The single representative of the family, *Anilius scytale,* is restricted in distribution to the Neotropics. It feeds primarily on the worm lizards of the family Amphisbaenidae but may accept caecilians as well.

Genus *Anilius;* Coral Pipesnake

The single species in this genus is a beautifully colored burrowing serpent with a specialized diet. It is often referred to as a coral snake mimic. The coral pipesnake is not often seen because of its persistent burrowing, and actual population densities at a given location are almost impossible to estimate. The species ranges southward from the northern-tier countries of South America to Brazil and Peru.

194. Coral Pipesnake

Anilius scytale scytale

Size: Adults may reach a total length of 3 feet (91 cm).

Identifying features: This beautiful, shiny, red and black–ringed snake might be mistaken for a coral snake. The snout is short and, when viewed from above, bluntly rounded. The tail is short and rather blunt tipped. The eyes are proportionally small and are covered by a transparent, irregularly edged scale rather than the normal specialized, rounded brille. The black rings may be entire, divided laterally, or offset vertebrally; or two otherwise separate rings may join vertebrally. The ventral scutes are only slightly widened.

Reproduction: This ovoviviparous species gives birth to one to three (perhaps more) large babies.

Similar species: The irregular scale covering the eye is diagnostic but difficult to determine if the snake is not in hand.

Habitat/Range: The coral pipesnake inhabits leaf litter or burrows. It makes its own burrow and does not inhabit other species' burrows. It is most common in primary forests but is occasionally found in recently cleared areas. In its overall distribution, the species seems restricted to regions of relatively high rainfall.

Thread Snakes: Family Leptotyphlopidae

Blind Snakes: Family Typhlopidae

These burrowing snakes are confusingly similar. To identify them to family it is necessary to check the positions and number of the teeth, something that is better done in the lab than in the field. Here we do no more than mention the identifying characteristics of each *family*.

195. Blind Snakes: Families Leptotyphlopidae and Typhlopidae

Size: Blind snakes may be only 3 inches (7.5 cm) long and as thin as a string, more than twice that size and a little heavier proportionally, or anywhere in between.

Identifying features: As a group, the slender blind snakes tend to be pinkish or light brown. Some species may be pinkish brown, but many are the color of dark earth. The lower jaw is countersunk, perhaps as an adaptation to facilitate burrowing. All of the species in these families lack functional eyes and have enlarged rostral scales to help them burrow. They have short tails and lack enlarged ventral scales.

The leptotyphlopids lack teeth in the upper jaw, and the maxillary bones are fused to the skull.

The typhlopids have no teeth in the lower jaw. The tooth arrangement can be checked only in dead specimens.

Reproduction: The leptotyphlopids are oviparous. Both egg-laying and live-bearing species of typhlopids are known. The reproductive biology of most Amazonian species is unknown.

Similar species: All of the small colubrines in the region have functional eyes. The amphisbaenids have scales arranged in annuli. Caecilians have slimy skin with no scales.

Habitat/Range: These burrowing snakes may be encountered in well-drained forest glades, clearing edges, beneath fallen trunks or other vegetational debris, or, rarely, in hollow twigs. They eat termites, ant pupae, and, more rarely, other small insects and their larvae.

Boas: Family Boidae

At least seven species of this family are found in Amazonas. Many tourists are already familiar with the various boas through television or the pet trade, as most are showy and are coveted by hobbyists. All are powerful constrictors. Infrared heat–sensory pits are present in the labial (lip) scales. Two species are essentially terrestrial, two are primarily arboreal, and one is aquatic.

The green anaconda (often called the water boa) is the longest of the New World snakes, and because of its immense girth has more body mass than any other living snake. Lengths in excess of 30 feet (10 m) have been reported for this aquatic giant.

The common (also called the red-tailed) boa and the Peruvian rainbow boa are the two essentially terrestrial forms. Both can, and do, climb well and will bite readily if carelessly restrained.

The Amazon tree boa is the more common of the two arboreal species. The strikingly beautiful emerald tree boa is seldom found, but this may be more because of its remarkably effective camouflage than a reflection of true rarity.

The boids are considered primitive snakes. All bear remnants of a pelvic girdle and external vestiges of the rear limbs in the form of spurs. The spurs are larger on males than on females and are used in precopulatory courtship.

It would seem that of the various species, the Amazon tree boa is the most frequently seen. It is often found on night walks, generally in trees along the edges of forest creeks, and especially in emergent trees in still-flooded oxbows.

Genus *Boa;* Common Boas

Only a single well-subspeciated species occurs in the Neotropics. It has recently been suggested that the Madagascar boas, long classified in sister genera, are also members of this genus. The Neotropical *Boa*s have been so popularized by the pet industry that they are often referred to *the* boa. This species and the related anacondas are the snakes that Neotropical rainforest ecotourists most wish, and expect, to see.

In one subspecies or another, the boa ranges from Mexico south to Argentina. The races at the northern and southern extremes of the range are the darkest. Those from the rainforests have the lightest ground color, the most contrasting dorsal and lateral markings, and the most brightly colored tail.

196. Red-Tailed Boa (Constrictor)

Boa constrictor constrictor

Size: This heavy-bodied snake attains a length of more than 8 feet (2.4 m).
Identifying features: The red-tailed boa epitomizes to all ecotourists the very essence of the Amazon. Babies are often offered for sale by street vendors in Iquitos, and at least one (usually large) specimen is kept for photo purposes in most tourist-oriented villages. The saddles are tan or gray anteriorly, darkening to reddish brown or maroon posteriorly; thus the common name "red-tailed boa." The dark bands are deeper brown anteriorly, paling to cream or off-white posteriorly. A dark longitudinal mid-cranial stripe, narrowest on the snout, extends onto the neck. A dark stripe, even-edged on top but often uneven below, is present on each side of the head. Despite the richness of its coloration—or perhaps because of it—the boa blends remarkably well with the fallen leaves on the forest floor.

Reproduction: Females may produce more than two dozen live babies. The largest and healthiest females produce the largest clutches, but not necessarily the largest neonates.

Similar species: It would be difficult to mistake this supple, heavy-bodied constrictor for any other snake. The maroon tail and tan anterior saddles are quite distinctive.

Habitat/Range: *Boa constrictor constrictor* occurs in both primary forest and disturbed areas, and individuals are often found near brush piles at the edges of cleared agricultural plots. This form ranges throughout the Amazon Basin.

Comments: Although seldom seen, boas are not uncommon in the Iquitos region. Their cryptic colors and quiet demeanor allow most to avoid detection. These boas are quite capable of climbing but are most often encountered on the ground. Some will strike savagely when approached while others are complacent and good-natured. Although boa skins, and occasionally live baby boas, are still offered for sale in the marketplaces of many villages, boas are now a protected species. Do not purchase these snakes or any parts thereof. In bygone years, boas were collected in the Iquitos region in considerable numbers for the pet trade.

197. Common Boa (Constrictor)

Boa constrictor imperator

Size: This heavy-bodied snake routinely attains a length of 6–8 feet (1.8–2.4 m) and occasionally exceeds 10 feet (3 m).

Identifying features: Readily recognized and eagerly sought, this race of the boa is common but seldom seen. The saddles are tan or gray anteriorly darkening to reddish gray or reddish brown on the tail. The dark bands are deep brown and most complete anteriorly, and pale to cream or off-white posteriorly. A dark longitudinal mid-cranial stripe, narrowest on the snout, extends onto the anterior neck; dark extensions often reach to the eyes. A dark postocular bar is present, as is a moderately dark preocular triangle. This snake blends remarkably well with the forest and savanna backgrounds against which it is often seen. Savanna specimens tend to be less vibrantly colored than those from the rainforest.

Reproduction: This large viviparous snake may produce more than two dozen babies.

Similar species: It would be difficult to mistake this supple, heavy-bodied constrictor for any snake other than the more richly colored red-tailed boa. The latter, which ranges farther south, usually has a maroon rather than brownish red tail and lacks extensions to the eyes from the mid-cranial stripe.

Habitat/Range: *Boa constrictor imperator* occurs in secondary forests and disturbed areas and is often found near brush piles at the edges of cleared agricultural plots. It ranges widely through northern Latin America to the northern Amazon Basin.

Genus *Corallus;* Tree Boas

Although they are occasionally encountered on the ground, the members of this genus are essentially arboreal. All are compressed laterally and are powerful constrictors. The tree boas seem perpetually ready to bite, and their long teeth leave painful wounds. Younger tree boas eat treefrogs and arboreal lizards; adults round out their diet with birds and small arboreal mammals. Despite their intolerance for being handled, Amazon and emerald tree boas have long been kept and bred by herpetoculturists and are eagerly sought for zoological displays. The several species in this genus (two occur in the Amazon Basin) range from northern Central America south to Brazil. They also occur on the Windward Islands.

Although they may stray far from water, tree boas seem most common (or are at least most commonly seen) along the perimeters of watercourses or in trees emerging from flooded areas.

198. Emerald Tree Boa

Corallus caninus

Size: Adults range in size from 4.5 to 6 feet (1.4–1.8 m).

Identifying features: This beautiful arboreal constrictor undergoes extensive ontogenetic changes. Neonates are *usually* terra cotta dorsally (more rarely pale green, brownish, or calico) with a broken to complete (but rarely absent) enamel white middorsal stripe with a series of well-separated, short lateral extensions. With growth, the dorsal ground color usually fades to yellow-green, then pale green, and finally intensifies to bright leaf green. Variations on this theme are known. The white markings (if present) remain constant throughout the snake's life. Variable amounts of black interstitial (the skin between the scales) coloration is often present dorsally. This may highlight the white dorsal markings. Small, discrete patches of black may be present on subadults. The venter is white to yellow and the iris is yellowish. The body is laterally compressed. All the labial scales have heat-sensory pits.

Reproduction: Females bear small clutches (5–12, rarely more) of live young.

Similar species: None. Other green arboreal snakes lack labial pits and a white vertebral pattern. Amazon tree boas, *Corallus hortulanus*, are never green and do not have the white vertebral stripe. The venomous forest pit viper *Bothriopsis bilineata smaragdina* lacks a white vertebral stripe and has only a single sensory pit on each side of the face, above the labials and between the eye and the nostril.

Habitat/Range: Although it occasionally descends to the ground, the emerald tree boa is more typically arboreal. It occurs in primary and secondary forests, often at the edges of clearings or tree falls. Emerald tree boas are found throughout most of the Amazon Basin.

Comments: Birds and small arboreal mammals seem to be the favored prey of adults. Juveniles may add lizards and amphibians to the diet. These snakes usually do not hesitate to bite.

Although no subspecies are scientifically recognized, hobbyist breeders of this spectacular snake differentiate between the Amazon Basin form and the more northerly form based on the degree of fragmentation of the crown scales.

199. Amazon Tree Boa

Corallus hortulanus

Size: This snake commonly attains a length of 5 feet (1.5 m), and occasional adults are considerably longer. Its size is often underestimated because of its slenderness and propensity for keeping its body in gentle curves when prowling the treetops or rather tightly coiled when resting draped on a branch.

Identifying features: The body is laterally compressed, and the color is very variable. The most commonly seen color phases are pearl gray to olive green and may be nearly unicolored or prominently saddled. Brick red and bright to pale yellow phases can also be found, and combinations of all of these colors occur as well. The iris color is nearly as variable as the ground color. Heat-sensory pits are present in the posterior labials of both upper and lower jaws.

Reproduction: Females produce clutches of five to more than a dozen live young. A given clutch may include a kaleidoscope of colorations. Although most Amazon tree boas will not hesitate to bite when disturbed, gravid females tend to have dispositions even more unpleasant than normal. The teeth are long, and the strike distance can be considerable.

Similar species: No other similarly colored arboreal snake in the region is a powerful constrictor or has labial pits.

Habitat/Range: In suitable habitats Amazon tree boas can be quite common. They may be encountered in any patch of primary or secondary forest, but are most often seen by ecotourists at night in trees along rivers and oxbows. They move easily through interlacing canopies and are often found in more or less isolated copses well out in flooded oxbows. These boas swim well and are also occasionally seen on the ground. Amazon tree boas may be encountered throughout the northern and eastern Amazon Basin.

Comments: This species was long known scientifically as *Corallus enydris*.

Genus *Epicrates;* Rainbow and West Indian Boas

These small to large boas are most speciated in the Bahamas and West Indies. They vary in size from the yard-long, very slender and graceful *E. gracilis* of Hispaniola to the hulking 12-foot-long Cuban boa, *E. angulifer*. Some insular forms are endangered. The moderate-sized (6–8 feet) rainbow boa, considered to be a single strongly subspeciated species by most authorities, is the mainland representative of the genus. The (approximately) nine races of this snake, named for the shimmering opalescence of the scales in the sunlight, range from Costa Rica south to Argentina.

Juvenile rainbow boas accept frogs and lizards as well as endothermic (warm-blooded) prey. Adults seem to prefer endothermic prey but may also accept large lizards.

Several races of this powerful constrictor are bred in captivity, among them the Colombian, Brazilian, Peruvian, and Argentine forms.

Rainbow boas are often encountered on forest trails, in trail edge shrubs, and in agricultural plots. They are primarily terrestrial but are not at all hesitant to climb or swim.

Rainbow boas undergo considerable individual day–night color changes. Many become quite pale at night, especially on the flanks. Heat-sensory pits are present in the anterior labials of both jaws.

200. Brazilian Rainbow Boa

Epicrates cenchria cenchria

Size: Adults range in total length from 6 to 7 feet (1.8–2 m).

Identifying features: The Brazilian rainbow boas bear rounded, dark-edged, orange to orange-brown middorsal saddles against a ground color of opalescent gray to pale orange. The flanks are lighter, often silvery gray, gray, or pale brown. There are two rows of dark lateral spots; each spot in the top row has a light half-moon in the upper third. Five dark longitudinal stripes appear on the head: two laterally (which pass through the bottom of the eye), two dorsolaterally, and one centrally.

Reproduction: Females produce 6 to more than 20 live babies. Larger females have larger clutches of larger babies.

Similar species: The Peruvian rainbow boa, *E. cenchria gaigei*, lacks the light spots in the lateral ocelli. See the account for that species, below.

Habitat/Range: These constrictors occur in secondary and primary forests in both terrestrial and arboreal situations, on trail edges, and at forested edges of newly cleared agricultural plots. They are found in the eastern Amazon Basin.

201. Peruvian Rainbow Boa

Epicrates cenchria gaigei

Size: Adults reach 5–6.5 feet (1.5–2 m).

Identifying features: The rainbow boas in the western part of the Amazon Basin are remarkably beautiful. They are similar to the Brazilian race, but the lateral ocelli lack light centers. The dorsal ground color may be opalescent gray to pale orange. There are rounded, dark-edged, orange to orange-brown middorsal saddles against a variably darker ground color. The flanks are lighter, often silvery gray, gray, or pale brown. There are two rows of dark lateral spots. Five dark longitudinal stripes appear on the head: two laterally (which pass through the bottom of the eye), two dorsolaterally, and one centrally.

Reproduction: Females produce 6–20 or more live babies. Larger females have larger clutches of larger babies.

Similar species: *Epicrates cenchria cenchria* has light half-moons in the lateral ocelli; see the account for that species, above.

Habitat/Range: Rainbow boas occupy terrestrial and arboreal situations in secondary and primary forests as well as clearings. They are sometimes encountered on trail edges and forest edges in agricultural plots. The range of this race includes lowland regions of eastern Peru and western Bolivia.

Comments: Although their dispositions vary, most wild specimens are ready and willing to bite. Many of the rainbow boas found in Peruvian Amazonia appear intermediate between the Peruvian and the Brazilian races.

Genus *Eunectes;* Anacondas

At least two species in this genus vie for the title of world's longest and heaviest snake. They have no equal among extant snakes in weight and girth. The green anaconda occasionally attains a length of 25 feet (7.5 m) (anecdotal reports claim lengths of 34–37.5 feet [10–11.5 m]!) and may weigh well in excess of 400 pounds. The Old World reticulated python may equal the largest anacondas in length but is comparatively more slender.

The anacondas are often collectively referred to as water boas. The forest folk know them as *boas negras* (black boas) because of their predominantly dark green color.

The four (up to six, according to some authorities) anaconda species are firmly associated with aquatic habitats from Venezuela and Colombia to Argentina. The green anaconda is the predominant species in the Amazon Basin.

202. Green Anaconda

Eunectes murinus murinus

Size: Adults usually reach 6–15 feet (2–5 m). With a reported maximum of more than 30 feet (10 m), this is unquestionably the largest *and* heaviest snake of the region.

Identifying features: The ground color is variable but darkest dorsally. Cold anacondas seem darker than optimally warm ones, and they are darker by day than by night. The dorsal ground color is olive drab to dull but distinct olive green. Paired or alternating large black oval spots extend from the neck to the tail tip. The ground color pales laterally, becoming a light olive. Dark-edged peach spots are visible ventrolaterally. These are brightest and most prominent on juvenile specimens. Peach spots lacking a dark edging are present on the sides of the neck. The top of the head is dark; the sides of the head are lighter, and a black stripe extends diagonally downward from the eye to a point just posterior to the head.

Reproduction: Like other Neotropical boas, the anaconda is a live-bearer, with larger females producing larger clutches of larger babies. Clutches of 8–35 seem normal, but some containing more than 50 young have been documented. Neonates are heavy bodied and often exceed 30 inches (75 cm) in length.

Similar species: None.

Habitat/Range: This riverine and oxbow species seems invariably associated with water. Water boas are often seen with one or more coils exposed, resting on anchored logs or vegetation or on exposed banks. The species occurs throughout the Amazon drainage.

Comments: The green anaconda usually resists familiarity by biting. Some can be intimidating when approached. A person alone should not approach a large anaconda. Size is subjective here, but I use a length of 8 feet (2.5 m) as my upper limit.

Harmless Snakes: Family Colubridae

This large and varied assemblage of snakes is badly in need of critical evaluation by systematists/taxonomists. At present the Colubridae includes a number of subfamilies, most of which, by today's standards, could probably be elevated to full family status.

It is impossible to make sweeping generalities about the colubrine snakes. Even the popularly assigned common name, "harmless snakes," is erroneous. Some rear-fanged species (with grooved teeth in the rear of their upper jaws) are known to be venomous, and others, although lacking specialized venom-carrying teeth, are known to have toxic saliva. Bites from snake species in the subfamilies Boiginae (the rear-fanged or opisthoglyphid snakes) and Natricinae (the garter and water snakes and allies) in Africa and Asia have caused human fatalities, and people bitten by species in other subfamilies have suffered toxic reactions. The toxic potential of many of these snakes remains unknown. Because of this we urge extreme caution when handling them.

Among the colubrine snakes are persistent arborealists, aquatic species, fossorial forms, and many with "normal" terrestrial habits, as well as nocturnal, diurnal, and crepuscular species. The species we discuss here depict an excellent cross section of the Amazon Basin colubrines. Some are easily identified; others present more of a challenge. For those requiring specialized identification processes such as counting scale rows, lip scales, and other such exacting comparative features, it will be necessary to have the snake in hand. Again, we urge extreme caution when handling all!

Genus *Atractus;* Earth Snakes

The small to medium-sized snakes of this huge genus vary from plain-colored species to those brightly ringed in black, red, and white; add to this equation polymorphism and occasional melanism, and the sum is potential confusion. While some species are easily differentiated, attempting to identify others can be an exercise in futility. This is especially true of the many nearly uniformly colored leaf litter forms.

These are fossorial snakes. Some seem content to root about in damp ground litter; others burrow into the earth. Most species eat earthworms. The approximately 70 species range from Costa Rica south to Brazil.

203. Wedge-Tailed Earth Snake

Atractus latifrons

Size: Adults are just over 2 feet (61 cm) long.
Identifying features: This remarkably beautiful small-headed, tricolored snake is brightest when young. Old adults may become suffused with black pigmentation and dull perceptibly in coloration. Some specimens may lack most or all of the white (or pale yellow) rings. The scales are in 17 rows, noteworthy when trying to differentiate this species from the ornate earth snake, *A. elaps*.
Reproduction: Three to six eggs seem to be the normal clutch size.
Similar species: *Atractus elaps* differs from this species in having only 15 scale rows and a more variable pattern, with the black rings containing either one, two, or three white rings—often on the same snake. When patterns vary, the anterior black rings usually contain fewer white rings than the posterior black rings. Consider also the calico snakes (genus *Oxyrhopus*), the false coral snake (genus *Erythrolamprus*), and the various coral snakes (genus *Micrurus*). The bands of *Xenopholis scalaris* are separated dorsally by a red vertebral stripe.
Habitat/Range: We have found this species in newly cleared areas bordered by primary forest and along forest trails. Most were seen following heavy rains. It is probable that this species is a leaf litter dweller in primary forests in the northwestern Amazon Basin.
Comments: Although *Atractus latifrons* is innocuous, do not handle any ringed snake before ascertaining its identification.

204. Collared Earth Snake

Atractus species cf. *collaris*

Size: Adults attain an overall length of about 8 inches (20 cm).
Identifying features: This undescribed species is remarkably similar to *A. collaris* in appearance. It is olive gray to slate gray or olive brown dorsally. A broad, light nuchal collar is present. The belly is coral red. Some specimens may display seven lighter longitudinal dorsal pinstripes.

Reproduction: The normal clutch size seems to be two or three eggs.

Similar species: Because of the similarity to *A. collaris*, it may be best simply to refer to these snakes as a species complex.

Habitat/Range: The collared earth snake seems most abundant in agricultural clearings and may also be found along the edges of trails, particularly when the ground is sodden. Those we found were active in the late afternoon and evening in Amazonian Peru.

205. White-Naped Earth Snake

Atractus species

Size: Adults may reach a length of about 15 inches (37.5 cm).

Identifying features: The scales are smooth and in 17 rows. The anal scale is normally not divided. The bellies vary from light to dark in a series found along the Rio Apiyacu in Peru's Departamento Loreto. If the belly is light, small dark spots are usually discernible and are most prominent posteriorly. The dorsal coloration is quite variable. Many specimens have a grayish ground color with reddish brown cross bands that are narrowly bordered with black. Advancing age usually brings with it a suffusion of melanin. Examples not yet suffused with melanin have a large white triangle on each side of the nape. The nose is rather sharply pointed. The preocular scale is about twice as long as it is high.

Reproduction: One 15-inch (38-cm) female found at trailside in primary forest along Peru's Rio Orosa contained four fully formed eggs. Other than this the reproductive biology is unknown to us.

Similar species: It is usually quite easy to designate the various *Atractus* forms to genus, but individual and age-related color and pattern variations make assigning them to species more difficult.

Habitat/Range: This snake may be found in a wide variety of habitats. It occupies primary and secondary forest situations, village edges, and agricultural plots. The exact range is unknown.

206. Rusty Earth Snake

Atractus torquatus

Size: Adults reach a total length of 14 inches (35 cm).

Identifying features: Although this is another of the earth snakes with a neck ring, the ring may be quite difficult to discern. Many specimens are a nearly uniform buff terra cotta dorsally. If you look closely, you can usually see some traces of well-separated dark dorsal markings. The belly is light—creamy yellow rather than bright yellow. At least one posterior upper labial scale may be a rather bright yellow. The scales are in 17 rows at midbody.

Reproduction: Clutches contain two to three eggs.

Similar species: Rusty earth snakes may be difficult to identify (see lead-in comments). The specimen of *A. torquatus* depicted herein is quite typical of the species. Compare your specimen with this photograph.

Habitat/Range: We found this burrowing snake along a wet path through primary forest following a rather lengthy rainstorm. The species is widely distributed (Bolivia, Peru, Colombia, and Brazil) in the Amazon Basin.

Genus *Chironius;* Whipsnakes

These fast, alert, big-eyed snakes are most often seen on the ground, in brush tangles, and low in shrubs. They often sleep at night a dozen or so feet up in small trees. They are typified by few (10–12) rows of large scales and a slender build. Most are quietly colored in hues of olive tan, olive brown, or olive green, and have yellow(ish) venters. A few undergo age-related color changes—from bright green hatchlings to brownish/reddish adults.

The genus comprises 13 species, some of which, because of overlapping characteristics, are confusingly similar and may require scale (or tooth) counts to differentiate.

All species in the genus are oviparous. Some specimens will bite readily when restrained, while others will indulge in a series of false strikes but will not actually bite. Frogs and lizards are the preferred prey.

Collectively, the species in this genus range from Honduras south to northeastern Argentina.

207. Common Whipsnake

Chironius exoletus

Size: Adults commonly attain a length of about 4.25 feet (1.3 m).

Identifying features: Both the anterior body and the midbody have 12 rows of scales; there are 8 rows posteriorly. The paravertebral rows are keeled. The anal plate is divided. Ventral scutes number between 123 and 162. Adult coloration is dusky olive green to olive brown dorsally. A brownish vertebral stripe is not usually present. The belly is variably yellow but brightest anteriorly. Juveniles tend to be darker (browner) than adults dorsally, and brighter yellow ventrally. Narrow, light-edged, but poorly defined cross bands are usually discernible. Cheeks are yellow.

Reproduction: One female being held temporarily for photography produced 5 infertile eggs. Up to 12 eggs have been documented.

Similar species: *Chironius carinatus* and *C. multiventris* are very similar but have different ventral scute counts. Other species of this genus in Peruvian Amazonia have a single anal plate.

Habitat/Range: This wide-ranging, adaptable snake may be encountered in secondary and primary forests as well as in clearings and agricultural areas. It is most often seen on or near the ground but has also been found in arboreal situations. It readily takes to the water and is frequently seen crossing forest rivers. *Chironius exoletus* (and other members of this genus) are often seen sleeping at night, loosely coiled, in small trees. The species ranges from Costa Rica south to Bolivia and southern Brazil.

Comments: The members of this genus can be difficult to identify. Consider all characters carefully.

208. Olive Whipsnake

Chironius fuscus

Size: This slender and very active snake is adult at about 5 feet (1.5 m) in total length.

Identifying features: The dorsal ground color is brownish black, gray, brown, olive, or dirty green. The belly is yellow. There may or may not be a dark postorbital bar. Body scales are in 10 rows; the scales in the paravertebral rows are keeled. The prominent cross bands of the juveniles are occasionally retained well into adulthood. A light vertebral stripe is usually present.

Reproduction: Five to 11 eggs seem to constitute an average clutch. Incubation duration is about 60 days. Hatchling size is unknown, but a juvenile found on the Rio Apayacu measured just over 13 inches (32.5 cm) in length.

Similar species: This is one of the more difficult species to identify, especially as certain criteria continue to change. Compare the accounts for *Chironius exoletus* and *C. scurrulus*.

Habitat/Range: The olive whipsnake is a common semiarboreal species in primary and secondary forests throughout most of the Amazon Basin—throughout much of the northern half of South America, in fact. Individuals may be found in small trees after dark sleeping loosely coiled across slender branches. They are often terrestrially active during the hours of daylight.

209. Rusty Whipsnake

Chironius scurrulus

Size: Adults average about 4.5 feet (1.3 m), although lengths greater than 6 feet (1.8 m) are known.

Identifying features: This pretty, slender, fast-moving snake undergoes extensive ontogenetic changes. Hatchlings are leaf green, but the color darkens with growth. Adults are deep brown to mahogany red, the head often being a shade or two darker than the body. Darker flecks may be present both dorsally and laterally. This snake has only 10 scale rows, and the paravertebral scales (the scales to each side of the middorsal line) are *not* keeled.

Reproduction: Clutch sizes ranging from 8 to 18 eggs have been reported. Incubation duration is about 60 days. A juvenile 14 inches (35 cm) in total length found in eastern Peru bore a healed umbilical scar, indicating it was a relatively recent hatchling.

Similar species: Although several of the species in this genus can be difficult to identify, the color and body scalation of this one afford a reasonable degree of accuracy.

Habitat/Range: These semiarboreal snakes inhabit secondary and primary forest habitats, and may be found in small trees after dark sleeping loosely coiled across slender branches. They are often terrestrially active during the hours of daylight. The species is common throughout most of the Amazon Basin and ranges from the basin north to northern Venezuela.

Genus *Clelia;* Mussuranas

The snakes of this genus have rear fangs and are powerful constrictors as well. Several species undergo dramatic age-related color changes—from red babies to jet black adults. They are secretive and terrestrial. Mussuranas feed on small mammals, lizards, and other snakes, including venomous species—to whose venom they have considerable resistance.

The genus ranges from tropical Mexico south to Argentina. One race of the common mussurana occurs on some islands of the Lesser Antilles.

210. Common Mussurana

Clelia clelia clelia

Size: Adults of this heavy-bodied snake reach a total length of 6 or 7 feet (1.8–2 m).

Identifying features: Hatchlings and juveniles are as different from adults as day is from night. Young snakes have a red dorsum with a tiny black spot in each scale, a black head and nape, and a prominent yellow-white collar. The red coloration fades quickly with growth, and by the time the snake is 2.5 feet (75 cm) long it has become dull brownish black. Beyond that point it quickly assumes the solid olive black to jet black adult coloration. The white venter remains unchanged. There are 19 scale rows.

Reproduction: Clutches of up to 40 eggs have been reported, but the normal clutch size is 15–30.

Similar species: The big black adult mussuranas with their stark white venters are rather easily identified. Only the very slender *Drymoluber dichrous* is similar in color. *Drymoluber*, however, has only 15 scale rows, compared with the mussurana's 19. Three Amazonian species may be easily confused with the black-headed red mussurana babies. *Drepanoides anomalus* (15 scale rows) and *Pseudoboa coronata* (17 scale rows) both have a wider white collar that starts just posterior to the eyes rather than on the anterior nape. *Oxyrhopus formosus* has 19 scale rows like the mussurana, but has a white nose tip (this is black on the juvenile mussurana).

Habitat/Range: This interesting snake may be encountered in clearings and along swamps, ponds, and oxbows in primary and secondary forests. It does not hesitate to swim rivers and other bodies of water. Mussuranas occur from Guatemala southward to Argentina, including all of the Amazon Basin.

Comments: The mussurana is a rear-fanged, "mildly venomous" snake. The virulence of its venom on humans is unknown, but it would be prudent to avoid being bitten, especially by a large individual. It is a powerful constrictor that feeds opportunistically on other snakes (including venomous ones), lizards, ground birds, and, occasionally, small mammals.

Genus *Dendrophidion*; Forest Racers

The beginning point in species determination with this genus is with the subcaudal (the scales on the underside of the tail) count. If there are more than 175 rows, you have *D. dendrophis* in hand. Although counting sub-caudal rows may sound like a tedious but straightforward task, that is seldom the case. The tail of the snakes in this genus breaks off so easily that many specimens do not have a full tail. This, of course, thwarts all counting efforts.

The forest racers are moderately slender, big-eyed, alert, and fast. They are most often seen on the ground or in brush piles or shrub thickets, but they also climb reasonably well. They are diurnal. Amphibians and lizards are the primary food items.

This genus ranges from Mexico south to northern South America. Only one species is present in the Amazon Basin.

211. Tawny Forest Racer

Dendrophidion dendrophis

Size: This moderately slender snake exceeds 4 feet (1.2 m) in total length.
Identifying features: Despite its subtle colors, the tawny forest racer is one of the most beautiful snakes of the Neotropics. Once seen, it is usually long remembered. The predominant color is warm toffee, tawny brown, or coffee brown. More than 50 cross bands, yellowish tan anteriorly and dark brown posteriorly, separate the brown of the dorsum into discrete blotches. The venter is yellow, sometimes lighter (whitish) anteriorly. The interstitial skin is bright yellow. A broad, smooth supraocular scale protrudes outward, shading the top of each eye.
Reproduction: The females of this oviparous species lay a maximum of about a dozen eggs.
Similar species: The large hooded eyes, blotched pattern, and brilliant yellow interstitial skin separate this species from the many other arboreal snakes in the region.
Habitat/Range: Although *Dendrophidion* is considered a snake of the primary forests, the several specimens we have seen were asleep at night on pathside or riverside vegetation 6–8 feet (2–2.5 m) above the ground. Individuals may also be seen atop fallen trunks and on the leaf litter of the forest floor. The species occurs over much of the Amazon Basin and from there ranges northward into southern Central America.
Comments: The long, slender tail is easily broken due to the presence of caudal fracture planes. Although a broken tail heals quickly, regeneration does not occur.

Genus *Dipsas;* Snail-Eating Snakes

These small, supple, nocturnal snakes are often found as they prowl slowly through low shrubs and brush piles or amid grasses in search of their prey—snails and slugs. Some species are clad in tans and browns; others are quite vividly colored in black, tans, creams, and white. They have vertically elliptical pupils.

The snail eaters extract snails from their shells by first biting the exposed foot of the snail and then—often with the lower jaw at least partially in the snail's shell, and working each of the jawbones independently—slowly drawing the snail outward. The snakes of this genus lack a mental groove (the expandable groove separating the two sides of paired chin shields).

This genus of more than 30 species ranges from tropical Mexico south to Argentina.

212. Ornate Snail-Eating Snake

Dipsas catesbyi

Size: Adults reach a length of about 28 inches (70 cm).
Identifying features: This abundant arboreal snake is slender, but *not* vine slender. It has a rather narrow head, and like others in the genus, only 13 rows of scales; the vertebral row is widened. This species looks quite unlike either of the other *Dipsas* species in the region. The head is black with a (partial to complete) white ring around the nose and a prominent white nape ring. The dorsal ground color is rich reddish brown. There are very large, very deep brown, generally rounded lateral blotches, which are outlined with white. These dark blotches may or may not touch dorsally. The venter is white marked with longitudinal dark streaks and spots.
Reproduction: Clutches seem small, perhaps one to five eggs.
Similar species: Color alone will preclude mistaking this snake for any other in the region.
Habitat/Range: Ornate snail-eating snakes inhabit primary forests, secondary forests, and agricultural areas. They seem especially abundant at night in shrubs along the edges of forest streams but are known to climb high into the canopy as well seeking the snails and slugs on which they feed.

213. Big-Headed Snail-Eating Snake

Dipsas indica indica

Size: Adults of this uncommon species may be 3 feet (91 cm) in length.

Identifying features: This robust, thick-headed snail eater is the darkest of the genus in the western Amazon Basin and the only one of the three *Dipsas* species with a predominantly dark venter. The dorsum is gray or gray-brown with darker dorsal blotches that are in the form of triangles with their tops cut off. Most of these dark triangles have a light ventrolateral blotch at the base. The labials are light with dark vertical scale sutures.

Reproduction: Females lay two to six eggs per clutch.

Similar species: None. Throughout much of its extensive range this is the only predominantly dark snake with scales in 13 rows *and* a precisely delineated pattern.

Habitat/Range: This quietly pretty snake utilizes all types of forests. It is persistently arboreal, and individuals are often quite high in trees when they are spotted. The heavy head structure suggests that this species may eat larger snails than its congeners. It ranges over much of northern South America.

214. Variegated Snail-Eating Snake

Dipsas variegata variegata

Size: Adults reach about 3 feet (91 cm) in length.

Identifying features: This busily and imprecisely patterned snail eater has a gray or gray-brown dorsum with darker rings, and sometimes has a brownish overwash that is strongest vertebrally. The rings have uneven edges that are lined with lighter pigment. The labials are gray with dark vertical scale sutures. The venter is black and white. The scales are in 13 rows.

Reproduction: Females lay two to six eggs per clutch.

Similar species: The several tones of gray and the uneven-edged markings are quite diagnostic. Compare the *Dipsas indica* account, above.

Habitat/Range: This quietly colored nocturnal snake utilizes all types of forest habitats. It is persistently arboreal and individuals are often seen cruising slowly through bushes and trees. The species ranges from Venezuela to Amazonian eastern Peru and Amazonian Brazil. Although it is seldom seen, *Dipsas variegata variegata* may actually be more secretive than rare.

Comments: This snake is remarkably similar in color and pattern to *Sibon nebulata* (also a snail eater), of the northern Amazon Basin, but *Dipsas* differs by having labial scales all of the same height and by lacking a mental groove.

Genus *Drepanoides;* Amazon Egg-Eating Snake

The single species in this monotypic genus ranges from Bolivia north to Colombia. Like the North American scarlet snakes, this snake eats lizard eggs. Several other Amazonian species, among them juvenile common mussuranas (*Clelia*) and Amazon scarlet snakes (*Pseudoboa*), share the red body color and the black and white head. Little is known about the life history and reproductive biology of *Drepanoides*.

215. Amazon Egg-Eating Snake

Drepanoides anomalus

Size: The adult size of this uncommon snake is thought to be about 22 inches (54 cm).

Identifying features: Very little is known about this beautiful little snake. The head is black from the tip of the snout to a point just posterior to the eyes, where a *broad*, creamy white collar rings the neck. This is followed by more black, but the nape quickly assumes the red coloration of the rest of the back and sides. A tiny black spot appears on the posterior edge of each scale, forming a netlike pattern. The venter, including chin and tail, is creamy white. The scales are in 15 rows.

Reproduction: Unknown.

Similar species: Hatchling mussuranas have black heads from the tip of the snout to the nape and have 19 scale rows. *Oxyrhopus formosus* has 19 rows of scales and a white-tipped nose. *Pseudoboa coronata* has a single subcaudal scale (it is divided in all look-alikes) and 17 scale rows.

Habitat/Range: Most Amazon egg-eating snakes found have been in clearings associated with primary rainforests. We found a single specimen crossing a newly paved section of the under-construction Iquitos–Nauta highway.

Comments: This species is thought to prey on lizard eggs.

Genus *Drymarchon;* Cribos and Indigo Snakes

Although this genus is currently under evaluation, we continue to consider it to consist of a single species with eight subspecies that range from Florida and Texas south to Argentina. Only the southernmost race, the huge, heavy-bodied, yellow-tailed cribo, is found in the Amazon Basin.

The scales are smooth and shiny. These big, fast-moving, and alert snakes are quite capable of catching and overpowering many kinds of prey, ectothermic and endothermic. The lack of both constriction capability and venom seems to be no hindrance. The cribo strikes and grasps the prey in its jaws, throws a loop of its body over the prey to hold it still, and swallows its meal alive.

216. Yellow-Tailed Cribo

Drymarchon corais corais

Size: Adults can exceed 7 feet (2 m) in length, and some measuring more than 8.5 feet (2.5 m) have been recorded.

Identifying features: This immense, fast, alert snake rapidly coils into a striking S if cornered and does not hesitate to bite. The head and anterior portion of the body are olive, olive brown, to olive gray. Dark lines radiate from each eye. The body color fades progressively from head to tail, and by midbody is taking on an olive yellow to yellow hue. The tail of some specimens is bright yellow.

Reproduction: Females lay 4–11 eggs per clutch. Hatchlings are 15–20 inches (38–51 cm) in length.

Similar species: The mussurana (*Clelia clelia*) equals the cribo in size but is all black dorsally. *Drymoluber dichrous* also lacks the yellow posterior, and is smaller and much slenderer.

Habitat/Range: This relative of the North American indigo snake is a species of secondary forest openings, agricultural areas, and other clearings. It can climb but seems to be essentially terrestrial. Widespread throughout South America.

Comments: Like the indigo snake, the cribo is an opportunistic feeder, eating other reptiles, amphibians, birds, and small mammals.

Genus *Drymoluber;* Glossy Racers

Of the two species in this genus, only *D. dichrous* is widespread in the Amazon Basin. These are fast, alert snakes of thickets and open woodlands. The 15 rows of scales are unkeeled. Vision appears to be acute. Glossy racers are capable of climbing but are most often seen on or near the ground. They feed primarily on lizards but also eat frogs. They are oviparous, but as is the case with many Amazonian herpetofauna, surprisingly little is known about their breeding biology.

217. Common Glossy Racer

Drymoluber dichrous

Size: Although most adults seen are in the 30–36-inch (75–90-cm) size range, occasional examples may near 48 inches (120 cm) in total length.
Identification: The age-related color and pattern changes are dramatic. Juveniles are gray to brown with about 40 light gray-white cross bands. The sides of the face and the central nape are also light. In older animals the color becomes uniform shiny brown, greenish brown, or nearly black. The venter, upper lips, and sides of the neck are rich cream to bright yellow. The scales are smooth (unkeeled), and the anal plate is entire.
Reproduction: Other than the fact that it is oviparous, very little is known about the breeding biology. A 34-inch-long (86-cm) female contained four posterior bulges that appeared to be eggs.
Similar species: Adult *Chironius scurrulus* are rust colored but have only 10–12 scale rows. *Liophis reginae* has a yellow and black–checked belly. *Pseustes poecilonotus* has 19 scale rows; *Mastigodryas boddaertii* has 17 scale rows.
Habitat/Range: This species is widespread in the northern Amazon Basin in both secondary and primary forests, and is most often seen along trail or clearing edges. The species ranges from Colombia and Venezuela south to eastern Peru and northern Brazil.
Comments: This alert, diurnal snake seems to use visual cues when foraging. Although lizards are the primary prey, our attention was drawn to one small adult that had captured a struggling crested toad.

Genus *Erythrolamprus;* False Coral Snakes

This genus of smooth-scaled, usually tricolored snakes comprises six variable species. All are rear-fanged, producing venom that is effective against their lizard and snake prey but seems to have virtually no effect on humans. The rings (or bands) are black, red, and white (or yellowish). The red is separated from the yellow by black. Throughout most of its range—

southward from Nicaragua to Brazil—*Erythrolamprus* mimics at least one coral snake species. Many of the species are most brilliantly colored and patterned when young. With advancing age, melanin often suffuses the posterior tips of both the red and the white scales.

218. Common False Coral Snake

Erythrolamprus aesculapii aesculapii

Size: Adults range in length from 25 to 29 inches (65–78 cm).

Identifying features: Rings of three colors encircle the body. The black rings tend to narrow ventrally. The color tends to darken with age. Even in juveniles, all (or most) of the scales in the red and cream bands are tipped with black. This creates an interesting, busy, sometimes netted pattern. The snout is white (or cream, rarely all red), followed by a ring of black over the eyes (sometimes lacking), another ring of white, a second ring of black, then the first of the red bands. The sequence of body banding is red-black-cream-black-red. The scales are nonkeeled, and the anal plate is divided. There is some geographical variability in coloration.

Reproduction: A captive female laid five infertile eggs, but virtually nothing is known of the reproductive biology in the wild.

Similar species: The color pattern on the head—white(snout)-black-white-black-red—will differentiate this snake from other tricolors in the region, including all the coral snakes save for *Micrurus spixii obscurus*. The latter, however, has much wider rings, with the first red band occurring posterior to the neck. *Micrurus lemniscatus helleri* has a similar pattern of rings, but its nose is black.

Habitat/Range: The common false coral snake seems restricted to primary forests, where it is considered a leaf litter species. It has been found along forest trails and in newly cleared agricultural areas. It is a secretive snake about which little is known. It is widespread in the Amazon Basin.

Comments: This snake often responds to prodding by elevating and coiling the tail in a manner similar to that of some coral snakes.

Genus *Helicops;* Neotropical Water Snakes

The more than one dozen species in this genus of semiaquatic snakes are restricted in distribution to South America. They range from Venezuela and Colombia south to Argentina.

The dorsal pattern may consist of prominent bands or of spots that are darker than the ground color. The eyes are comparatively small, and the nostrils are dorsally oriented. When threatened these snakes flatten the body and will strike viciously. The saliva contains sufficient enzymes and peptides to produce an itchy welt on a bitten human.

Fish and amphibians are the favored prey. The mode of reproduction is either questionable, variable, or both. Some species have reportedly produced both eggs and live young; others seem to be exclusively viviparous.

219. Banded South American Water Snake

Helicops angulatus

Size: Although most examples seen are smaller, a total length of 2 feet (61 cm) is possible.

Identifying features: This prominently banded snake has a ground color of olive gray, tan, or olive brown. The bands are reddish, purplish red, or purplish brown to dark brown. They may be narrowly edged in black and may extend either partially or entirely across the cream to light tan (occasionally with an orangish haze, and sometimes red) belly. The underside of the tail is gray(ish). The subcaudal scales are *keeled*. The top of the head and the irises are dark.

Reproduction: Knowledge of the reproductive biology of this snake is muddled. One captive female produced six infertile egg masses; a museum specimen contained 11 ovarian eggs (Duellman, 1978); and a reptile dealer claimed that a large female gave birth to five live young. Additional research is needed.

Similar species: *Helicops pastazae* and *H. polylepis* have spotted, not banded, dorsa.

Habitat/Range: These are essentially aquatic, primarily nocturnal snakes. Most specimens found have been in or next to shallow water in riverine situations at night. They have also been reported from forest pools and streams. The species ranges widely in northern South America; it has been recorded from Venezuela, Colombia, Ecuador, Peru, Brazil, and Bolivia.

Comments: My initial thought when I (RDB) saw my first specimen of this snake nosing at night through submerged grasses in search of prey was that a small northern water snake (*Nerodia sipedon*) had somehow been teleported to the Amazon. That impression has remained with me over the years. This snake has enlarged teeth in the rear of its upper jaw, and the saliva should be considered at least weakly toxic. It bites readily if carelessly restrained, and bites have resulted in tingling, some tenderness, and swelling.

220. Spotted Water Snake

Helicops leopardinus

Size: Adults reach 15 or so inches (38 cm) in total length.

Identifying features: This small, aquatic snake has keeled scales, an obscurely colored back, and a brightly colored belly. The dorsum is some shade of gray and has four longitudinal rows of darker spots. Some or all of the dorsal spots may be vaguely interconnected by narrow, dark projections. The venter is a checkerboard of black and red, a similarly colored pattern of bands, or a combination of checkers and bands.

Reproduction: Little is known about the reproductive biology of any member of this genus. It is thought that most lay eggs in an advanced state of development, and that the incubation period is abbreviated as a result. However, records exist of at least one live birth.

Similar species: Other species of *Helicops* from Peruvian Amazonia lack the crispness of the red and black belly pattern of this species. *Liophis breviceps* can be of very similar appearance but has a banded rather than spotted dorsum and has nonkeeled scales.

Habitat/Range: Small forest pools; quiet, periodically intermittent streams; and lagoon edges are the habitats of this snake. The species ranges from the Guianas and Peru to Argentina.

Comments: Like other members of this genus, the spotted water snake will bite savagely if carelessly restrained.

Genus *Hydronastes*; False Water Cobras

One of the two species in this genus is among the largest "nonvenomous" snakes in South America. *Hydronastes gigas* has been documented at more than 9 feet (2.7 m) in length. The genus ranges from French Guiana south to Argentina. Both species are oviparous.

These semiaquatic snakes spread a cobralike hood when threatened, but do not elevate the head and neck while doing so. The water cobras have "mildly toxic" saliva that seems quite effective on ectothermic prey items, but less so on endothermic prey. The effects on humans are variable. Some bites produce few signs of typical envenomation; others produce lividity and edema. Avoid being bitten.

221. Giant False Water Cobra

Hydronastes gigas

Size: This is an immense snake. Adults in excess of 9 feet (2.7 m) in total length have been found.

Identifying features: The ground color is buff, tan, or yellowish. Broad, dark brown to black bands, either entire or broken into spots, cross the dorsum and may continue onto the venter. The scales are smooth and shiny. The belly color of males is yellowish; that of females is olive brown to brown.

Reproduction: Females lay 20–30 eggs per clutch. The eggs hatch after approximately 60 days' incubation. Hatchlings are large (about 12–15 inches [30–37.5 cm]), heavy bodied, and often very defensive.

Similar species: None.

Habitat/Range: This large snake is a resident of slow-moving or quiet waters in the eastern Amazon Basin. From there the species ranges far southward on the continent.

Comments: This snake flattens its neck (but does not rear up) like a cobra when frightened. Some are very approachable; others strike and bite at the least provocation. This rear-fanged species should be treated with more than usual caution.

Genus *Hydrops*; Neotropical Mud Snakes

This genus contains two predominantly aquatic species. They are considered mildly venomous by some researchers, and harmless by others. Both are coral snake mimics. Both species are oviparous.

Synbranchid eels appear to be the preferred prey. Little is known about the life history or reproductive biology of either *Hydrops*. Both are largely restricted in distribution to the Amazon Basin.

Although they are considered diurnal by some herpetologists, we have seen them prowling amid aquatic vegetation after dark.

222. Coral Mud Snake

Hydrops martii

Size: Females attain a length of about 40 inches (1 m); males are noticeably smaller than females.

Identifying features: This is an interesting, rather flat-headed, aquatic snake. Between the white-tipped snout and broad white temporal band (incomplete dorsally), the small-eyed and flattened head is largely black. Following the temporal band the colors are, sequentially, black-white-red-white-black all the way to the tail tip. All of the bands are narrow, the white especially so. The black and white bands may be entire or broken and offset vertebrally. The smooth scales are in 17 rows at *midbody*.

Reproduction: The reproductive biology is largely unknown. Dixon and Soini (1976) report a hatchling found in November.

Similar species: The rather similar (but usually more broadly banded) *Hydrops triangularis bassleri* usually lacks red dorsally and has scales in 15 rows. The Amazonian coral snake, *Micrurus s. surinamensis*, has much broader bands (each black band contains two well-separated yellow bands) and a red head.

Habitat/Range: *Hydrops* are thoroughly aquatic snakes. They seem most common in areas of shallow, quiet or slowly flowing water.

Comments: The specimen pictured here was disgorged, still alive, by a small spectacled caiman that we had detained at the river's edge for photographs. It is not known whether the saliva of this snake is toxic, but it is probably best to use caution when handling one. *Hydrops* are thought to be specialist feeders on tropical (synbranchid) eels and, perhaps, aquatic caecilians.

Genus *Imantodes;* Blunt-Headed Tree Snakes

Two of the five or so species in this primarily Latin American genus occur in the Amazon Basin. On first viewing a blunt-headed tree snake, most ecotourists are not only awed that a snake this attenuate can exist, but that it can span a distance of 2 feet, unsupported, when moving from limb to limb in the shrub in which it is foraging. In their proportions the *Imantodes* are at least as slender, and perhaps even more so, than the better-known vine snakes of the genus *Oxybelis*.

Their mild venom helps these slender snakes to overcome the frogs and tiny lizards on which they feed. In our experience, they cannot be induced to bite humans. They are nocturnal; have vertically elliptical pupils in their very large eyes; and have a short, rounded snout. The largest among them attains a length of about 3 feet (91 cm).

223. Common Blunt-Headed Tree Snake

Imantodes cenchoa

Size: To 3 feet (91 cm).

Identifying features: One of the nocturnally active "cat-eyed" snakes, this tree snake is of extreme slenderness and has a truncated snout. The ground color is cream to grayish cream, sometimes with an orangish blush. The dorsal blotches are dark brown, more rarely purplish brown. The venter is light with dark speckles. The irises of the large, protuberant eyes are greenish tan, and the pupil is vertically elliptical.

Reproduction: Females produce one to five elongate eggs. This species apparently breeds year-round in the Iquitos region.

Similar species: Although the dorsal blotches are large and dark brown, this species is sometimes confused with *I. lentiferus,* which has smaller, buff blotches. Separating the two species may require counting scale rows. *Imantodes cenchoa* has 17 rows; *I. lentiferus* has 15.

Habitat/Range: This is one of the most abundant and frequently seen of the arboreal nocturnal snakes. It is easy to find at night as it hunts small frogs and anoline lizards in shrubs and low trees. Its very slight build allows it to move easily along the slenderest of twigs. We found several by day coiled vertically against the trunks of trees, propped in place by the roots of epiphytic plants. *Imantodes cenchoa* may be found in primary and secondary forests and is commonly seen along paths, trails, and clearing edges where anoles are often most abundant. The species ranges from southern Mexico south to Argentina.

224. Amazon Blunt-Headed Tree Snake

Imantodes lentiferus

Size: This *very* slender snake attains a length of about 45 inches (114 cm).

Identifying features: Superficially, *Imantodes lentiferus* is a paler version of the more common *I. cenchoa.* However, *I. lentiferus* has only 15 rows of scales (*I. cenchoa* has 17), and the dark dorsal blotches seldom reach the ventral scales. Each of the dark dorsal blotches has a small dark dot on its central leading edge and its central trailing edge. The nose is very short, the eyes are bulbous, and the pupils are vertically elliptical. This and the common blunt-headed tree snake are the two slenderest snakes in the region.

Reproduction: Females produce two or three eggs in each clutch. The incubation duration is unknown, but a juvenile specimen with what appeared to be a still fresh umbilical scar measured almost 11 inches (27.5 cm) in total length.

Similar species: See the account for *Imantodes cenchoa,* above.

Habitat/Range: This nocturnal shrub dweller is widely distributed in the Amazon Basin. Look for it in small trees and large shrubs along trail edges in primary forests and where forest meets newly cleared agricultural areas.

Genus *Leptodeira;* Cat-Eyed Snakes

It is strange how common names for some snakes are based on a trait or characteristic shared by many. For example, although the eight or nine *Leptodeira* species certainly do have elliptical, catlike pupils, this adaptation to nocturnal activity is certainly not restricted to the genus. Elliptical pupils are found in many other snake genera worldwide. In the Neotropics these include the bug-eyed, short-nosed members of the genus *Imantodes* and the many species of pit vipers. Be that as it may, the name "cat-eyed" has long been applied to the snakes of the genus *Leptodeira*. These relatively small and quite slender snakes are found from Texas to Argentina, and some of the species display quite variable colors and patterns.

Leptodeira are mildly venomous, oviparous snakes that preferentially accept ectothermic prey. Some, including the Amazonian *L. annulata*, search out and consume the egg clusters of hylid frogs. They can seldom be induced to bite humans.

225. Common Cat-Eyed Snake

Leptodeira annulata annulata

Size: This slender (but not vinelike) snake is a little more than 2 feet (61 cm) in total length.

Identifying features: The dorsum is tan or some shade of brown (sometimes quite dark) with a series of irregularly shaped, dark dorsal blotches from nape to tail tip. The blotches may be entire or broken and staggered vertebrally. The belly is tan to light pinkish brown, lightest anteriorly. The head is unmarked except for a dark postocular stripe. The eyes are large and have a brownish iris and a vertical pupil. The scales are in 19 rows; the vertebral row is at least slightly enlarged.

Reproduction: Females lay three to six (perhaps more) eggs per clutch. Amazonian populations probably lay throughout the year.

Similar species: Other similarly colored and patterned snakes of this region are of vinelike thinness or lack vertically elliptical pupils.

Habitat/Range: This snake prospers in secondary forests, is more rarely encountered in primary forests, and is especially abundant near the edges of ponds, swamps, and oxbows where frogs are most numerous. It feeds on both frogs and their eggs, and is well known for seeking out and consuming the egg clutches of the various leaf frogs. The cat-eyed snake is a nocturnal species that is most frequently found in low vegetation but is also active terrestrially. The species ranges from Amazonian Bolivia north to Venezuela.

Genus *Leptophis;* Parrot Snakes

This genus comprises eight species of slender, semiarboreal snakes that indulge in intimidating threat displays. The genus may be encountered from Mexico southward to Argentina. The adult length is about 4 feet (1.2 m), and the color of most species is a beautiful leaf green, either with or without tan and yellow highlights. When threatened and unable to flee, these snakes S the forward half of the body, open the mouth widely, and make feinting strikes. If an escape route opens, the snake will quickly avail itself of the opportunity.

The parrot snakes are diurnal and prey on resting arboreal frogs and anoline lizards. Their saliva contains anticoagulants and perhaps other enzymes and peptides. It is best to avoid a bite. Insofar as is known, all are oviparous.

226. Black-Skinned Parrot Snake

Leptophis ahaetulla nigromarginatus

Size: Adults are a slender 3.5–4 feet (1.1–1.2 m) long.
Identifying features: The black-skinned parrot snake is leaf green dorsally and burnished bronze on the lower sides. The interstitial skin is black. The throat is white; the venter may vary from white to pinkish. The irises are gold. There are 15 rows of scales.
Reproduction: Clutches are small, usually one to five eggs. The smallest specimen we have found was 13 inches (32.5 cm) in total length.
Similar species: The black-margined green scales, gold sides, and rounded snout separate this species from all others in its range.
Habitat/Range: This rather common snake blends so well with its leafy habitat that it is often overlooked. It is primarily arboreal, but we have seen some specimens in terrestrial situations. It seems to be a diurnal species and has been found coiled and sleeping in shrubs at night. This race of the common parrot snake occurs in Amazonian western Brazil, Colombia, Ecuador, and eastern Peru.

Genus *Liophis;* Swamp Snakes

Many of the species in this large genus (approximately 50 species) are still in taxonomic dispute. The genus ranges pretty much throughout South America, and in many regions several species are sympatric. Swamp snakes are known to eat amphibians and amphibian eggs; some species reportedly eat fish as well. Some species are apparently crepuscular and nocturnal; others are diurnal. Many species are polymorphic. Some are very brightly colored; others are nondescript. Insofar as is known, all *Liophis* are oviparous. Many species are present in the Amazon Basin.

Some swamp snakes, *L. typhlus* among them, indulge in a neck-flattening defense display. Many species bite readily. The saliva apparently contains an anticoagulant, for bleeding from even a minimal wound can be considerable.

227. Tricolored Swamp Snake

Liophis breviceps breviceps

Size: About 2 feet (61 cm).
Identifying features: This small-headed, shiny-scaled snake has six or seven supralabial scales. It is olive brown dorsally and has a lateral pattern of olive and red wedges. The red wedges *may* be buffy dorsally. The venter is primarily bright coral red but may be patterned with thin olive cross bands.
Reproduction: Females lay up to six eggs; virtually nothing else is known about the reproductive biology.
Similar species: *Liophis cobella* (not pictured) is quite similar in appearance, but its light marks tend to be buff laterally and of a less intense red ventrally, and it has eight supralabials.
Habitat/Range: Tricolored swamp snakes seem partial to the muddy, heavily vegetated edges of ponds, swamps, and oxbows, and may be seen moving through the shallows at night. We found one moving slowly through a shallow pond in which dozens of treefrogs were singing. This is a species of the northern Amazon Basin from Peru to Suriname and Brazil.

228. Common Swamp Snake

Liophis reginae semilineatus

Size: This moderately heavy-bodied snake is adult at a length of about 22 inches (55 cm).
Identification: The ground color of the dorsum is grayish, olive, or gray-green, with the anterior being the greenest. Narrow and often poorly defined irregular dark bars are present along the length of the dorsum. The

upper lip is creamy yellow. A dark postorbital stripe extends to the angle of the jaw. The 17 rows of scales are smooth (unkeeled), and the interstitial color is cream, yellow, or pale green. The belly is yellow with irregular black checkers or bars. The anal plate is divided.

Reproduction: The normal clutch size is three to six eggs, sometimes as many as eight.

Similar species: Other members of this genus may flatten the neck as a defensive display, but they lack the dark dorsal bars, have more prominent dorsal bands, or lack the black and yellow–checked/barred venter.

Habitat/Range: In keeping with its name and prey preferences, this snake is most commonly seen in damp to wet habitats. It is primarily diurnal, but we have found several individuals active in shallow water well after dark. Although it seems to prefer shallow water with floating or emergent vegetation, *L. reginae* swims well. It is a common snake of the northwestern Amazon Basin.

Comments: When startled, this snake holds its head and neck flat against the ground, flattens its head, and spreads the anterior of its neck in a cobralike manner.

229. Velvety Swamp Snake

Liophis typhlus typhlus

Size: Adults are about 25 inches (63.5 cm) long.

Identifying features: This wide-headed snake may be brilliant green, olive green, or olive gray. The chin is yellowish, and the venter is lighter than the dorsum. The anal plate is divided. The interstitial skin is whitish. The irises are often reddish gold. There are 19 scale rows at midbody; these reduce to 15 rows posteriorly.

Reproduction: The clutch size is two to seven eggs. Nothing more is known about the reproductive biology.

Similar species: *Philodryas viridissimus* is arboreal, has a white chin and venter, and has 17 rows of scales posteriorly. *Oxybelis fulgidus* is very slender and has a pointed snout.

Habitat/Range: *Liophis typhlus* is primarily terrestrial and seems most common near the edges of swamps and oxbows where frogs are plentiful. It is commonly seen in the northern Amazon Basin.

Comments: When startled, this snake holds its head and neck flat against the ground, flattens its head, and spreads the anterior of its neck in a cobralike manner. One specimen we caught regurgitated a considerable number of freshly ingested frog eggs.

Genus *Mastigodryas;* Neotropical Racers

This genus comprises 11 species of alert, fast-moving, diurnal, semiarboreal snakes. None is brightly colored, and most (all?) undergo ontogenetic pattern changes. Juveniles are usually strongly banded dorsally and laterally. Some adults retain at least vestiges of the juvenile pattern, but others lose the juvenile bands and develop longitudinal stripes. The Neotropical racers are oviparous. They eat all types of smaller creatures, from mammals and birds to frogs and lizards. They hunt largely by sight but are fully capable of trailing prey. Species of this genus range from Mexico south to Argentina.

230. Tan Racer

Mastigodryas boddaertii

Size: Adults are slender and may be somewhat more than 4 feet (1.2 m) long.

Identifying features: There is nothing particularly memorable about this alert, fast-moving snake. The adult is nearly uniform tannish gray to reddish gray for most of its length, but does have a poorly defined lighter dorsolateral stripe on scale rows 4 and 5 on each side. The supralabial scales are often yellowish, and a darker eye stripe is usually visible. Juveniles, on the other hand, are strongly patterned, with about 70 light dorsal bands, best defined anteriorly, against a reddish gray dorsum. The sides are also barred vertically, with the lateral bars offset from the dorsal ones and also best defined anteriorly. Juveniles usually have well-defined eye stripes and gray lips. The belly of adults and juveniles is cream to yellow, brightest on juvenile specimens. There are 17 scale rows.

Reproduction: Oviparous; one female, freshly killed by villagers, contained five eggs.

Similar species: The glossy racer (*Drymoluber dichrous*) has light dorsolateral stripes (except on its neck). The various whipsnakes (*Chironius*) have 10 or 12 scale rows.

Habitat/Range: This snake is often seen near the ground in shrubs in secondary forests or at the edges of agricultural clearings. It ranges widely from Colombia and Trinidad to Bolivia and Brazil.

Genus *Oxybelis;* Vine Snakes

Three of the four species in this genus are found in the Amazon Basin. They are very appropriately named, being both of vinelike slenderness and inhabitants of vines and shrubs. Vine snakes are diurnal and arboreal lizard hunters that occasionally take treefrogs as well. The largest species, *O. fulgidus,* also consumes small mammals and birds. All species are oviparous.

The vine snakes have rear fangs and produce venom that quickly overcomes their lizard and frog prey but seems less effective on endothermic prey. Humans bitten by the smaller species have described symptoms varying from none to lividity and a stinging sensation at the bite site similar to that of a bee sting. The effect on a human of a bite from the much larger *O. fulgidus* is unknown.

When frightened, a vine snake faces the threat and opens the mouth widely, displaying the black interior, and inflates the neck in what seems an effort to appear larger and more formidable. Following this, if hardpressed, the snake will sometimes make half-hearted strikes.

As a group, the vine snakes range from southeastern Arizona (USA) south to Brazil and Peru.

231. Brown Vine Snake

Oxybelis aeneus

Size: Adults are more than 4 feet (1.2 m) long and pencil thin.
Identifying features: The dorsum is tan to grayish brown, the venter is white. A vague dark ocular stripe is present. Dark lines may be scattered over the dorsum. The nose is sharp but not truly pointed.
Reproduction: Females lay one to six elongate eggs. Hatchlings are a little over 1 foot (30 cm) in length.
Similar species: None. Other vine snakes are green or have green stripes. The pencil-thin snakes of the genus *Imantodes* have blunt noses and bands.
Habitat/Range: This arboreal, diurnal snake is commonly seen in low shrubs and is a familiar sight in sunny patches along paths, trails, and agricultural openings. It is also seen in many forest locations. The range is immense—from Arizona to the Amazon.

232. Green-Striped Vine Snake

Oxybelis (Xenoxybelis) argenteus

Size: Adults of this slender, attenuate snake reach or exceed 4 feet (1.2 m) in total length.

Identifying features: The dorsum and sides are tan or light brown. The venter is pale green anteroventrally, fading to white posteroventrally, where there are two green stripes. There are three dull green stripes: a vertebral stripe down the back and a lateral stripe on each side. The body becomes rigid, often in odd positions, when frightened. The green and tan tongue may be protruded, tips together, and held motionless for several seconds.

Reproduction: Females lay as many as six eggs per clutch. Nothing more is known about the reproductive biology.

Similar species: None. The slender build and pattern of the three dull green lines are diagnostic.

Habitat/Range: This arboreal, diurnal snake is more frequently met with in secondary forests and disturbed habitats than in primary forests. Although abundant, it is very easily overlooked during the day when it is foraging for frogs and lizards. It is most often found at night when it is sleeping, loosely coiled, on low shrubs and trees. The species occurs in northern South American lowland forests and clearings.

233. Green Vine Snake

Oxybelis fulgidus

Size: At 5.5 feet (1.7 m), this is the largest of the three *Oxybelis* species in the Amazon Basin.

Identifying features: The dorsum is dark leaf green; the venter is somewhat lighter. A white ventrolateral line parallels each outer edge of the ventral scutes. The lips and chin are noticeably lighter than the rest of the head. The nose is *sharply* pointed.

Reproduction: Females lay up to eight eggs. Hatchlings are a very slender 14 inches (35 cm) in length.

Similar species: None. The slenderness, white ventrolateral lines, and sharp nose are diagnostic. The green vine snake is of proportionally greater girth than its two Amazonian congeners.

Habitat/Range: Although the two smaller Amazonian members of this genus coil up for the night almost before dusk, we have found *O. fulgidus* still active in tangled vegetation (perhaps seeking somewhere to coil for the night?) shortly *after* sunset. Green vine snakes seem to be more common where frogs and lizards are abundant. They are persistently arboreal, but may occasionally descend to the ground. Look for this snake from Mexico south to the Amazon Basin.

Comments: This species is reluctant to gape when disturbed, but will do so if hard-pressed. It is more apt to inflate the throat and neck vertically and strike at the disturbing object. It is considered a mildly venomous species. Green vine snakes take small mammals and nestling birds along with lizards and frogs. They are nearly impossible to see unless they are moving.

Genus *Oxyrhopus*; Calico Snakes

Another good common name for the snakes of this genus would be "confusing snakes." Color and pattern vary by individual, by age, and by geographic location. Individuals of many of the 11 species that comprise the genus are either black and white banded or tricolored early in life. Some remain so, intensifying in color; others become suffused with a patina of melanin that may, in extreme cases, virtually obscure the pattern. Others lose the bands, assuming an overall orange body color that usually has an overlying pattern of interstitial black. The belly may be devoid of markings anteriorly but strongly patterned posteriorly, or virtually devoid of markings altogether.

All of these rear-fanged snakes produce venom that helps them overpower their lizard prey. They are oviparous, nocturnal, and primarily terrestrial.

234. Yellow-Headed Calico Snake

Oxyrhopus formosus

Size: Adults are about 3 feet (91 cm) long.

Identifying features: The color and pattern are variable, but the snout and cheeks are always yellow to buff. This snake may be banded with black and orange-red (belly light and unpatterned), or the pattern may fade, producing an orange snake with dark scale tips, a dark crown, and a pearl white belly.

Reproduction: A clutch of four eggs has been reported; other than that, the reproductive biology is virtually unknown.

Similar species: Even though the other features are extremely variable, the yellow nose and cheeks are diagnostic.

Habitat/Range: We have found this beautiful snake along watercourses in secondary and primary forests as well as in villages and agricultural plots. The species is common and widely distributed over much of Amazonia, and from there northward to Venezuela.

235. Black-Headed Calico Snake

Oxyrhopus melanogenys melanogenys

Size: Adults are about 3 feet (91 cm) in total length.

Identifying features: We have encountered this snake in two dramatically different color phases. The normal coloration is a pretty banded pattern: typically, a black nose (not spotted with white) is followed by a broad red band, then by a sequence of black-yellow(or white)-black-red-black bands. Atypically, the anterior half of the body may be a series of black and white rings; on the posterior half of the body red rings are incorporated into the pattern in a black-white-black-white-black-red (or, alternatively, a black-white-black-red) sequence. Both sequences may appear on the same snake. Some pale specimens have yellow bands rather than red ones. Dorsal melanism may prevail with advancing age. Juveniles can be significantly paler than the adults. The belly is off-white to cream, and the underside of the tail is gray or black. There are fewer than 100 rows of subcaudal scales.

An aberrant phase we found on several occasions has an all-black head and red-orange body with each scale edged narrowly with black, creating an attractive netted pattern. Occasionally a narrow, poorly defined white band may be present on the neck. Again, the belly is creamy white and the subcaudals are black.

Reproduction: Up to 12 eggs per clutch have been verified. Beyond this, nothing is known about the reproductive biology.

Similar species: The netted pattern of the aberrant morph coupled with the black face and snout and the lack of a white neck ring are diagnostic. Compare the accounts for *Pseudoboa coronata, Drepanoides anomalus,* and *Clelia clelia.* Positive field identification of the ringed morph to more than genus may prove quite difficult. See especially the accounts for other *Oxyrhopus.* Other ringed snakes are more regularly and evenly colored.

Habitat/Range: This tricolored snake may be encountered in primary and secondary forests, in agricultural clearings, and at the edges of villages. The species ranges widely through Amazonian Bolivia, Brazil, Ecuador, and Peru.

Comments: The black-headed calico snake is an opportunistic feeder on small mammals, birds, amphibians (especially frogs), and other reptiles (especially lizards).

236. Banded Calico Snake

Oxyrhopus petola digitalis

Size: About 3 feet (91 cm). Females seem to be noticeably smaller than males.

Identifying features: This usually bicolored, occasionally tricolored snake is typically banded in black and red (sometimes black and orange or yellowish). The bands may be broken and offset middorsally. The anterior of the first red band is often the palest of the red bands, but on some specimens several of the light anterior bands are cream or yellow. Rarely, this species may be tricolored posteriorly. The belly is yellow or cream. The top of the head and the *nose* are black. There are more than 100 rows of subcaudal scales.

Reproduction: The clutch size is 3–10 eggs. Nothing more is known about the reproductive biology.

Similar species: The pattern of black and red (or yellow or orange) bands and black nose of typically colored specimens is diagnostic. See also the accounts for other *Oxyrhopus* species.

Habitat/Range: Although considered primarily nocturnal, this snake is occasionally active by day, especially in canopy forests. It also occurs in well-grown secondary forests and in the clearings associated with forest villages and agriculture. It is at least partially arboreal. The species occurs in scattered areas from Amazonian Brazil and Bolivia northward to Panama.

Comments: This calico snake seems to prey preferentially on lizards.

237. Brazilian Calico Snake

Oxyrhopus trigeminus

Size: Up to about 3.5 feet (1.1 m).

Identifying features: Because they exhibit overlapping characteristics, including color and pattern, the Amazonian *Oxyrhopus* species can be very difficult to differentiate. This is especially true of the typically banded forms of *O. trigeminus* and *O. melanogenys*. Typically, *O. trigeminus* displays a regular sequence of black, white, and red rings, beginning with a white-spotted black nose and a red neck ring followed by a yellow ring. Black-yellow-black-red sequences may follow, but the red is often suffused (sometimes entirely so) with melanin. Juveniles can be much paler than adults and may lack red entirely. There are fewer than 100 rows of sub-caudal scales.

Reproduction: One female, imported gravid by the American pet trade, laid eight eggs.

Similar species: It may not be possible to determine the species in the field. Some species may be eliminated because they have a white snout. See the accounts for *Oxyrhopus melanogenys, O. petola digitalis, Erythrolamprus aesculapii,* and the various coral snakes of the genus *Micrurus.*

Habitat/Range: Brazilian calico snakes are habitat generalists and may be encountered in a wide variety of situations ranging from forest villages and city edges to agricultural plots, secondary forests, and primary forests. This species occurs primarily in Amazonian Brazil.

Comments: *Oxyrhopus trigeminus* seems to be active both day and night and takes both ectothermic and endothermic prey.

Genus *Philodryas;* Palmsnakes, Pampas Racers

The 15–20 species in this genus vary widely in appearance and habits. All are fast-moving and alert rear-fanged snakes that are not at all reluctant to bite when confronted by a human. The venom is relatively virulent; it quickly immobilizes prey animals and may cause lividity, edema, and localized pain in humans. The palmsnakes should be considered dangerously venomous. Do not attempt to handle them.

Amphibians, lizards, nestling birds, and small mammals are the prey. The semiarboreal species are usually some shade of green; terrestrial forms may be green-brown or a combination of these colors.

Snakes of this genus occur over much of South America.

238. Emerald Palmsnake

Philodryas viridissimus viridissimus

Size: Females may be 3 feet (91 cm) long; males seem to be several inches shorter.

Identifying features: Lithe and agile, this often-defensive snake is brilliant green both above and below. The chin is somewhat paler than the belly.

Reproduction: Up to seven eggs have been reported in a clutch, but little else is known about the reproductive biology.

Similar species: The green vine snake has a sharply pointed nose. The brilliant green, velvety swamp snakes will spread a hood if frightened. Forest pit vipers have well-developed labial pits.

Habitat/Range: The palmsnake is arboreal, but its preferred level in the forest is not completely understood. Its brilliant green color would stand it in good stead in the canopy, where it is thought to spend most of its time, but numerous specimens have been found in rather low shrubs. Perhaps it is actually less specialized than we believe. The species is widely distributed, but apparently nowhere common, throughout most of the Amazon Basin.

Comments: If frightened this snake will stand its ground, flatten its head, and strike fiercely. It has relatively toxic venom.

Genus *Pseudoboa;* Scarlet Snakes

This genus ranges southward from Panama to Brazil and also occurs on Grenada. There are four species. Although all are rear-fanged (opisthoglyphids), virtually nothing is known about the composition or virulence of their venom; it is not thought to be dangerous to humans. As a group, these nocturnal snakes are secretive, terrestrial constrictors that feed on small mammals.

239. Amazon Scarlet Snake

Pseudoboa coronata

Size: Adults occasionally exceed 3 feet (91 cm) in total length.

Identifying features: The head from the tip of the snout past the eyes is black. The back of the head and the anterior part of the neck may be white. The white may become suffused with black pigment and may nearly disappear on old adults. A narrow band of black follows the white. The dorsum is mahogany red with each scale tipped with black. The black tipping expands in area with advancing age, and some adults are quite dark. The venter is cream. There are seven supralabials.

Reproduction: This oviparous species lays two to six eggs per clutch. Nothing more is known about its reproductive biology.

Similar species: The fact that the scales are in 17 rows and the anal plate is entire will differentiate this snake from the mussurana (*Clelia*) and the egg-eating snake (*Drepanoides*), which have similar colors. *Pseudoboa neuweidii* has eight (rather than seven) supralabial scales.

Habitat/Range: *Pseudoboa coronata* seems most abundant in secondary forests and cleared areas and is most often seen near the edges of ponds and oxbows. It feeds on lizards and small rodents, and is probably diurnal. The species may be encountered from Colombia to the Guianas and from Bolivia to Brazil.

240. Eastern Scarlet Snake

Pseudoboa neuweidii

Size: Adults are 2–2.5 feet (60–75 cm) in total length.
Identifying features: This beautiful constrictor has a rich red-orange body (somewhat duller in older snakes) with a black head and nape and a broad white ring at the back of the head. There are eight supralabial (upper lip) scales.
Reproduction: The clutch size is three to nine eggs. Incubation takes about 65 days. The hatchlings are about 7 inches (18 cm) in total length.
Similar species: See the account for *Pseudoboa coronata*, above.
Habitat/Range: This terrestrial forestland species may also be found near villages and agricultural plots. It ranges from the Brazilian Amazon north to Panama.

Genus *Pseudoeryx;* Dusky Mud Snake

The dusky mud snake is primarily aquatic, feeds on fish, and is most often encountered near weedy edges of ponds and oxbows. It is a heavy-bodied, small-headed snake that may reach 4.5 feet (1.4 m) in length. The body is mud colored with darker sides. Juveniles have a peach or orange suffusion on the belly. Although nonvenomous, this snake will not hesitate to bite if carelessly restrained. It is oviparous and is said to be diurnal.

The single species ranges from Colombia and Venezuela to northern Argentina.

241. Dusky Mud Snake

Pseudoeryx plicatilis

Size: Adults may reach a length of 4.5 feet (1.4 m) long.
Identifying features: All the scales of this large aquatic snake are smooth and shiny. The dorsum of adults is dark—primarily dark olive green, olive brown, or olive black—with only a vague indication of a broad, dark lateral stripe. The labial scales are brown to yellowish, with the sutures

being darkest. Some indication of a light partial collar may be visible. The belly is cream to yellowish (occasionally with the slightest blush of red) and bears a row of small black spots along each side. The dark spots are most prominent on the subcaudal scales. The overall appearance is merely of a big, shiny, light-bellied, dark snake.

Juveniles, on the other hand, are quite prettily colored. The broad, dark olive green middorsal area is separated on each side from the similarly colored sides by a prominent stripe of medium pink that begins on the snout and continues to the tail tip. At the outer edge of the dark middorsal area is a row of small black spots. A row of similar black spots is present along each side of the bright orange-red belly. A dark orbital stripe is bordered above by light olive pigment, below by yellow, and is separated from the lateral body stripe by a broad, dorsally interrupted, olive yellow collar. The labial scales are yellowish. The snout is short and rounded; the nostrils are directed noticeably forward.

Reproduction: All that is known about this species is that it is oviparous and that a single apparently newly hatched baby measured only 5.5 inches (14 cm) in total length.

Similar species: None. The water snakes of the genus *Helicops* have keeled scales.

Habitat/Range: Weedy oxbow lake edges and the edges of slow moving watercourses seem to be the preferred habitats. This species is widespread throughout the Amazon Basin.

Comments: The dusky mud snake undergoes a considerable ontogenetic change in coloration, dulling greatly in both color and pattern with advancing age. Fish seem to comprise most, if not all, of the diet.

Genus *Pseustes;* Bird Snakes

The four species in this genus of nonvenomous, oviparous snakes are large, fast, alert, and, if pestered, feisty. They are quite arboreal and are often seen in trees and shrubs, and even along the ridgepoles in the thatched roofs of forest dwellings. In most respects, the bird snakes are very much like the better-known tiger rat snake, *Spilotes pullatus*. When threatened they draw the neck back into an impressive S, inflate and distend the throat and neck vertically, and strike fiercely.

Even well-fed individuals have a ridged back and appear thin. Adults of the giant bird snake may near 9 feet (2.75 m) in length, but an adult size of about 5 or 6 feet (1.5–1.8 m) is typical of the other species. Hatchlings are strongly banded; adults tend to have a uniformly colored dorsum.

The genus is distributed from Mexico to Argentina.

242. Common Bird Snake

Pseustes poecilonotus polylepis

Size: Adults commonly exceed 5 feet (1.5 m) in length, and occasionally near 6.5 feet (2 m).

Identifying features: This agile arborealist may vary in color from almost black both above and below, with throat and anterior belly lighter; to greenish gray with a cream belly and throat; to mahogany red dorsally with a yellow chin and belly. Juveniles are gray to gray-green, strongly banded, and have a dark peppering on the head scales.

Reproduction: Females lay up to nine eggs. Incubation takes about 65 days. Hatchlings are comparatively large, up to 18 inches (45 cm) in total length.

Similar species: See the accounts for *Pseustes sulphureus* and *Spilotes pullatus,* below.

Habitat/Range: This snake is a forest and clearing dweller that often takes up residence in the thatched roofs of forest dwellings. It climbs well but also spends considerable time on the ground. The species ranges widely throughout most of the Amazon Basin.

Comments: When on the defensive the common bird snake inflates its throat on a vertical plane, hisses loudly, and strikes savagely.

243. Giant Bird Snake

Pseustes sulphureus sulphureus

Size: Adults often exceed 7 feet (2.1 m) and occasionally exceed 9 feet (2.75 m) in total length.

Identifying features: This big, fast, and always defensive snake is olive tan to olive green dorsally and laterally, but may have a wash of sulfur yellow on the sides. There are darker transverse marks posteriorly. The chin and anterior venter are a sulfur yellow that takes on an overcast of olive as it progresses posteriorly. The labials are yellow with dark vertical interstitial sutures. The scales are keeled. There are three postocular scales and one anterior temporal scale (see diagram page 202).

Reproduction: Females lay 6–15 eggs. Nothing more is known about the reproductive biology.

Similar species: *Pseustes poecilonotus* is similar in appearance but has only two postocular scales and two anterior temporals. *Xenodon severus* is much smaller and heavier bodied, and has smooth scales. *Spilotes pullatus* is prominently patterned with black and yellow.

Habitat/Range: *Pseustes sulphureus sulphureus* lives in primary and secondary forests. It is often seen on the ground in clearings and especially in agricultural areas—drawn, perhaps, by the rodents that are attracted to such sites. We found two large specimens in the thatched roof of Amazon Camp, an ecotourism lodge, on the Rio Momon. The range of this species includes Peru, Brazil, the Guianas, and Trinidad.

Comments: This slender, alert snake often periscopes its head high above its body when actively hunting. When frightened it inflates the throat vertically, lolls the pink tongue out, draws back into a loose S, and, if not able to escape, makes sweeping strikes. It has powerful jaws and can bite quite hard.

Genus *Rhinobothryum;* Ringed Snakes

There are two species in this poorly known genus of oviparous, rear-fanged snakes. The species that occurs in the Amazon Basin is thought to be nocturnal and largely arboreal. Ringed snakes are 3–4 feet (90–122 cm) long and feed on frogs and lizards. Although they are venomous, their bite is not considered harmful to humans.

The two species range from Costa Rica south to Paraguay but seem nowhere common.

244. Amazon Ringed Snake
Rhinobothryum lentiginosum

Size: Adults are up to 4 feet (1.2 m) long.

Identifying features: This beautiful, slender, chunky-headed snake has red, black, and white rings. The black rings are the widest, the reds are next widest (but much narrower than the blacks), and the white rings are the narrowest. The black head scales are outlined with red. Although the colors continue onto the belly, they are very irregular. The pupils are vertically elliptical and the tail is only weakly prehensile.

Reproduction: This species is oviparous, but virtually nothing else is known about its reproductive biology.

Similar species: The red-edged black head scales of this species are diagnostic.

Habitat/Range: This beautiful ringed snake is an arboreal resident of primary rainforest habitats. The species ranges widely from Suriname to Paraguay but seems to be uncommon throughout its range.

Comments: This rear-fanged snake is not considered dangerous to humans, but the composition of its venom is unknown.

Genus *Siphlophis;* Liana Snakes

There are five snakes in this poorly known genus. They are considered uncommon at best, and most researchers consider them actually rare. It may be that they are simply overlooked when resting quietly in their arboreal rainforest retreats.

The liana snakes are oviparous and rear-fanged. They feed on nestling birds and small mammals, and perhaps lizards. Virtually nothing is known about the composition of the venom, but their bites are not thought to be dangerous to humans.

Four of the five species are restricted to various areas of Brazil. The fifth, *S. cervinus,* ranges from Bolivia and central Brazil north to Panama.

245. Common Liana Snake

Siphlophis cervinus

Size: Adults are about 2.5 feet (75 cm) long.

Identifying features: This pretty, slender snake is one of Amazonia's least known species. Its color is brightest (red-orange to orange) vertebrally, and it has yellow (or cream) and black bands laterally. The chunky head is brownish or brownish red with the scales outlined in cream or yellow. The belly is whitish spotted with black, giving a checkered appearance. The pupils are vertically elliptical.

Reproduction: Clutches of up to a dozen eggs have been reported. Other than this, nothing is known about the reproductive biology.

Similar species: None. The orange vertebral area and checkered belly are diagnostic.

Habitat/Range: In a dichotomy of terms, the common liana snake is thought to be uncommon but has been found in a variety of habitats in primary and secondary forests as well as in agricultural clearings and villages. It appears to be both arboreal and terrestrial. The species ranges from Trinidad and Colombia to Bolivia and Brazil.

Comments: This little snake may be more secretive and difficult to find than actually uncommon. Although it is reported to eat baby birds and small mammals, lizards seem to be the primary prey. It has rear fangs, but this species is not considered dangerous to humans.

Genus *Spilotes;* Tiger Rat Snake

This magnificent snake may be more than 8 feet (2.5 m) long and is tiger-like in both appearance and disposition. The shiny black body has yellow markings. Although it is often seen on the ground, the tiger rat snake is an accomplished climber that may hunt for birds and small mammals in the trees and shrubs. Like the racers, it is alert and very vision oriented. It watches closely for its prey, immediately changing direction on spotting a potential meal to one side or the other. Youngsters eat lizards; adults prey on birds and mammals.

The tiger rat snake is nonvenomous, but nonvenomous definitely does not mean nonbiting. If threatened, it draws its neck into an S and strikes fast and repeatedly. It does not hesitate to bite.

The single species ranges from Mexico south to Argentina.

246. Tiger Rat Snake

Spilotes pullatus pullatus

Size: Commonly more than 7 feet; occasionally 8 feet or more (2.1–2.5 m).
Identifying features: Despite its common name, this fast, alert snake is more closely allied to the racers than to the rat snakes. The dorsal and lateral ground color is black. There is a variable amount of yellow patterning in the form of many small spots, narrow or broad bands, or blotches. Some specimens are more yellow than black or even virtually all yellow; some lack most or even all of the yellow; and others lack cross bands but have a well-defined yellow vertebral stripe. The sides of the face are yellow with black labial sutures. The venter is primarily yellow but may be profusely patterned with black.
Reproduction: The clutch size is 5–17 eggs. Females—at least captive females—may produce two clutches per year. Hatchlings are about 17 inches (43 cm) long.

Similar species: This is the only shiny jet black *and* yellow arboreal snake in the region.

Habitat/Range: Like the species in the allied genus *Pseustes*, *Spilotes pullatus* is rather a habitat generalist. It occurs in primary and secondary forests, clearings, trash heaps, and village edges—anywhere rodents and lizards can be found. The species ranges from Costa Rica to northern Argentina.

Comments: When threatened, the tiger rat snake inflates its neck vertically, faces the source of its displeasure, and makes sweeping strikes. It bites hard and chews when contact is made, leaving many more wounds than a simple bite would leave.

Genus *Taeniophallus;* Leaf-Litter Snakes

This is a Neotropical genus of about eight small, earth-colored snakes. They are seldom seen unless turned up from under a log or moist leaf litter. A favored habitat is among the tangles of fibrous roots and decaying leaves between the buttresses of ceiba and other giant trees. These nonvenomous, oviparous, easily overlooked snakes probably eat earthworms and other invertebrates.

247. Short-Nosed Leaf-Litter Snake

Taeniophallus brevirostris

Size: Adults are 12–15 inches (30–38 cm) in length.

Identifying features: The five longitudinal brown stripes against a ground color of gray to brownish gray are easily seen in even moderately good light. The venter may vary from cream to pale green. The chin often has a reddish blush but may also be cream. The brown head bears spots of tan to reddish tan. The upper labial scales are cream to tan and variably speckled with brown. The smooth scales of this burrowing snake are in 17 rows. The anal plate is divided.

Reproduction: Both Dixon and Soini (1977) and Duellman (1978) mention finding a female containing two eggs. Nothing else is known about the reproductive biology.

Similar species: *Tantilla melanocephala,* another small burrowing snake, looks superficially like *Taeniophallus brevirostris* but has only 15 rows of scales.

Habitat/Range: This forest floor species is occasionally found crossing trails in all types of forests—secondary and primary—as well as in clearings and agricultural areas. More often it is found by raking leaf litter and turning decomposing logs. It is said to be primarily diurnal. The species ranges throughout most of the Amazon Basin.

Comments: This is a common to abundant but secretive snake.

Genus *Thamnodynastes*; Mock Vipers

If a lichen-covered stick begins to crawl across the forest floor, the chances are pretty good that you have been fooled by a mock viper. The half-dozen species in this genus are among the most cryptic of the New World serpents. They occur in the Neotropics and the West Indies.

When threatened the mock vipers either assume an unmoving, rigid position or strike savagely. Fortunately, a nonvenomous snake that is adult at just over 15 inches (37.5 cm) is not dangerous to anything other than its prey—which consists of frogs and invertebrates. These little snakes are found amid the leaf litter or behind bark and other such habitats in both cleared areas and primary rainforest.

248. Common Mock Viper

Thamnodynastes pallidus

Size: Adults are about 16 inches (40 cm) long.

Identifying features: The dorsal ground color of this slender and admirably camouflaged snake is tan, pinkish tan, or buff. Anterior markings may be in the form of partial bands that become spots posteriorly. The belly is darker than the dorsum and may be spotted with very dark brown. The top of the head is darker than the dorsum; the chin and throat are lighter than the belly.

Reproduction: This species bears live young, but its reproductive biology is poorly understood.

Similar species: None, other than congenerics. This is the only mock viper in the Amazon Basin with dorsal scales in 17 rows.

Habitat/Range: The common mock viper inhabits leaf litter and pond edges in primary rainforest. It can and occasionally does climb. The species is widely distributed in the northern Amazon Basin.

Comments: The common mock viper's usual response to harassment is to straighten out and become rigid, showing no signs of life. Sometimes, however, the same snake will strike and bite fiercely with little provocation.

Genus *Tripanurgos;* Red Vine Snake

Currently this is a monotypic genus. Some taxonomists doubt its validity and think that the red vine snake actually belongs in the genus *Siphlophis.* This beautiful, translucent, very slender rear-fanged snake attains a length of a little more than 2.5 feet (76 cm). It is oviparous and nocturnal, has large eyes with vertical pupils, and feeds on lizards and frogs. The potency of the venom is unknown, but this small snake, which is reluctant to bite anything other than a prey item, probably poses no danger to humans.

249. Red Vine Snake

Tripanurgos (Siphlophis) compressus

Size: The total length is 30–36 inches (76–91 cm).
Identifying features: The ground color is almost translucent rose to red. There are 40 or more well-separated dark bars along the body and tail. The top of the head, from the tip of the snout to the parietals, and the neck are dark, separated by a wide cream to yellow collar that is wider laterally. The venter is cream. The scales are in 19 rows. The vertebral scales are noticeably enlarged.
Reproduction: A large preserved female contained three eggs.
Similar species: No other vine snake has a red ground color. Other species with a dark head, white collar, and red ground lack the black saddles.
Habitat/Range: The red vine snake occurs in both primary and secondary forests. It has been found high in trees, low in bushes, and in grasses at the edge of swamps. Most specimens have been found at night. Most of those we have seen were in shrubs between 4 and 10 feet (1.2–3 m) above the ground, but one individual was found among the grasses of a small seep. The species is found from Bolivia and Brazil northward through the Amazon Basin.
Comments: It is probable that this snake feeds on frogs, and perhaps eats small lizards as well. This does not seem to be a common species.

Genus *Xenodon;* False Vipers

This genus contains about five species, all diurnal amphibian eaters of stout build and irascible disposition. The false vipers are terrestrial but are often found in the proximity of water. They do not hesitate to swim.

Considered by some to be the ecological counterparts of the North American hog-nosed snakes, the false vipers have many of the same defensive ploys. When threatened, they hiss and strike; if the perceived threat continues, they open the mouth, roll over, and play dead. One notable difference between the false vipers and the hog-nosed snakes is that the false vipers will bite (something that hog-noses seldom do), and will do so repeatedly.

The common name refers to these snakes' similarity in color and pattern to the venomous vipers of the genera *Bothrops* and *Bothriopsis*.

The genus ranges from Mexico south to Argentina.

250. Common False Viper

Xenodon rhabdocephalus rhabdocephalus

Size: Adults are generally 30–40 inches (76–102 cm) in total length, but some exceed a heavy-bodied 4 feet (1.2 m).

Identifying features: This pretty, hooded snake may be uniformly colored or banded; if the latter, it retains much of the pattern and color throughout its life. The banded false viper resembles the venomous fer-de-lance in color and body pattern, although the former usually has fewer dark bands. The dorsal and lateral ground color is variable brown to russet. The bands are wide, of a darker brown, and may contain obscure lighter areas ventrolaterally. A dark blotch, bifurcate posteriorly, is present on the top of the head. The arms of this blotch extend onto the neck. A dark, diagonal postocular stripe is usually visible. The anal scale is not divided. Although the pattern is usually visible throughout life, the contrast on old, large adults may be reduced.

Reproduction: This oviparous species may produce 5–15 eggs in a single clutch. Nothing else is known about its reproductive biology.

Similar species: See the accounts for *Xenodon severus* and *Bothrops atrox*, below.

Habitat/Range: This diurnal snake is most frequently seen in forested areas where its favored prey, toads and frogs, is abundant. This species ranges from northern Central America south to Amazonian Bolivia.

Comments: Like other members of the genus, *Xenodon rhabdocephalus* is able to eat the very toxic giant toad, *Bufo marinus*, with impunity. When frightened, this interesting snake may distend its neck laterally. If very frightened it will include the anterior portion of its body in the distension, and may strike and bite. If very hard-pressed, it will roll onto its back and play dead.

The nongrooved teeth in the rear of the upper jaw are greatly enlarged, and the saliva probably contains toxins. If it is necessary to handle this snake, do so with care.

251. Giant False Viper

Xenodon severus

Size: Adults may exceed 4 feet (1.2 m) in total length.

Identifying features: The babies and juveniles of this heavy-bodied snake are prominently banded on both the head and dorsum. The ground color is gray, and the bands and markings are dark olive gray to brownish. With growth the bands tend to fade and the ground color changes to olive gold, brownish, or olive tan. Some large old individuals become a nearly uniform olive gold dorsally, with the ventral aspect of each scale paler or brighter than the rest of the scale. This produces a pretty spangled effect. The ventral scales are yellow to pale orange. The smooth scales are arranged in 21 oblique rows. The anal scale is divided.

Reproduction: The clutch size is 9–26 eggs. It is not known whether this species produces multiple clutches.

Similar species: The false vipers can be difficult to identify. *Xenodon r. rhabdocephalus* has only 19 rows of scales and usually retains at least traces of a posteriorly bifurcate head spot.

Habitat/Range: This terrestrial, diurnal snake occurs in primary and secondary forest habitats. It is most commonly encountered where the toads (including the very toxic giant toad) and leptodactylid frogs on which it feeds are most common. The range of this species encompasses most of the Amazon Basin.

Comments: This species is capable of taking comparatively large prey items. Most specimens are quite ready to bite if carelessly restrained. The teeth in the rear of the upper jaw are enlarged, and the saliva is thought to contain toxins of unknown composition and virulence. When frightened this snake flattens its head and neck horizontally and distends the neck into an impressive hood.

Genus *Xenopholis*; Flat-Headed Snake

The single species in this genus is a small, fossorial snake occasionally seen at trailside or amid damp leaf litter during wet weather. Some of the few specimens found have been near water holes. The flat-headed snake apparently feeds on small frogs and is nocturnal. The genus is restricted in distribution to Amazonian Peru, Ecuador, Colombia, and western Brazil.

252. Flat-Headed Snake

Xenopholis scalaris

Size: Adults are about 14 inches (35 cm) long.

Identifying features: The most definitive part of this burrowing snake's pattern is the (sometimes very obscure) zigzag terra cotta–colored vertebral stripe that starts on the nape and continues onto the tail. The dorsal and lateral ground color is reddish brown. More than 20 partial black bands extending downward from the dark vertebral stripe overlie the ground color. These may be straight across on both sides or offset vertebrally. The belly is off-white to cream. There are 17 rows of smooth scales. The prefrontals, paired on most snake species, are fused into a single large scale.

Reproduction: The reproductive biology of this oviparous species is unknown.

Similar species: The single prefrontal scale and terra cotta middorsal stripe should differentiate the flat-headed snake from other colorful species, but the earth snake *Atractus schach* can be very similar in appearance.

Habitat/Range: This burrowing snake is considered an uncommon resident of secondary and primary rainforests. It is restricted in distribution to the northwestern Amazon Basin.

Comments: Like many snakes, when it feels itself threatened this little colubrine flattens its body to almost ribbon thinness. Thus flattened, it appears much larger to a predator viewing it from above.

Venomous Snakes

Although greatly outnumbered by the "harmless" colubrine snakes, the venomous snakes are always of immense interest to Amazon travelers. Two families are represented in the region: the coral snakes, members of the cobra family Elapidae; and the pit vipers of the family Viperidae. Because of their potential significance to ecotourists, we discuss a fair percentage of the species present in the Amazon Basin.

Except for three predominantly black species—*Leptomicrurus n. narducci, L. scutiventris,* and *Micrurus putumayensis*—the coral snakes are brightly ringed in red, black, and white or yellow; on some ringed species, the dark colors predominate. Most coral snakes are terrestrial and secretive. A few readily enter the water. Coral snakes have fixed, hollow front fangs; can move quickly; will bite readily if carelessly restrained; and should be considered extremely dangerous.

More than half a dozen species of pit vipers occur in the Amazon Basin. Two are primarily arboreal; the others are primarily terrestrial. The arboreal forms are occasionally found in terrestrial situations, and the terrestrial species occasionally climb. The fer-de-lance, *Bothrops atrox,* is abundant and commonly encountered even near habitations. The other pit vipers are much less frequently seen, perhaps due as much to their remarkable camouflage as to their actual rarity. The bushmaster, *Lachesis muta muta,* is an uncommon species that attains a greater length than any other viperine species.

There are no rattlesnakes in the western Amazon Basin, but several races of the widely distributed tropical rattlesnake, *Crotalus durissus,* occur to the east in savannas north and south of the actual limits of the basin. We include an account of these two snakes to satisfy ecotourists' interest in them.

All vipers must be considered dangerously venomous. They have movable, hollow fangs and strike—rather than bite—when frightened, injured, or feeding.

Cobra Relatives: Family Elapidae

The venomous coral snakes, all in the subfamily Micrurinae, are the only New World members of the cobra family. Two genera (the validity of one, *Leptomicrurus,* is disputed) occur in Amazonia.

Collectively, these are secretive burrowing snakes that possess rigidly affixed front fangs. The venom is strongly neurotoxic. The common belief that coral snakes can bite only appendages such as fingers and toes or areas of exposed skin is entirely erroneous. Large specimens can bite through a layer of clothing. A bite from any coral snake can be a devastating, even lethal, experience.

Genera *Leptomicrurus* and *Micrurus;* Coral Snakes

Because these two genera are often synonymized, we treat them together. People in the United States learn to recognize coral snakes in one of two ways. They either recite the rhyme "red to yellow, kill a fellow; red to black, venom lack" (or some variation), or they think of the two caution colors of a traffic signal; the red and yellow abut on both the signal and the snake. These prompts are often *not* valid in the Neotropics. Some Neotropical coral snakes are predominantly black, and others are narrowly ringed with black and white; on those that are tricolored, the yellow is often replaced by white and is separated from the red by a ring of black. Albinism is known. The black-white-black-white-black rings present on many of the tricolored species are often referred to as triads. The number of triads is used in species identification.

Collectively, coral snakes consume onychophorans (peripatus), fish (especially synbranchid eels), caecilians, amphisbaenids, lizards, and other snakes (including venomous species).

Some coral snakes of the Amazon Basin, including the heavy-bodied, water-loving *Micrurus surinamensis*, may be active day or night, are reasonably alert while surface active, and can exceed 5 feet (1.5 m) in length. The smallest species, the pygmy black coral snake, *Leptomicrurus scutiventris*, seldom exceeds 14 inches (35 cm) in total length. All are oviparous.

A note of caution: Although there are more tricolored nonvenomous snakes than tricolored coral snakes in Amazonas, we urge you not to tempt fate by approaching and handling any tricolored snake. Remember that not all of the Amazonian coral snakes are tricolored! Use common sense at all times.

253. Northwest Black-backed Coral Snake

Leptomicrurus narduccii melanotus

Size: Occasional large specimens slightly exceed 3 feet (91 cm) in length, but most are about 24 inches.

Identifying features: Viewed dorsally, this is a black snake with a yellow head ring, yellow to orange lateral spots, and one or two rather bright red tail rings. Viewed ventrally, the snake has a yellow chin and a variable number (37–62) of yellow to orange (or orange-red) belly bands. The upward extensions of the bands form the pattern of spots on the otherwise black sides. Two to four red subcaudal spots are present, and some may continue around the dorsum to form the tail rings.

Reproduction: This snake is oviparous, but little else is known about its reproductive biology. The clutch size is suspected to be two to four or perhaps five eggs.

Similar species: See the species accounts for *Leptomicrurus scutiventris* and *Micrurus putumayensis*.

Habitat/Range: The northwest blackbacked black coral snake is a secretive denizen of primary and secondary forests and rainforests at elevations ranging from 500 to 4000 feet (150–1300 m). Its range includes southern Colombia, eastern Ecuador, northern Peru, and northwestern Brazil.

Comments: This most "uncoral snake–like" coral snake is rarely seen. It is thought to feed on gymnophthalmid lizards.

254. Pygmy Black Coral Snake

Leptomicrurus scutiventris

Size: Among the smallest of the coral snakes, adults are usually between 14 and 17 inches (35–43 cm) in total length.

Identifying features: This predominantly black coral snake may occasionally have some very narrow reddish rings dorsally. Ventrally, the color is black with 26–35 reddish, usually rounded, ventral spots. The chin and throat are red, sometimes with black spotting. A prominent yellowish to orange head ring is present. At least one of the two to four red subcaudal spots forms a complete ring.

Reproduction: This snake is oviparous, but virtually nothing else is known about its reproductive biology.

Similar species: See the accounts for *Leptomicrurus narduccii melanotus* and *Micrurus putumayensis*.

Habitat/Range: This diminutive micrurine is a denizen of the rainforests and their associated clearings. Its range extends eastward in a wide swath from eastern Ecuador and northern Peru to eastern Colombia and northeastern Brazil.

Comments: *Leptomicrurus scutiventris* was long known as *L. schmidti* and *Micrurus karlschmidti*. The diet is thought to consist primarily of microteiids.

255. White-Banded Coral Snake

Micrurus albicinctus

Size: Adults range from 16 to about 21 inches (40–53 cm) in length.

Identifying features: Dorsally and laterally the white rings on this otherwise all-black snake are one scale long and made up of white spots. The white markings are longer than one scale in length on the tail. Ventrally, the white markings may be spots or may consist of entirely white ventral scutes. The approximately 85 white rings create a busy pattern. The head is predominantly black but also bears white spots. The chin is light.

Reproduction: Virtually nothing is known about the breeding biology of *Micrurus albicinctus*.

Similar species: None.

Habitat/Range: This secretive and poorly known snake inhabits forested areas in the Amazonian region of western and central Brazil.

Comments: *Micrurus albicinctus* was initially considered a subspecies of *M. ornatissimus*.

256. Black-Headed Coral Snake

Micrurus averyi

Size: The average adult length is 20–28 inches (60–70 cm).

Identification: Typically, this pretty coral snake has about 12 very broad orange-red rings separated by narrow black rings edged with white spots (or rings) so narrow that they are barely discernible. The short tail is also tricolored, but a heavy suffusion of black all but obscures the red bands. There are no triads of black and white. Like the body pattern, the white rings on the tail are very narrow and usually consist of spots. The head is predominantly black, often with obscure red markings on the snout and some light markings on the upper labial scales beneath the eyes.

Reproduction: Other than the fact that this coral snake is oviparous, the reproductive biology is unknown.

Similar species: *Micrurus remotus* has much narrower red rings.

Habitat/Range: The forested Amazon lowlands of Brazil and adjacent Suriname are home to this snake.

257. Slender Coral Snake

Micrurus filiformis

Size: Adults occasionally near 3 feet (91 cm) but are more typically in the 22–28-inch (56–70-cm) size range.

Identifying features: This tricolored coral snake is small, slender, and supple. The typical pattern of ringing, beginning with the snout, is black-white-black-red-black-white-black-white-black-red. The red rings are the widest, and the white (sometimes yellowish) rings are the narrowest. There are up to 20 body triads.

Reproduction: The clutch size is probably two to five elongate eggs.

Similar species: Although its extreme slenderness may help identify this coral snake, the excitement of finding a tricolored snake in the field is often enough to muddle one's judgment. Besides the obvious similarities of the other tricolored coral snakes, some harmless snakes such as *Erythrolamprus*, *Hydrops*, *Oxyrhopus*, and some *Atractus* also mimic the colors and patterns of coral snakes. Compare the ringing patterns of all before making an identification.

Habitat/Range: This nocturnal snake seems to be most often associated with trash heaps and surface debris near human habitations but is also found near forest rivers and streams. The species is found throughout much of the northern and eastern Amazon Basin.

Comments: The preferred foods are unknown.

258. Orange-Ringed Coral Snake

Micrurus hemprichii ortonii

Size: Large adults may be 3 feet (91 cm) long, but most are in the 1.5–2-foot (45–61-cm) range.

Identifying features: This coral snake bears very wide black rings and very narrow white rings (the black and white are in triads) separated by moderately wide rings of rather dull orange. Including those on the head and the tail, this species has only six or seven orange rings (five or six black and white triads). This is the only coral snake with an undivided anal plate.

Reproduction: Like all coral snakes, this species is oviparous and, being of moderate length, probably produces between one and eight eggs per clutch.

Similar species: The undivided anal plate and very wide rings are diagnostic.

Habitat/Range: The orange-ringed coral snake inhabits rainforests in the Amazonian lowlands and moderate elevations from southern Colombia and southern Venezuela to Bolivia, Peru, and Brazil.

Comments: The diet consists largely of peripatus, but also includes amphisbaenids and small snakes. Because of the elongate, wormlike form of the peripatus, *Micrurus hemprichii ortonii* is occasionally called the "western worm-eating coral snake."

259. Langsdorff's Coral Snake

Micrurus langsdorffi

Size: Adults are generally about 20 inches (50 cm) long; some reach about 30 inches (75 cm).

Identifying features: This is one of the most variably colored coral snakes in the western Amazon Basin. The dorsum may be normally tricolored (red-white-black-white-red) or reddish black to brownish red with broad, dull (but brighter than the ground color) strawberry red rings. The red rings are separated from the ground color by very narrow rings of white. The venter may have only two colors, with the brownish red ground color rings becoming white or off-white and alternating with the strawberry rings (some black ringing may be present). Alternatively, the belly may be virtually all black or all white. There may be white spots on the head shields as well as a variable amount of white (or black) scale edging dorsally and laterally. Melanin may suffuse the normally darker dorsal colors, creating the impression of a black and white snake.

Reproduction: Like other coral snakes of moderate size, this species probably produces eight or fewer eggs per clutch, but no records are available.

Similar species: The fact that the black rings are single rather than in triads will differentiate this species from sympatric coral snakes. *Erythrolamprus aesculapii* often has double black rings, and tricolored *Oxyrhopus* may have triads of black and white.

Habitat/Range: This species is associated with forestlands and adjacent clearings in southern Colombia and adjacent Ecuador, northern Peru, and Amazonian Brazil.

Comments: Because of the polymorphism exhibited by this species, the common name "confusing coral snake" is occasionally applied.

260. Western Ribbon Coral Snake

Micrurus lemniscatus helleri

Size: Adults may be about 3.5 feet (1 m) long, but many (most?) specimens are at least somewhat smaller.

Identifying features: This coral snake has very wide red and black rings, and narrow white rings. Because of the ring width, the number of body triads is low—usually between 9 and 11 (very rarely to 12). The tip of the snout is narrowly black followed by white-black-red-black-white-black-white-black-red.

Reproduction: The clutch size is probably three to eight elongate eggs.

Similar species: Compare the species accounts, pictures, and literature for all other tricolored coral snakes of Amazonian Peru as well as those for

Atractus latifrons, A. elaps, and all species of *Oxyrhopus, Hydrops,* and *Erythrolamprus* before deciding which snake you have.

Habitat/Range: Besides secondary and primary forests, *M. lemniscatus helleri* has also been found in agricultural and other cleared areas, where it is active both day and night. Rather a habitat generalist, it occupies an immense area of west-central South America from southern Colombia to Bolivia.

Comments: The western ribbon coral snake is known to feed on caecilians, smaller snakes, and synbranchid eels.

To reiterate our earlier warning: Until its identification has been confirmed, use caution when approaching *any* tricolored snake in this region.

261. Eastern Ribbon Coral Snake

Micrurus lemniscatus lemniscatus

Size: Adults reach lengths near 3.5 feet (1 m), but the specimens seen are usually somewhat smaller.

Identifying features: This coral snake has very wide red and black rings and narrow white rings. The eastern subspecies is more busily patterned than the western form, *M. l. helleri.* Because the black rings are narrow, *M. l. lemniscatus* usually has between 13 and 15 (very rarely 12) triads. The tip of the snout is narrowly black followed by white-black-red-black-white-black-white-black-red.

Reproduction: The clutch size is thought to be three to eight elongate eggs.

Similar species: Compare the species accounts and pictures for the other tricolored coral snakes of Amazonian Peru as well as *Atractus latifrons, A. elaps,* and all species of *Oxyrhopus, Hydrops,* and *Erythrolamprus.*

Habitat/Range: Besides secondary and primary forests, *M. lemniscatus helleri* may also be found in agricultural and other cleared areas, where it is active both day and night. This habitat generalist occupies an immense area of west-central South America from southern Colombia to Bolivia.

Comments: Some populations of the eastern ribbon coral snake apparently feed exclusively on the marbled swamp eel, *Synbranchus marmoratus.* Other populations also incorporate caecilians and smaller snakes into the diet.

Use caution when approaching *any* tricolored snake in this region.

262. Sooty Coral Snake

Micrurus putumayensis

Size: Adults are about 32 inches (80 cm) long.

Identifying features: This snake does not look like the typical coral snake because it is ringed in black and yellow only. With increasing age, most (if not all) of the yellow body rings become suffused with melanin dorsally, occasionally to the point of being nearly obscured. The nuchal and tail rings remain best defined. There are 7–11 yellow body rings, including the nuchal ring. The yellow remains rather well defined ventrally.

Reproduction: The breeding biology is entirely unknown.

Similar species: The very slender (and uncommon) black coral snakes (genus *Leptomicrurus*) also lack dorsal cross bands on the body but have red spots ventrally.

Habitat/Range: The sooty coral snake is thought to inhabit leaf litter in old secondary and primary forests. It is very infrequently encountered, but whether that is due to rarity or reclusiveness is unknown. Although most specimens encountered have been seen during the morning hours, it is probable that, like other coral snakes, *M. putumayensis* is at least occasionally active after dark. This species occurs in northeastern Peru and adjacent Brazil.

Comments: Nonvenomous snakes seem to be the primary food items.

263. Remote Coral Snake

Micrurus remotus (=psyches)

Size: Adults are between 2 and 3 feet (60–91 cm) long.

Identifying features: Because an age-related suffusion of melanin often occurs, this coral snake can be of variably intense color and pattern. The red rings are the widest, but on some specimens they are only moderately wider than the black rings. The white rings are very narrow. The head is largely black, but a white postocular (occipital) triangle (occasionally an actual ring) is usually visible. There is only a single black ring between each pair of red rings. There are no triads in the pattern.

Reproduction: Like all coral snakes the remote is oviparous, but virtually nothing more is known about its breeding biology.

Similar species: Many other coral snakes and many mimics have the black and white bands in triads.

Habitat/Range: Look for this snake under surface debris. This species is distributed through the Amazonian provinces of Venezuela, Colombia, and adjacent Brazil. Its actual range remains imperfectly delineated.

264. Western Amazon Coral Snake

Micrurus spixii obscurus

Size: Adults may be more than 5 feet (1.5 m) long and have a considerable girth.

Identifying features: The suffusion of black intensifies with age, and some specimens may show even less contrast between the ground color and rings than the one pictured. Ring widths and arrangements, and hence color sequences, can be quite variable on the head and anterior neck. The black rings are narrowest. The white and red rings are about equal in width. The tip of the nose is white, but often has a heavy suffusion of black. The black eye ring is narrow and may be discontinuous laterally. Red is usually next in the sequence, but it may be reduced to a rosy suffusion on the cheeks. The white ring at the back of the head is usually best defined laterally and ventrally. A wide black ring follows that is about eight scale rows wide and may project forward vertebrally, narrowing or even interrupting the first white neck ring dorsally. Following this, the pattern becomes more stable—white, black, red, black, etc. Juveniles are more cleanly patterned than old adults, which have black pigment suffusing the posterior parts of many of the white and red scales. The rings encircle the body. The white rings may be pale yellow ventrally.

Reproduction: Little is known about the reproductive biology of this oviparous snake. The clutch size could be as big as a dozen eggs.

Similar species: The white (yellow) body rings of both *Micrurus lemniscatus helleri* (black nose) and *M. s. surinamensis* (red nose) are much narrower than the black and red rings.

Habitat/Range: The western Amazon coral snake inhabits humid, canopied primary forests. It is most often found beneath ground debris such as leaves and fallen logs. The species ranges from southern Venezuela and southern Colombia south to the Peru–Bolivia border.

Comments: Some specimens are quiet and inoffensive, even when provoked, but many are irascible. The diet consists of other snakes, some lizards, and caecilians. If restrained, this beautiful coral snake will flatten its body and tail and coil the tail upward while hiding its head beneath its coils.

265. Central Amazon Coral Snake

Micrurus spixii spixii

Size: Adults may exceed 5 feet (1.5 m) in total length.

Identifying features: The color patterns can be quite variable, especially on the head and neck. The snout may be largely black but usually has at least traces of white laterally. The top of the head may be so suffused with black as to appear uniformly colored. The cheeks are rosy red; the chin is a brighter red. The anterior edge of the first black ring is often imprecise, but the posterior edge is well defined. Except for on the neck, the black and white rings are in triads. The black body rings are narrowest. The white and red rings, which may be variably suffused with black, are about equal in width.

Reproduction: Little is known about the reproductive biology of this oviparous snake. Like the more westerly race and other large members of the genus, the clutch size could be as large as a dozen eggs.

Similar species: The white (yellow) body rings of both *Micrurus lemniscatus helleri* (black nose) and *M. s. surinamensis* (red nose) are much narrower than the black and red rings. The various races of *M. hemprichii* have a black snout. *Micrurus isozonus* (not pictured) usually has very discernible red on the crown of the head.

Habitat/Range: This burrowing snake is found under surface debris. This species occurs in Amazonian central Brazil.

Comments: Confusingly patterned intergrades occur in areas where ranges of the various subspecies abut.

266. Aquatic Coral Snake

Micrurus surinamensis surinamensis

Size: Specimens more than 4 feet (1.2 m) long have been reported, and some individuals may exceed 5 feet (1.5 m).

Identifying features: This is one of the prettiest of the Amazonian snakes, and one of the largest and most robust of the coral snakes. From the tip of the snout, the colors are red (nearly the entire head), black (narrow), yellow (narrow), black (wide), yellow (narrow), black (narrow), red (wide), etc. The black ring between the yellow rings is wider than the black rings that abut the red. The head scales are outlined narrowly in black. The yellow rings are narrow. The pattern is rather precise. The colors are usually clearly defined, but some black tipping may occur on the red scales. The colors encircle the body.

Reproduction: Clutches of up to 13 eggs have been documented.

Similar species: *Micrurus spixii obscurus* has a white nose and very broad white body rings. The slender *M. lemniscatus helleri* has a black nose and the black and white body rings are about similar in width.

Habitat/Range: This brightly colored coral snake inhabits the edges of ponds, streams, rivers, and oxbows, and is often seen actually in the water. One that we surprised on a streamside path at night dove into the water and almost immediately burrowed out of sight into the glutinous mud of the stream bottom.

Comments: The diet includes tropical (synbranchid) eels. It is not known whether amphibians are also consumed.

Pit Vipers: Family Viperidae

Six species of these intriguing, evolutionarily advanced venomous snakes may be encountered in the Peruvian upper Amazon (the current ecotour epicenter), and additional species are found elsewhere in the Amazon Basin. The pit vipers vary in size from the 18-inch (45-cm) forest tree vipers of the genus *Bothriopsis* to the slender 8-plus-foot (2.4-m) bushmaster, *Lachesis muta muta*.

The pit vipers derive their name from the heat-sensing pit between the eye and the nostril that enables the snake to home in on warm-blooded prey. Although the composition of the venom differs from one species to the next, all pit viper venom contains complex and varying proteins and enzymes that not only kill the prey animal but also begin a predigestive tissue breakdown. A venomous snake can control the amount of venom expended in a bite.

After envenomating the prey, many pit vipers (especially the terrestrial species) release it. The prey animal runs off and dies, and the snake finds it by following the trail of chemical cues it left behind. Arboreal pit vipers often hold the envenomated prey until it dies.

Genera *Bothriopsis* and *Bothrops;* Lanceheads

These two closely allied genera are still considered congeneric by some taxonomists. The *Bothriopsis* species are primarily arboreal and have a strongly prehensile tail. The *Bothrops* species are essentially terrestrial but are fully capable of climbing, especially when young. In fact, juvenile *Bothrops* often position themselves in an alert hunting coil several feet above the ground on the leaves of broad-leaved plants (such as ginger or heliconia), where they seem to be awaiting a foraging treefrog or arboreal lizard.

Because of their cryptic coloration, all members of both genera are amazingly well camouflaged against their normal backgrounds.

All juvenile lanceheads accept cold-blooded prey such as frogs and lizards; the adults round out their diets with warm-blooded prey species. Juveniles of many species have contrasting tail tips, which they use to lure prey. Such "caudal luring" involves extending the writhing, usually brightly colored, tail tip upward from the coil in hope of attracting a hungry frog or lizard. When the prey animal approaches within striking distance, it is seized and envenomated, and it becomes the meal.

All species in both genera bear live young.

Representatives of the genus *Bothriopsis* (eight species) range from eastern Panama and northern Venezuela south to northern Bolivia and central Brazil. The 40-plus species of *Bothrops* range from northern Mexico southward to Argentina. Several species live on islands in the Caribbean.

Although jungle lore greatly overestimates the probability of encountering a venomous snake in the forest, use care when pushing through vegetation overhanging forest trails or walking through shrubby, overgrown areas.

267. Eastern Striped Forest Pit Viper

Bothriopsis bilineata bilineata

Size: Females often approach 30 inches (75 cm); the substantially smaller males are about 20 inches (50 cm) long.

Identifying features: The markings of this subspecies are rather well defined and constant. A dark (russet) postocular stripe is present. The lips are yellowish green. There are small, widely separated tan to pale orange dorsal markings. Black peppering of variable intensity is also present on the dorsum and is most intense anteriorly. The sutures between the labial scales are black. The ventral scutes are yellow centrally and pale green at their outer edges. A pale yellow(ish) stripe separates the ventral scutes from the smaller scales of the sides. The irises are bronzy green. Juveniles may be paler than adults. The tail is strongly prehensile and has an orang(ish), whitish, or yellow tip.

Reproduction: Clutches seem to consist of two to six babies.

Similar species: None in the immediate area.

Habitat/Range: This arboreal snake may be found in shrubs a yard or two above the ground. Because of the color and persistent immobility of the coiled snake, it is easily—and probably often—overlooked. This race is found in the eastern Amazon Basin.

Comments: Some reports claim that the venom is extremely toxic. Certainly, captive snakes can kill a lab mouse quickly. This nocturnal snake is more prone to bite after dark. It may sit quietly and allow close approach by day. It seems most common near water.

268. Western Striped Forest Pit Viper

Bothriopsis bilineata smaragdina

Size: Females often approach 30 inches (75 cm); males are substantially smaller, about 20 inches (50 cm).

Identifying features: The markings of this subspecies are variable but always muted. There may be small, widely separated, tan to pale orange dorsal markings. Black peppering of variable intensity is also present on the dorsum and is most intense anteriorly. The postocular stripe is either very pale or absent. The sutures between the labial scales (which are pale yellowish to greenish) are vague. The ventral scutes are yellow centrally and pale green at their outer edges. A pale yellow(ish) stripe often separates the ventral scutes from the smaller scales of the sides. The irises are bronzy green. Juveniles may be paler than adults. The tail is strongly prehensile and has an orang(ish), whitish, or yellow tip.

Reproduction: Clutches of this live-bearing species seem to consist of two to six young.

Similar species: None in the immediate area.

Habitat/Range: This nocturnal, arboreal pit viper positions itself in shrubs a few feet above the ground, often near standing water. This race occurs in the western Amazon Basin.

Comments: The western striped pit viper is more prone to bite after dark. It may sit quietly and allow close approach by day.

269. Speckled Forest Pit Viper

Bothriopsis taeniata taeniata

Size: Adults are 30–50 inches (75–151 cm) long.

Identifying features: The coloration varies and appears to change with age. Juveniles are grayish with a variable degree of black speckling and band intensity. Half-grown specimens may have a ground color of brown or pinkish brown. With advancing age the ground color changes to olive (never bright) green or gray, and the primary bands deepen to dusky forest green. Obscure secondary bands, often most visible dorsolaterally (but broken vertebrally), are present between the primary bands. A broad, dark postorbital stripe is present. A row of discrete white blotches is present along each lower side. The venter is light with a variable amount of scattered dark pigment. The irises are speckled forest green and yellow. The strongly prehensile tail may be dark tipped or orangish, brightest on young specimens. The tail color does not contrast strongly with the body color of adult snakes. The overall appearance of this snake might best be likened to that of a stout lichenate branch bearing a variable number of mosses.

Reproduction: The reproductive biology of this viviparous snake is largely unknown. The single reported clutch had six babies.

Similar species: None. The white ventrolateral spots are diagnostic.

Habitat/Range: Little is known about this big arboreal pit viper. It seems to be uncommon but may simply be so well camouflaged that it is often overlooked. Exercise caution when pushing through trailside and overhanging vegetation in its preferred primary forest habitats. The species is sparsely, but widely, distributed in the northern Amazon Basin.

Comments: This nocturnal snake is far more apt to bite after dark than during the day. A full bite from a large specimen could have serious consequences. The species was long known scientifically as *Bothrops castelnaudi* and is still occasionally referred to by that name.

270. South American Lancehead (Fer-de-Lance)

Bothrops atrox

Size: Most specimens encountered are 1–4 feet (30–120 cm) long, but specimens in excess of 6 feet (1.8 m) are occasionally seen.

Identifying features: This is a slender to robust snake with a prominent, lance-shaped head. While variable, the ground color is usually some shade of brown (light to very dark or russet), often with an olive tinge. Nineteen or more darker, light-edged cross bands are variably prominent. These may be complete across the dorsum or broken and staggered vertebrally. The top of the head may be patterned posteriorly. A well-defined to obscure broad or narrow postorbital stripe is present. The belly is yellowish with few to many dark spots. Neonates and juveniles have a yellow tail tip. The irises are gold to amber.

Reproduction: This fecund live-bearer produces 9–26 (rarely more) babies per clutch.

Similar species: *Bothrops brazili* is typically less busily patterned and has a narrower (or absent) postorbital bar, a less heavily marked venter, and grayish spots at the outer edges of some ventral scales. The bushmaster, *Lachesis m. muta,* has strongly keeled scales that are particularly rough vertebrally.

Habitat/Range: *Bothrops atrox* is an abundant and greatly feared species throughout most of the Amazon Basin. Although it climbs rather well (and is often found coiled a few feet above the ground on broad-leaved plants), the fer-de-lance is considered a terrestrial snake. The species is common in primary and secondary forests as well near human habitations. We have found them to be particularly common at the edges of swamps (they swim well and do not hesitate to take to the water) and at dumping sites.

Comments: This irascible snake has virulent venom. The fer-de-lance may be active by day but seems more crepuscular and nocturnal.

271. Velvety Lancehead

Bothrops brazili

Size: This is another of the large lanceheads. Adults are commonly 3–5 feet (0.9–1.5 m) and more rarely up to 6 feet (1.8 m) in length.

Identifying features: The velvety lancehead resembles the fer-de-lance in overall appearance. There are typically fewer than 18 cross bands, however, so it generally appears lighter overall with a less busy pattern than the fer-de-lance. The ground color can be pinkish, tan, or variably brown. The dark bands are grayish to brown, darkest at the edges. The venter is light but may have dark blotches and grayish spots at the outer edges of some of the ventral scutes. The top of the head is often light in color and may be entirely unmarked. The postorbital stripe is usually thin and may be entirely absent. Babies are slender but adults are often quite heavy bodied.

Reproduction: Captive females have produced 4–14 babies.

Similar species: The fer-de-lance, *Bothrops atrox,* usually has 19 or more dark cross bands, a more heavily patterned venter, and a broader and more prominent postorbital bar than *B. brazili.* The bushmaster, *Lachesis m. muta,* has protuberant and prominently keeled vertebral scales.

Habitat/Range: This species is less common than *B. atrox.* It seems restricted to upland primary forests. The species ranges from eastern Ecuador eastward to southern Venezuela and central-eastern Brazil.

272. Amazonian Hog-Nosed Lancehead

Bothrops hyoprora

Size: The adult is the smallest of the terrestrial pit vipers of Amazonian Peru. Most specimens are between 14 and 18 inches (35–45 cm) long, occasionally up to 26 inches (65 cm).

Identifying features: There is some degree of sexual dichromatism, with the female being the less prominently banded, especially anteriorly. The dorsal ground color is gray to brown and may be darker anteriorly. There are usually fewer than 20 wide, reddish brown bands (often brightest or most contrasting posteriorly). The bands, often edged with at least a few whitish or buff scales, may continue unbroken across or may break and alternate along the dorsal midline. The sides of the face are often darker than the crown. Vestiges of a light ventrolateral line may exist anteriorly, and a terra cotta vertebral stripe may be weakly evident. The canthus is upturned and strongly delineated. The belly is palest midventrally.

Reproduction: Females produce small clutches of live young.

Similar species: This is the only one of the terrestrial lanceheads of Amazonian Peru to have an upturned canthus rather than a rounded snout.

Habitat/Range: This hog-nosed viper is associated with leaf litter in streamside and wooded habitats in well-drained lowland forests of eastern Ecuador, southern Colombia, northern Peru, and western Brazil.

Comments: Like all of the Amazonian lanceheads, this small viper blends almost perfectly with its background. It does not seem to be a common species, but use care when walking forest trails.

Genus *Crotalus*; Rattlesnakes

Rattlesnakes in one form or another are widespread through much of North, Central, and South America, but their ranges skirt the Amazon Basin. The only rattlesnakes found in or near the basin—and then at only the outermost northern and southern extremes—are the two races of the widespread and dangerously toxic tropical rattlesnake. We have included these snakes in this book primarily because visitors want so badly to see them that they often insist, erroneously, that they have. Both races of the tropical rattlesnake have stripes on the neck and diamonds along the back.

273. Amazonian Rattlesnake

Crotalus durissus dryinas

Size: Up to 4.5 feet (1.4 m) long.
Identifying features: The scales are coarsely keeled. The ground color is grayish brown to rich brown. The colors are lightest anteriorly and darkest posteriorly. A pair of broad (more than a single scale row wide), dark stripes begin at the rear of the head, transverse the neck, and terminate about one-fifth of the way down the body. From that point rearward the markings are light-edged, dark, brown-centered rhomboids. The pattern becomes increasingly obscure posteriorly, and the tail is very dark. Unless broken off, a rattle is present.
Reproduction: Up to 20 (but often fewer) live babies are born in each litter.
Similar species: Although other snakes, including nonvenomous species, may vibrate the tail and produce a whirring buzz in vegetation, no other snake has a tail-tip rattle.
Habitat/Range: This is a snake of savannas and other dry, often scrubby habitats in the Guianas. It is not associated with the Amazonian lowlands.
Comments: When disturbed, this rattlesnake lifts its head high above its body coils, often lolls the tongue, and faces its adversary. It may remain this way, rattling furiously or silent, for long durations. Beware! The venom is very toxic.

274. Tropical Rattlesnake

Crotalus durissus terrificus

Size: This impressively heavy-bodied snake may attain a length of up to 4.5 feet (1.4 m).
Identifying features: The scales are coarsely keeled, and the ground color is grayish brown to rich brown. The colors are lightest anteriorly and darkest posteriorly. A pair of broad (more than a single scale row wide), dark stripes begin at the rear of the head, transverse the neck, and terminate about one-fifth of the way down the body. From that point rearward the markings are light-edged, dark, brown-centered rhomboids. The pattern becomes increasingly obscure posteriorly, and the tail is very dark. Unless broken off, a rattle is present.
Reproduction: Up to 20 (but often fewer) live babies are born in each litter.
Similar species: Although other snakes, including nonvenomous species,

may vibrate the tail and produce a whirring buzz in vegetation, no other snake has a tail-tip rattle.

Habitat/Range: This is a snake of savannas and other dry, often scrubby habitats throughout much of Brazil to Argentina. It is not associated with the Amazonian lowlands.

Comments: When disturbed, this rattlesnake lifts its head high above its body coils, often lolls the tongue, and faces its adversary. Although not as prone to bite as many believe, this snake is extremely dangerous.

Genus *Lachesis*; Bushmasters

The bushmaster is the largest and most distinctive of the terrestrial Neotropical pit vipers. It is also one of the most infrequently seen, but that is probably due more to its secretive habits and remarkably cryptic coloration than to actual rarity. The relatively slender build, strongly keeled back, very coarsely keeled scales, and distinctive pattern of dark dorsal diamonds containing a light spot on each side are distinctive.

The snakes in this genus are the only oviparous pit vipers in the New World.

Once a single species with four races, some taxonomists have now elevated at least one of the races to full species status.

Bushmasters range from Nicaragua (questionable records) south to Brazil and are found throughout much of the Amazon Basin.

275. Bushmaster

Lachesis muta muta

Size: Specimens 7 feet (2 m) long or more are often seen, and 8.5-foot (2.6-m) individuals are not truly uncommon. The largest authenticated size is 11 feet, 10 inches (3.57 m).

Identifying features: The vertebral scales bear knoblike keels; the lateral scales are less prominently keeled. The dorsum is tan to pinkish with black rhomboidal markings. Light spots/blotches occur in the lateral sections of the rhomboids. The belly is a nearly immaculate off-white. A prominent diagonal postorbital bar is usually present. Distally, the tail scales are spinous. When nervous, this snake produces a rattling sound by vibrating its tail in the leaves.

Reproduction: This is the only oviparous pit viper in the Amazon Basin. Females lay 6–19 eggs, often in a burrow, with the largest females tending to produce the largest clutches. Females reportedly often remain with their clutches.

Similar species: The rugose, prominently keeled vertebral scales are diagnostic.

Habitat/Range: The bushmaster is generally associated with primary forest habitats. It is an inactive snake that may remain in or near a particular spot for days at a time. It is most active at night. Bushmasters spend a good deal of time in the burrows of small mammals, in seclusion beneath the roots of toppling trees, or in other such retreats. They may seek sunny patches on the forest floor in which to coil and thermoregulate. The species ranges over much of northern South America.

Comments: Despite their formidable reputation and devastating potential, bushmasters are not always easily riled. It would seem that incubating females and males during the breeding season are the most irascible. Bushmasters are also more prone to strike at night, when they are alert and active, than during the hours of daylight, when they are quiescent.

Glossary

Amplexus	The breeding embrace of anurans (in pelvic amplexus the male grasps the female around the waist; in inguinal amplexus the female is grasped immediately posterior to the forelimbs).
Anurans	The tailless amphibia: frogs, toads, and treefrogs.
Aquatic	Dwelling in the water.
Anterodorsal	Toward the front of the upper surface.
Anteroventral	Toward the front of the belly.
Arboreal	Living in trees.
Autotomy	The breaking off of the tail by certain tailed amphibians and reptiles as a defense mechanism.
Axilla	The armpit.
Barbels	As used here, fleshy projections on the chin or neck of turtles and aquatic anurans.
Bridge	The part of a turtle's shell connecting the carapace and plastron.
Brille	The transparent scale protecting the eye of most snakes and some lizards.
Calcar	A fleshy projection (often referred to as a spur) on the heels of some frogs.
Canthus/canthal	A physical demarkation between the top and the side of the snout/pertaining to the canthus.
Carapace	The upper shell of a turtle.
Cirri	Fleshy downward projections from the nostrils of some salamanders.
Cloaca	The common chamber into which the digestive, reproductive, and urinary canals discharge, and which opens to the exterior through the anus.

Confamilial	Belonging to the same family.
Congener(s)	Species in the same genus.
Conspecific(s)	Individuals of the same species.
Co-ossified	Skin that is firmly attached to the bony skull.
Costal grooves	Vertical grooves along the sides of caecilians and salamanders.
Cranial crests	The raised ridges between or posterior to a toad's eyes.
Crepuscular	Active at dawn and dusk.
Cryptic	Concealed or camouflaged by color or structure.
Dermal flap	An extension of skin (such as that on each side of the cloaca of some of the hatchet-faced treefrogs).
Dewlap	The throat fan of some lizards.
Diapause	Temporary cessation of development.
Dichromatic	(Often) sexually related differences in color.
Dimorphic	(Often) sexually related differences in form (this can include color).
Distal	The area (of an appendage) furthest from the body.
Diurnal	Active by day.
Dorsolateral	The upper side.
Dorsolateral fold (or **ridge**)	The ridge of skin along the upper sides of some frogs.
Emarginate	Jagged, toothed.
Femoral pores	Openings in the scales under the thighs of some lizards.
Flank	The side.
Flash mark	Brightly colored markings, normally concealed, that are revealed when the animal is alarmed.
Fossorial	Burrowing.
Fracture planes	Weakened areas in the caudal bones of some lizards and salamanders. This is the point where autotomy occurs.
Genus (pl., **genera**)	A taxonomic classification in which a group of related species is placed.
Granules	As used here, small, flattened scales.
Gravid	The herpetological equivalent of pregnant.
Groin	The posterior part of the side near the juncture of the hind legs.
Gular	Pertaining to the throat.

Heterogeneous	Used here to indicate the presence of variably sized and/or textured scales.
Hidden surface	As used here, the portion of the legs that is not visible when a creature is in a normal, leg-folded, resting position.
Homogeneous	Used here to indicate scales of similar size and texture.
Infralabials	Lower lip scales.
Interorbital	Between the eyes.
Interspecific	Between two or more species.
Interstitial	As used here, referring to the skin between the scales.
Intraspecific	Within a species.
Keel	A longitudinal ridge. This may be on the shell of a turtle or on the scales of other reptiles.
Labial	Pertaining to the lip; lip scales.
Lamellae	The divided or complete transverse pads on the underside of the toes of most anoles and some geckos.
Lateral	Pertaining to the side.
Median	Toward the center.
Melanism	A suffusion of black.
Middorsal	The middle of the back.
Midventral	The middle of the belly.
Monotypic	Containing a single species.
Nape	The back of the neck.
Nasolabial groove	The groove from the nostril to the edge of the upper lip on some salamanders.
Neonates	Newborn young; usually used in conjunction with live-bearing species.
Neotropical	Referring to the New World Tropics.
Neural spines (or processes or projections)	A series of vertebrae that protrude through the dorsal muscles forming visible projections along the midline of the back of some toads and treefrogs.
Nocturnal	Active at night.
Nuchal	Pertaining to the neck.
Nuptial pad	A rough excrescence on the thumbs and/or chest of some frogs.

Oblique	Diagonal.
Ocelli (sing., ocellus)	Eyelike spots.
Occipital scale	The crown scale containing the porelike delineation of the pineal eye.
Odontoid process	A bony toothlike process on the upper and lower jaws of some frogs.
Ontogenetic	Age related.
Oviparous	Egg-laying.
Ovoviviparous	Birthing full-term live young in a membranous sac, but providing no placental nutrition.
Papillae	Conical (nipplelike) projections.
Papillate	Bearing papillae, or fleshy projections.
Paravertebral	On both sides of the vertebral line.
Parotid glands	The (usually toxin-secreting) neck or shoulder glands of toads and some treefrogs and salamanders.
Patagium	An axillary membrane.
Pelvic girdle	The part of the skeleton to which the hind limbs are attached.
Plastron	The bottom shell of a turtle.
Posterodorsal	Toward the rear of the back.
Posterolateral	Toward the rear of the side.
Posteroventral	Toward the rear of the belly.
Posterior	The rear.
Postocular	To the rear of the eye. When used with snakes and lizards this can refer to specific scales (see diagram page 202).
Preanal pores	Pores in the scales anterior to the vent.
Prehensile	Grasping, as the tail of certain snakes and lizards.
Preocular	Ahead of the eye (see diagram page 202).
Primary forest	Pristine, unlogged climax forest.
Proximal	The part (of an appendage) closest to the body.
Pustulate	Covered with roughened elevations, or pustules.
Race	Subspecies.
Reticulate	Netlike.
Rugose	Wrinkled or rough.
Scutes	The belly scales of snakes; enlarged scales such as those on a turtle's shell.
Secondary forest	Logged or otherwise disturbed forest.
Serrate	Toothed.

Setae	The hairlike bristles in the lamellae on the toes of anoles and geckos.
Shields	Large scales.
Species	(abbrev. **sp.**; pl., **spp.**) A taxonomic division of similar creatures that produce viable young when they mate.
Spiculate	Spinous.
Subcaudal	Beneath the tail.
Subgular	Below the throat.
Subspecies	(abbrev. **ssp.**) The subdivision of a species; a race.
Superciliary	Above the eye.
Supralabials	Upper lip scales.
Supraocular	Above the eye.
Supratympanic	Above the eardrum.
SVL	Snout-to-vent length.
Sympatric	Occurring together in the same area.
Taxonomy	The science of classification.
Tibia	The leg between the heel and the knee.
Toe pad	An expansion of the toe, a disc.
Transverse	Diagonal.
Truncated	Foreshortened, squared off.
Tubercles	Knoblike warts.
Tympanum	The external eardrum.
Venated	Veined, as with colors or by furrows.
Venter/ventral	The belly/pertaining to the belly.
Ventrolateral	The lower side.
Vertebral	Along the middle of the back.
Viviparous	Bearing live young.
Vocal sac	The distensile, air-filled resonating pouch on the chin of most male frogs, toads, and treefrogs.
Web	The skin between the fingers and the toes.

Additional Reading

Avila-Pires, T. S. C. 1995. *Lizards of Brazilian Amazonia (Reptilia: Squamata)*. Leiden: Nationaal Natuurhistorisch Museum.

Bartlett, Richard D. 1988. *In Search of Reptiles and Amphibians*. New York: E. J. Brill.

Campbell, Jonathan A., and William W. Lamar. 1989. *The Venomous Reptiles of Latin America*. Ithaca: Cornell University Press.

Castner, James L. 2000. *Amazon Insects: A Photo Guide*. Gainesville, Fla.: Feline Press.

———. 2000. *Explorama's Amazon: A Journey through the Rainforest of Peru*. Gainesville, Fla.: Feline Press.

Cochran, Doris M. 1955. *Frogs of Southeastern Brazil*. Washington, D.C.: Smithsonian Institution Press.

Cochran, Doris M., and Coleman J. Goin. 1970. *Frogs of Colombia*. Washington, D.C.: Smithsonian Institution Press.

Crump, Martha L. 1971. *Quantitative Analysis of the Ecological Distribution of a Tropical Herpetofauna*. Occasional Paper 3. University of Kansas Museum of Natural History.

Dixon, James R., and Pekka Soini. 1975. *The Reptiles of the Upper Amazon Basin, Iquitos Region, Peru. I. Lizards and Amphisbaenians*. Publication 4. Milwaukee Public Museum.

———. 1977. *The Reptiles of the Upper Amazon Basin, Iquitos Region, Peru. II. Crocodilians, Turtles and Snakes*. Publication 12. Milwaukee Public Museum.

Duellman, W. E. 1978. *The Biology of an Equatorial Herpetofauna in Amazonian Ecuador*. Publication 65. University of Kansas Museum of Natural History.

Kornacker, Paul M. 1999. *Checklist and Key to the Snakes of Venezuela*. Rheinbach, Germany: Pako-Verlag.

Lamar, William W. n.d. *A Checklist of the Reptiles of the Iquitos Area, Northeastern Peru*. Privately printed.

Lancini, Abdem R. 1986. *Serpientes de Venezuela*. Second edition. Caracas: Armitano.

Lutz, Bertha. 1973. *Brazilian Species of Hyla*. Austin: University of Texas Press.

Murphy, John C. 1997. *Amphibians and Reptiles of Trinidad and Tobago*. Melbourne, Fla.: Krieger.

Perez-Santos, Carlos, and Ana G. Moreno. 1988. *Ofidios de Colombia*. Torino: Museo Regional di Scienze Naturali.

―――. 1991. *Serpientes de Ecuador*. Torino: Museo Regionale di Scienze Naturali.

Peters, James A., and Braulio Orejas-Miranda. 1970. *Catalogue of the Neotropical Squamata: Part I. Snakes*. Washington, D.C.: Smithsonian Institution Press.

―――. 1970. *Catalogue of the Neotropical Squamata: Part II. Lizards and Amphisbaenians*. Washington, D.C.: Smithsonian Institution Press.

Renjifo, Juan Manuel. n.d. *Ranas y Sapos de Colombia*. Medellín, Colombia: Instituto Humboldt.

Rodriguez, Lily O., and J. E. Cadle. 1990. "A Preliminary Overview of the Herpetofauna of Cocha Cashu, Manu National Park, Peru." In *Four Neotropical Rainforests*, ed. A. H. Gentry. New Haven: Yale University Press.

Rodriguez, Lily O., and William E. Duellman. 1994. *Guide to the Frogs of the Iquitos Region, Amazonian Peru*. Special Publication 22. University of Kansas Museum of Natural History.

Roze, Janis A. 1996. *Coral Snakes of the Americas: Biology, Identification, and Venoms*. Malabar, Fla.: Krieger.

Spix, Johann Baptist von, and Johann Georg Wagler. 1981. *Herpetology of Brazil*. Reprint. Oxford, Ohio: Society for the Study of Amphibians and Reptiles.

Starace, Fausto. 1998. *Guide des Serpents et Amphisbenes de Guyane*. Guadaloupe, Guyane: Ibis Rouge Editions.

Vanzolini, P. E. 1986. *Addenda and Corrigenda to the Catalogue of Neotropical Squamata*. Washington, D.C.: Smithsonian. Herpetological Informational Service no. 70.

Zug, George R., Laurie J. Vitt, and Janalee P. Caldwell. 2001. *Herpetology*. Second edition. San Diego: Academic Press.

Index

Richard D. Bartlett is a self-taught herpetologist who has, over the span of a 40-year career, published hundreds of articles as well as many full-length field guides and other books on reptiles and amphibians in North America. He has also co-authored numerous books with his wife, Patricia Bartlett, a museum director in Gainesville, Florida.